Culture and Customs
of Ireland

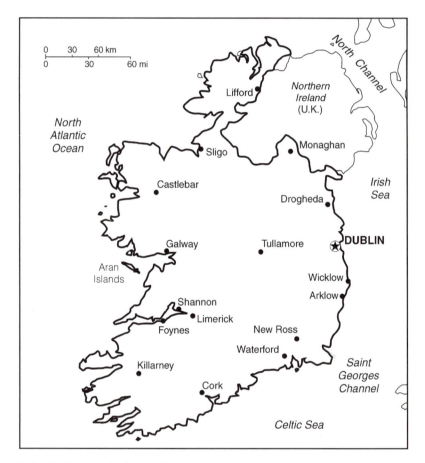

Ireland. Cartography by Bookcomp, Inc.

Culture and Customs of Ireland

MARGARET SCANLAN

Culture and Customs of Europe

GREENWOOD PRESS
Westport, Connecticut • London

Library of Congress Cataloging-in-Publication Data

Scanlan, Margaret, 1944–
    Culture and customs of Ireland / Margaret Scanlan.
        p. cm. — (Culture and customs of Europe)
    Includes bibliographical references and index.
    ISBN 0–313–33162–6 (alk. paper)
    1. Ireland—Civilization—21st century. 2. Northern Ireland—Civilization—21st century.
3. Ireland—Social life and customs—21st century. 4. Northern Ireland—Social life and customs—21st
century. 5. Ireland—Intellectual life—21st century. 6. Northern Ireland—Intellectual life—21st century.
I. Title. II. Series.
    DA925.S33 2006
    941.50824—dc22   2005031499
        SCANLAN
British Library Cataloguing in Publication Data is available.

Library of Congress Catalog Card Number: 2005031499
ISBN: 0–313–33162–6

First published in 2006

Greenwood Press, 88 Post Road West, Westport, CT 06881
An imprint of Greenwood Publishing Group, Inc.
www.greenwood.com

Printed in the United States of America

The paper used in this book complies with the
Permanent Paper Standard issued by the National
Information Standards Organization (Z39.48–1984).

10   9   8   7   6   5   4   3   2   1

Contents

Series Foreword   vii

Preface   ix

Chronology   xi

1   **The Land, People, and History**   1

2   **Religion and Thought**   33

3   **Marriage, Gender, Family, and Education**   65

4   **Cuisine, Holidays, and Leisure Activities**   89

5   **Literature**   109

6   **Media and Cinema**   133

7   **Performing Arts**   161

8   **Art and Architecture/Housing**   187

Glossary   219

Bibliography   223

Index   235

Series Foreword

THE OLD WORLD AND THE NEW WORLD have maintained a fluid exchange of people, ideas, innovations, and styles. Even though the United States became the de facto leader and economic superpower in the wake of a devastated Europe after World War II, Europe has remained for many the standard bearer of Western culture.

Millions of Americans can trace their ancestors to Europe. The United States as we know it was built on waves of European immigration, starting with the English who braved the seas to found the Jamestown Colony in 1607. Bosnian and Albanian immigrants are some of the latest new Americans.

In the Gilded Age of one of our great expatriates, the novelist Henry James, the Grand Tour of Europe was de rigueur for young American men of means, to prepare them for a life of refinement and taste. In a more recent democratic age, scores of American college students have Eurailed their way across Great Britain and the Continent, sampling the fabled capitals and bergs in a mad, great adventure, or have benefited from a semester abroad. For other American vacationers and culture vultures, Europe is the prime destination.

What is the New Europe post–Cold War, post–Berlin Wall in the new millennium? Even with the different languages, rhythms, and rituals, Europeans have much in common: they are largely well educated, prosperous, and worldly. They also have similar goals and face common threats and form alliances. With the advent of the European Union, the open borders, and the euro and considering globalization and the prospect of a homogenized Europe, an updated survey of the region is warranted.

Culture and Customs of Europe features individual volumes on the countries most studied and for which fresh information is in demand from students and other readers. The Series casts a wide net, inclusive of not only the expected countries, such as Spain, France, England, and Germany, but also countries such as Poland and Greece that lie outside Western Europe proper. Each volume is written by a country specialist, with intimate knowledge of the contemporary dynamics of a people and culture. Sustained narrative chapters cover the land, people, and brief history; religion; social customs; gender roles, family, and marriage; literature and media; performing arts and cinema; and art and architecture. The national character and ongoing popular traditions of each country are framed in an historical context and celebrated along with the latest trends and major cultural figures. A country map, chronology, glossary, and evocative photos enhance the text.

The historied and enlightened Europeans will continue to fascinate Americans. Our futures are strongly linked politically, economically, and culturally.

Preface

Now the second wealthiest country in the European Union, the Republic of Ireland has undergone remarkable transformation since the 1980s. At the same time, embattled Northern Ireland has taken key steps toward security and peace. This book surveys the cultural and political heritage of the Irish people, north and south. It highlights the remarkable accomplishments of Ireland's artists, writers, musicians, and performers. It investigates the role of religion in Irish life, and the ways in which prosperity, feminism, and scandals within the churches have weakened that role. It looks at the impact of immigrants and refugees on contemporary society, at the increasing visibility of women on both sides of the border, and at the growing acceptance of gay people. It also looks at daily life in Ireland, at people going to work, shopping, and finding someone to care for their children. In particular, it shows the challenges of maintaining Irish identity in the face of globalization.

Chronology

7000 B.C.	Mesolithic age. Human-made structures appear in County Derry.
4000 B.C.	Agriculture begins.
3200–2500 B.C.	Great stone tombs built in Dowth, Knowth, and Newgrange.
2100 B.C.	Large circular structures, "Mound of the Hostages," built at Tara.
600 B.C.	Iron-using Celtic tribes from central Europe settle in Ireland.
300–500 A.D.	Ogham inscriptions, showing influence of Roman alphabet, appear on stones.
432–461	Patrick begins converting Ireland.
500	Scholars from Europe study at Irish monasteries.
800	Book of Kells, illuminated Latin Gospel, created.
841	Vikings build settlement in Dublin.
1014	Irish forces commanded by Brian Boru defeat the Vikings at the Battle of Clontarf.

1170	Richard of Pembroke, Strongbow, marries Aoife, the daughter of Dermot MacMurchada, Lord of Leinster, one day after Pembroke helps Leinster seize Waterford.
1171	On MacMurchada's death, Strongbow claims his kingdom. England's Henry II sends an army.
1200–1400	Dublin and an area extending about 20 miles around it, known as the Pale, become anglicized. Outside Dublin, "beyond the Pale," invaders assimilate, adopt the Irish language.
1297	Anglo-Irish Parliament (nobles loyal to king) formed.
1500	First "plantation" of English in Ireland begun; Irish land granted to English farmers to secure loyalty to the crown.
1531–1534	King Henry VIII breaks away from the Pope, establishing the Church of England.
1541	Dublin Parliament proclaims Henry VIII King of Ireland.
1609	Plantation of Ulster; land in six northern counties granted to Scottish Protestants settlers.
1642–1649	English Civil War pits Puritans and republicans against Anglicans and monarchists.
1649	King Charles I executed. Oliver Cromwell invades Ireland.
1653	All Catholic gentry and landowners ordered to move west of the Shannon.
1660	English Restoration; Charles II becomes king.
1685–1689	James I, a Catholic, is English King.
1689	"Glorious Revolution," Parliament deposes James II and invites Protestant William and Mary of Orange (the Netherlands) to succeed him. James II comes to Derry with a French army; with the aid of Irish Catholics, he besieges the city for 105 days.
1690	King William of Orange defeats James II at the Battle of the Boyne.
1699	First Penal Laws.

1795	United Irishmen (coalition of Protestants and Catholics advocating reforms) founded.
1798	Year of the French. United Irishmen rebel, aided by French revolutionaries; British suppress rebellion.
1801	Act of Union abolishes Irish Parliament.
1829	Catholic Emancipation permits Catholics to be elected to Parliament.
1846–1849	Worst years of Potato Famine.
1858	Irish Republican Brotherhood founded in Dublin; Fenian Brotherhood founded in the United States.
1867	Hanging of the "Manchester Martyrs," three Fenians who had killed an English policeman. Irish Catholic hierarchy condemns the Fenians.
1870	First Irish Land Act recognizes tenant rights.
1873	Home Rule League founded.
1879	Land League formed to secure rights for tenant farmers; decade of rural unrest sparked by bad harvests and evictions.
1880	Charles Stuart Parnell elected chair of Irish Parliamentary Party, which advocates land reform and Home Rule.
1881	British Prime Minister William Gladstone's Second Land Act guarantees fair rent, fair land sales, and fixed leases.
1886	First Home Rule Bill defeated in Parliament.
1890	Parnell loses leadership of party after divorce suit exposes his long-term affair with a married woman.
1891	Parnell's funeral in Dublin is attended by 250,000 people.
1893	Second Home Rule Bill is defeated.
1893	Douglas Hyde founds the Gaelic League.
1905	Arthur Griffith founds republican party Sinn Fein.
1913	Third Home Rule Bill passes House of Commons but is stalled in House of Lords. Ulster Protestants form Ulster Volunteer Force (UVF) to resist Home Rule.

1914   UVF imports large arms shipments. World War I breaks
            out; Parliament suspends Home Rule for the duration of
            the war.

1916   Easter Rising; on July 1, 2,000 members of the Ulster
            Division die at the Somme.

1919   Sinn Fein wins majority of Irish parliamentary seats, but
            members refuse to take up their seats in Westminster.

1919–1921   Irish War of Independence.

1920   English boundary commission establishes six predomi-
            nantly Protestant Ulster counties as Northern Ireland; the
            rest is Southern Ireland.

1922   Treaty with England establishes Irish Free State along 1920
            boundaries; requires members of Irish parliament to take
            loyalty oath to the Crown.

1922–1923   Civil War in Free State between pro-Treaty forces and
            anti-Treaty forces. Pro-Treaty forces win.

1937   New Irish constitution adopted; Free State renamed
            "Eire."

1939–1945   The Emergency. World War II; Eire remains neutral;
            Northern Ireland fights on the British side.

1949   Eire is renamed Republic of Ireland.

1955   Republic joins the United Nations.

1967   (Catholic) Northern Ireland Civil Rights Association
            formed.

1968   Civil Rights marches; in October, marchers who defy a
            ban in Derry, Northern Ireland, attacked by police.

1969   Prime Minister of Northern Ireland, Terence O'Neill,
            resigns; August 14, British troops sent to Derry to protect
            Catholics.

1971   Northern Ireland begins internment without trial for
            suspected Republican terrorists.

1972   Republic joins the European Economic Community;
            reference to "special status" of Catholic Church removed
            from Constitution.

1972	Bloody Sunday in Derry; 13 civil rights marchers are shot by British; Stormont (Northern Ireland's Parliament) suspended.
1973	Sunningdale power-sharing agreement negotiated.
1974	Ulster Workers' Strike (Protestant) brings down Prime Minister Brian Faulkner. British impose direct rule on Northern Ireland.
1981–1982	Hunger strikes in North leave 10 Republican prisoners dead.
1993	Downing Street Declaration: British government accepts Irish right to self-determination.
1994	First Irish Republican Army (IRA) cease-fire.
1996	Cease-fire breaks down; IRA bombs London's Canary Wharf.
1997	Cease-fire resumed; three-party talks include Republic, British government, and representatives of all of Northern Ireland's political parties.
1998	Belfast, or Good Friday Agreement, accepted by majority votes in Northern Ireland and the Republic.
2005	Sinn Fein and Democratic Unionist Parties win majorities in Northern Ireland parliamentary election, displacing the moderate parties that negotiated the Good Friday Agreement.

1

The Land, People, and History

EVERY YEAR, SOME 6 MILLION TOURISTS visit the Republic of Ireland, a country with just less than 4 million citizens. Most are drawn to Ireland by the beautiful rural landscapes they have seen in films such as *The Secret of Roan Inish* (1994), and by plangent songs and poems that celebrate, for example, the vale of Avoca, whose waters are mingled in peace, or evoke William Butler Yeats's "white swan upon a darkening flood." Doubtless many hope to find a tranquil landscape of thatched cottages where women knit heavy Aran sweaters as their men dig peat for the evening's fire. They expect a devoutly Catholic country, peopled with poor but honest farming folk whose weakness for the drink only makes them more hospitable. They may well be shocked to find themselves in twenty-first century Dublin, where an expanding economy that owes much to new technology and foreign investment has created "Dublin 4," an urban upper-middle class known by the suburban postal zone in which many of its members live. Like their counterparts in Marin County, California, they wear Roloflex watches and Armani suits; they drive Porsches and ski in St. Malo. Like New York's Greenwich Village, the recently renovated Temple Bar district offers a range of international films and cuisines. Dublin 4 is the luxuriant coat of the Celtic Tiger, the swift and sure-footed new global Ireland where per capita income has been higher than England's since 1996. In contemporary Ireland, divorce, birth control, and sex education are freely available; gay people are constitutionally protected from job discrimination; and popular icons include an Afro-Celtic rock band.

Grafton Street, Dublin, attracts affluent shoppers. Courtesy of Linda Sichenze.

The traveler who ventures beyond the Temple Bar will also see that the Celtic Tiger, like its namesake, slashes and claws. Traditionally a poor country, Ireland has become an economically polarized one. Although the new economy benefits the young and well educated, it discards the unskilled: "next to the USA, Ireland has the highest percentage of low-paid workers in the developed world."[1] In 2000, 28.3 percent of the population lived on weekly incomes below $210; just over a fifth, 20.9 percent, lived on weekly incomes below $175.[2] Alcoholism is increasing; hard drugs have become a big business. Veronica Guerin, an investigative reporter who publicized the activities of a multimillionaire crime boss, John Gilligan, was killed in 1996. Two of his associates were jailed for her murder, and Gilligan himself received a long sentence on charges of trafficking in marijuana. But the drug trade, and attempts to police it, continue: a headline story in the *Irish Examiner*, on April 3, 2003, announced a "million-euro heroin bust"; on February 13, 2004; a similar operation netted a more modest quarter of a million. With poverty and drug addiction come rising crime figures: the number of "headline," or serious, offenses reported by Ireland's police, the Garda Siochana, increased from 86,633 in 2001 to 106,415 in 2002 (23%). These figures include a dramatic increase in assaults, from 3,802 to 5,995, and thefts, from 45,652 to 58,180. Even more distant from the imaginary land of shamrocks and fiddles than Dublin 4, this grim underworld, and the underclass on which it feeds, closely resembles the inner cities of Chicago and London.

To understand contemporary Ireland requires distinguishing between Ireland's reality and the sentimental ideas of "Irishness" many acquire as children celebrating St. Patrick's Day. This chapter looks at the place, the people, and the harrowing history that shape contemporary life.

THE LAND AND ECONOMY

Ireland is a small island roughly the size of Maine, 302 miles from north to south, only 171 miles from east to west. Set in the North Atlantic, Ireland is divided from its larger neighbor, Great Britain, by a channel that at its narrowest is no more than 14 miles wide. Although only about 11 percent of the Irish Republic's citizens are employed on farms, 80 percent of its land is still cultivated or grazed. Ireland has little available coal or iron, and no petroleum, hard facts that contributed to the nation's past poverty but also keep it relatively unpolluted.[3] Rain, however, has always been abundant—anywhere from 30 to 50 inches annually in most of the country, with up to 250 rainy days a year in the West and 190 even in the relatively sunny southeast. In most parts of the country, average temperatures fall below 42 degrees Fahrenheit—the level grass requires to keep growing—only in January.[4] Visitors to the South, even to Dublin, are often surprised to see the imported palm tree flourishing. On the other hand, as the average temperature in July, the hottest month, is only 60 degrees, few heat waves scorch the native heather, fuchsia, or shamrock. The highest temperature ever recorded was 92 degrees, at Kilkenny Castle, in 1887.

Generations of Irish schoolchildren have been taught that their nation is a limestone "saucer with a highland rim and a lowland heart."[5] The coastal gaps in these highlands have been Ireland's harbors for centuries: at New Ross in the south, at Galway and Westport in the west, and in the east for 100 miles between Dublin and Dundalk. The "lowland heart" contains the nation's best farmland, a landscape of gently rolling hills through which the Shannon River runs for 240 miles. Glaciers, the last of which melted only 10,000 years ago, deposited rich soil in the lowlands but had a more visible effect on highlands, stripping the soil and leaving a dramatic coastline of mountains and cliffs. While the coast is extraordinarily beautiful, nearby soil is so thin that the underlying limestone breaks through, most dramatically in the 350 square miles of County Clare's moonscape, the Burren, where Arctic plants survive. Especially in the west, generations of Irish farmers have dug up stones and deposited them at the edges of fields. The result is a picturesque landscape broken up with stone walls. In places such as the Aran Islands, much of the soil was created by men and women hauling huge baskets of seaweed up from the beaches.

One-sixth of Ireland is covered in bog, which people dig up in blocks, dry, and burn as that most Irish of fuels, peat.[6] The state-run Bord na Mona ("turf board") produces it on an industrial scale, more than 4 million tons annually. Although the "raised bog" of central Ireland is a naturally occurring phenomenon, the more extensive "blanket bog" of the north and west developed after early farmers arrived. They began to clear land in high areas, where the forest was less dense. As rains washed minerals in the fields downhill, a hard layer formed beneath the surface, preventing full drainage. As the land became waterlogged, its soil grew acidic; the remaining trees died and were replaced with heather, rushes, and moss. Cool, wet conditions retarded decay, and thick layers of peat accumulated. Abandoning this exhausted land, farmers simply moved to lower ground, repeating the process and enabling blanket bog to spread. To this day, Ireland has fewer trees per square mile than any other country in the European Union, although a government reforesting project increased the percentage of wooded land to 5 percent in 2000 from a low of 1 percent at the turn of the previous century.[7] The bog lands have been a great benefit to archaeologists, however, because they preserved what they covered, including, remarkably, Ceide Fields, a Neolithic farm in Mayo buried for more than 5,000 years.

POLITICAL DIVISIONS

Ireland is divided into 32 counties comprising the four traditional provinces of Ulster, Leinster, Munster, and Connaught. Between 1920 and 1922, it split into two political entities, the Irish Free State, established in 1922, and Northern Ireland, consisting of six Ulster counties. The Free State renamed itself the Republic of Ireland in 1949; Northern Ireland continues as part of the United Kingdom. Geographical names are often a sensitive matter in Ireland and confusing to outsiders, who find it odd that part of Donegal in the Republic is north of Northern Ireland or wonder why some people in Northern Ireland refer to their homeland as "Ulster." The answer is that those who use "Ulster" are Unionists, those who wish to preserve their political link to the United Kingdom, and prefer a name that suggests separation from the rest of Ireland. Republicans, who would like to see the North join the Republic, sometimes emphasize their historical link by referring to Northern Ireland as "the six counties."

NORTHERN IRELAND

Northern Ireland's six counties (Fermanagh, Armagh, Down, Tyrone, Londonderry, and Antrime) include almost 1.6 million inhabitants. Its population density, then, is double that of the Republic, with 65 percent of the population living in urban areas and only about 5 percent actually engaged in farming.[8] Greater Belfast, at 360,000, is the largest of these; Derry (or Londonderry, as Unionists call it), at 73,000, is the second largest. Belfast was settled in 1613; its harbor, so accessible to ships carrying English coal, enabled it to burgeon during the Industrial Revolution. By the nineteenth century, Belfast was a great manufacturing town dominated by ship-building and textiles. In 1951, Harland-Wolff, the shipyard that built the *Titanic,* still employed more than 21,000 workers and Belfast's linen mills employed another 76,000 people. Only 10 years later, however, new Third World producers and new products, such as the commercial jet and polyester, had severely damaged both industries.[9] After 1969, Northern Ireland's Troubles, three decades of armed conflict involving Protestant and Catholic paramilitaries, the police, and the British army, discouraged investment. In 2000, a failed bid to build the *Queen Mary II* spelled Harland-Wolff's death as a shipbuilder. In 2004 its Web site described what remained of the company as a "single, technically-led project management organization." Belfast's major linen mills are now museums, although Northern Ireland's surviving textile industry employs approximately 20,000 workers.

Northern Ireland's economy continues to move away from reliance on manufacturing. The February 2004 edition of *Northern Ireland Labour Market Statistics* reported a 6.3 percent unemployment rate for the previous quarter. Of 669,470 people employed, only 91,720 had manufacturing jobs in September 2003, compared with 107,070 in March 1998. On the other hand, 522,640 people were listed as having jobs in the service industries and 35,440 in construction. One potential growth area is tourism, unthinkable during the "Troubles," which cost 3,200 lives. Since the first cease-fire in 1994, the Northern Irish Tourist Board has tried to substitute images of urban renewal, of concerts, museums, and theater, for the grim televised images of warring Derry and Belfast, with their squalid slums. The Board highlights the splendid Mountains of Mourne in County Down and Antrim's spectacular Giant's Causeway, which formed 65 million years ago when lava from a volcanic explosion hit sea water. This mass of 40,000 hexagonal basalt columns, packed closely together, and rising from the sea, appears to bear out the old folkloric explanation that the giant Finn McCool built it as an overland path from Scotland. New sites designed with the American tourist in mind include the Ulster-American Folk Park, which tells the story of emigration, and the Andrew Jackson Centre at Carrickfergus. And although tourism is not the economic mainstay it is in the Republic, in 2002 tourists from outside Northern Ireland spent close to $500 million there.[10]

THE PROVINCE OF LEINSTER AND COUNTIES CAVAN AND MONAGHAN

Leinster, on the east coast, is the Republic's most populous province, with more than 2 million inhabitants, or 53.7 percent of the nation's total population, many living in Dublin or its suburbs. The adjacent Ulster counties of Cavan and Monaghan add another 107,188. Dublin, nearly 2,000 years old, was invaded by Vikings in 841 and by England in 1170. The English Pale, an area extending 100 miles north from Dublin, was the most Anglicized and later the most Protestant part of Ireland. Massive building projects in the eighteenth century made Dublin one of the most elegant cities in the world, with broad streets and spacious green squares. Beautiful examples of Georgian architecture can be found in Dublin at Trinity College, in public buildings such as the old Parliament and the Customs House, and in the houses of Merrion Square, with their distinctive doors and fanlights. Meanwhile, the native Irish laborers lived in the wretched conditions that satirist Jonathan Swift's "A Modest Proposal" (1729) addressed. By the early twentieth century, their descendants, still living miserably, had moved into the crowded tenements into which many Georgian houses had been converted.

Today Dublin is the Republic's capital and its cultural and economic center. It is home not only to Trinity College Dublin but to the national university, University College Dublin. It is the headquarters of brewer Guinness and whiskey distiller Jameson, of the Abbey Theater and the National Museum It is where the country's leading newspaper, *The Irish Times,* is published; it is home to major art galleries and book publishers. The national television company, RTE (Radio Telefís Éireann) has its headquarters there and films are made at Ardmore Studios in nearby Bray. The foreign invaders have left, but the city remains the most cosmopolitan in Ireland, the one with the most immigrants, the most international restaurants, the most gay and lesbian bars, and the most tolerance for the unconventional and the nonmonogamous. But with crime and drug abuse, the colonial tradition of Dublin as a city of polar extremes, divided between a ruling elite and a large underclass, also persists. Commentators note that the residents of poor neighborhoods have fewer resources than they would in other European countries: one public housing project "has one shop to serve 15,000 inhabitants; another ... of over 5,000 people has no school, doctor's surgery, phone box or mail box."[11]

THE PROVINCE OF MUNSTER

Munster is Ireland's southernmost province, home to more than a million people, 28.1 percent of the Republic's population. It contains the cities of Limerick, Cork, and Waterford and, along with neighboring Leinster, has much of Ireland's best farmland. Irish farms generally seem small by North American standards, averaging 76.6 acres, but farms in the south and east are generally larger and more profitable than those in the north and west.[12] A relatively low 9 percent of Irish farmland, mostly in Leinster and Munster, is devoted to crops; these include barley, wheat, oats, corn, sugar beets, and, of course, potatoes. The rest is devoted to grazing and growing grasses for farm animals, with the beef and milk industries alone accounting for about 58 percent of farm income; sheep, pigs, and poultry are also raised. Rural west Cork and Kerry also contain spectacular scenery, including the lakes of Killarney, the Dingle Peninsula, and Bantry Bay. The proximity of this landscape to Shannon International Airport makes it a magnet for visitors. To drive around the Ring of Kerry, a 126-mile scenic road from Kenmare to Killorgan, in bumper-to-bumper traffic is to understand why Irish people worry about tourism destroying the environment.

The urban center of Munster is Cork, Ireland's second largest city, located on the River Lee only 15 miles from the Atlantic harbor at Cobh. Under the British, Cork developed some manufacturing, including famous gin and whisky distilleries, and was a shipping and trade center. Cobh (then known as Queenstown) was a major port of call for ships to Britain and America. More Irish emigrants left from its docks than from any other. Contemporary Munster is also a showcase for some of the greatest successes of Irish economic and technological development. The first of these was the hydroelectric engineering feat called the Shannon Scheme. Completed in 1929 after four years of hard labor, its turbines supplied 96 percent of the nation's electricity by 1931. Recognized in 2002 by the American Society of Engineers as an International Landmark, the Scheme served as a model for large-scale electrification projects elsewhere; at home it made rural electrification feasible, reduced dependence on British coal, and boosted confidence in the nation's scientific and technological know-how. Also in Munster, 15 miles west of Limerick, Shannon Airport opened for international flights in 1945. To promote its use, the world's first duty-free shopping zone was opened at the airport in 1947. The Shannon Free Zone, a 600-acre business park with easy access to the airport, opened in 1958; in 2004, the Zone and its companies provided jobs for more than 7,500 people. In the private sector, Waterford Crystal offers another success story. In 1947, local businessmen reopened the workshop, which had been closed since 1851; today it employs 1,600 people, and busloads of tourists arrive daily to watch craftspeople make the crystal and carve it by hand.

THE PROVINCE OF CONNACHT AND COUNTY DONEGAL

When Donegal, which was separated from the rest of Ulster in 1922, is added to the five Connacht counties, this area of the Republic is usually known as "the West." With Connacht having 464,050 residents and Donegal adding another 137,383, the West is Ireland's least populous region, the one with its best scenery and poorest farmland. Modernization came slowly in the West; parts of rural Donegal remained without electricity until the 1950s. In the early 1970s, the horse-drawn "jaunting cart" was the only transportation available on the Aran Islands. As Dublin and the Pale were the most English, the West was the most Gaelic part of Ireland. Its past is embedded in its land-scape; even today prehistoric forts and tombs, along with the ruins of early Christian monastic settlements, lie open in fields near the abandoned cottages of nineteenth- and twentieth-century emigrants. Like the ruins around them, the West's people, particularly those in the Gaeltacht, the Irish-speaking areas, are often seen as survivals of a lost culture. Yet twenty-first century cars, appliances, technology, and music pervade life in the Gaeltacht, and the tenuous survival of the native language owes much to the taxpayer in Dublin and Cork.

Today approximately 86,000 people speak Irish as a first language; 11 of the 12 majority Irish-speaking voting districts are located in the West. Irish is required at all state-sponsored schools in the country, and preserving Irish-speaking communities seems crucial for keeping the spoken language from being lost to English. In Shakespeare's time, there were approximately as many speakers of the Celtic languages (Irish, Welsh, Scots Gaelic, Cornish, Manx) in the British Isles as there were English speakers. By the nineteenth century, English had become the principal language of Leinster and Ulster, but about half the population, largely in Munster and Connaught, spoke only Irish. Famine, deaths, and emigration destroyed many traditional Irish-speaking communities; for people who remained, English, already a world language, became an essential survival skill. By the end of the nineteenth century, only about 1 percent of the population spoke Irish. Today, Udaras na Gaeltachta, a government agency with a budget of more than $54,500,000, promotes the region's economic and cultural development. Udaras makes grants, low-interest loans, and other incentives available to businesses willing to employ Irish speakers. It also directly employs 7,800 full-time workers and some 4,000 additional seasonal or part-time workers. There is a state-sponsored Irish language radio network and television channel; besides textbooks, a state-sponsored Irish press annually publishes another hundred or so books. Irish-language summer schools for secondary and university students, long catering to students facing examinations, have become popular with foreigners.

THE PEOPLE: RELIGION, FAMILY, AND EDUCATION

Most people in the Republic are native-born (89.6%). Nonetheless, the 1990s saw real demographic change; in 1996, only 26,100 Irish residents claimed birth outside Ireland, the United States, or the European Union. By 2001, the Republic had nearly 97,2000 such residents, mostly immigrants from Eastern Europe, Asia, and Africa. The Republic is a predominantly Catholic (88.4%) country, with the rest roughly divided between those who either have no religion or refuse to state one (217,400) and those who belong to "other" religions (186,500). The 2002 census found 19,100 Muslims in Ireland, four times as many as in 1992. Orthodox Christians, who numbered 400 in 1992, were up to 10,400 in 2002; 167,000 Irish residents described themselves as Protestant. All of the older Irish churches have seen declining attendance and practice. An Associated Press story noted that weekly mass attendance was down to 48 percent in 2003; in the 1960s, the figure was upward of 90 percent.[13]

Along with the new prosperity, this weakening of Ireland's Catholic identity has contributed to major changes in the family and society. One frequently cited statistic is the 24.5 percent increase in the number of single-parent families between 1996 and the 2002 census. By 2002, one-third of births were taking place outside marriage; in the early 1960s, the figure was lower than 2 percent.[14] Similarly, the number of unmarried couples living together increased from 31,300 in 1996 to 77,600 in 2002. In spite of a falling birth rate, at 1.6 percent the nation's lowest ever, the country remains the youngest in the European union, with 41.2 percent of the population under 26. More people have jobs than ever before. For women alone, the employment rate increased by 40 percent between 1994 and 2003; for men, the increase was 15 percent. If any further evidence of modernization or prosperity is needed, Ireland is the largest software exporter in the world and, per capita, has the largest number of video game owners. Its citizens go to more movies than the citizens of any other country in the European Union, and 80 percent own mobile phones.[15]

The high educational level of its citizen attracts foreign investors. Although free elementary education was available throughout the twentieth century, free secondary education began only in 1967. By 1998, the percentage of young people successfully completing the "leaving certificate," roughly the equivalent of a high school diploma, was 80 percent. The number of students enrolled in higher education grew dramatically, "by more than a factor of six," between 1964 and 1997.[16] The Central Statistics office reported in 2003 that 23.1 percent of the population had achieved a "third-level" qualification such as a degree from a university or technical institute, up 17.3 percent in the previous four years. Ranked first in the European Union in 1997 in the number of students ages 25 to 27 with third-level qualifications, today Ireland consistently ranks above such countries as Australia, the United Kingdom, Austria, and Switzerland in most measures of educational success.[17]

ETHNIC MINORITIES: THE TRAVELLERS

The prosperity, modernization, and high educational levels characteristic of the Republic's ethnic majority do not extend to the economic underclass noted earlier, which includes a disproportionate percentage of its ethnic minorities. The largest native-born minority are the travellers, a people easily confused with Europe's Roma, although the two are ethnically separate. Travellers make up only about 0.6 percent of Ireland's population, or about 24,000 persons, but their frequent conflicts with the "settled population" give them a visibility disproportionate to their numbers. In addition to English, travellers speak their own language, so they can converse privately in front of outsiders. Like Roma, they acquired a reputation for dishonesty and disrespect for property values. Traditionally travellers used horse-drawn caravans, staying on the edges of rural communities and working as "tinkers," mending metal items such as pots and farm tools. Some also did casual farm labor, traded horses and donkeys, and bought and sold rags. When these occupations became obsolete, most travellers lacked skills required for new jobs. Nomadic life declined precipitously because of a requirement that those expecting government aid produce fixed addresses and because the expanded highway system displaced traditional campsites. In 1960, 95 percent of travellers lived in caravans; by 1980, the number in mobile housing was down to about 60 percent, and today it is closer to 50 percent.[18]

As the settled population grew more prosperous, its complaints about travellers—their large families, their filth, their destructive behavior in pubs—multiplied. Merchants refusing service to travellers paid little heed to arguments that poverty itself creates many problems. On virtually any measure, travellers are much poorer than other Irish people; the 2002 census showed, for example, that the group's male unemployment rate was 45.1 percent. In 1995, a writer in the *Irish Times* wrote that the most damning indictment of the Republic's treatment of travellers was that 95 percent of them died before age 55.[19] Anti-traveller bias in the media, as illustrated by a 1996 article in the widely circulated *Irish Independent* headlined, "Time to get tough on tinker terror culture" does nothing to improve conditions.[20] More hopefully, voices have arisen within the traveling community articulating its traditions and arguing for its basic civil rights. Sean Maher's *The Road to God Knows Where: A Memoir of a Travelling Boyhood* (1972) provided an early and compelling account of the author's struggle for education. Activist travellers, such as the town commissioners Ellen Mongan and Martin Ward; and Nan Joyce, who campaigned for a seat in the Irish Parliament (Dail), won support from settled people. As a result, the Republic started providing approved camping sites equipped with modern services for travellers, although public resistance has caused delays. The Employment Equality Act (1998) and the Equal Status Act (2000) define travellers as an ethnic group and forbid discrimination.

ETHNIC MINORITIES: THE REPUBLIC'S NEW IMMIGRANTS

Traditionally a country with a huge rate of emigration, Ireland had little experience assimilating outsiders. The 1984 census revealed that only about 20,000 people, or 0.6 percent of the population, identified themselves as Asian or black.[21] In the 1990s, however, not only did Irish emigrants return, but the government actively recruited specialist workers from Europe. At the same time, war, ethnic cleansing, and famine created hundreds of thousands of new refugees, and Ireland began to accept some. By many standards, the numbers were low: in 1997, for example, 9 percent of the immigrants, or 4,000, were asylum seekers. Through the 1990s, a total of 10,000 asylum seekers came to Ireland; in 2000 and 2001, the figure was up to 10,000 a year.[22] In a largely homogeneous society, refugees from countries such as Nigeria, Romania, Libya, and the Congo were highly visible. The government banned asylum seekers from taking jobs before their cases were heard,

In a demonstration against racism, a Nigerian man in Irish hat holds sign that says "Welcome to Ireland! Unless you're Nigerian." © *Irish Times* 4/15/2005.

providing them with basic necessities and a small amount of spending money. Intended to discourage refugees from putting down roots before their asylum claims were verified, and to reassure natives that refugees were not taking jobs away from them, the policy nonetheless generated widespread resentment of idle foreigners living at government expense. This resentment carried over to people of color more generally: a 1998 survey of international students revealed that 90 percent of "non-white" students reported some form of racial harassment when they left campus.[23]

Public and political responses to refugees and immigrants range widely. At one extreme, Aine Ni Chonaill, a schoolteacher from West Cork, founded the Immigration Control Platform. "Irish people," Ni Chonaill argues, "have no wish to emulate the British experience, the German, the French experience ... they have to pretend it's wonderful because that's what you do when you have failed to control your borders."[24] But others were struck with the irony that the Irish, who faced so much discrimination in England and the United States, now found themselves confronting their own prejudices. Such critics argued that the Irish had acquired racist attitudes while serving as soldiers and civil servants in the British colonies, and pointed out that Republicanism has traditionally identified Irishness in ethnic terms. Others preferred to emphasize more positive signs, such as the popularity of Afro-Irish athletes and performers and the new cultural influences in Irish art and life. For the distinguished scholar Declan Kiberd, the "marvelous fusion of Latino elements with native forms in Riverdance" and the "Caribbean collaboration of [poet] Seamus Heaney with [poet and playwright] Derek Walcott" enable "some element of Irish culture to present itself more stunningly to a modern world audience."[25] Most would agree with Kensika Monshengo, a Congolese immigrant working with Ireland's National Consultative Committee on Racism and Inter-culturalism, that the Irish must "learn to live with diversity."[26]

ETHNIC MINORITIES: PEOPLE OF COLOR IN NORTHERN IRELAND

Violence aimed at ethnic minorities also increased in recent years in Northern Ireland, even as a cease-fire offered hope of reconciliation between Catholics and Protestants. The perpetrators have usually been fringe members of loyalist paramilitaries who expanded their enemies' list as a result of closer ties to white supremacist groups in Britain. When attacks began in the early 1990s, most people of color in Northern Ireland were Chinese and South Asian, many well-established second- and third-generation descendants of immigrants from British Commonwealth countries, and officials initially attributed the violence to robbery. By 1996, when Albert Leung of Antrim and

Simon Tang of Carrickfergus died from beatings, few in Northern Ireland's Asian community were willing to accept that explanation. The Northern Ireland Council for Ethnic Minorities, a citizens' group established in 1994, urged action. In 1997 Northern Ireland's Race Relations Order offered specific protections to ethnic minorities, and today an Equality Commission for Northern Ireland investigates incidents. Yet the situation remains difficult; Northern Ireland's police force listed 226 racially motivated attacks in 2002.[27] And there were new victims; although people of Asian descent still constituted 75 percent of those attacked in 2000, a new generation of African refugees has also suffered assaults and harassment.

HISTORY: INVADERS AND OPPRESSORS

The proximity of a large and powerful neighbor often seems to ordain a small nation's destiny. Ireland's modern history takes its shape from British incursions and invasions that began in the middle of the twelfth century, when Dermot McMorraugh, King of Leinster, invited Strongbow to bring his Welsh-Norman knights and archers over to help protect his kingdom. Not liking to see potential rivals in league, England's King Henry II followed, using for justification a document from history's only English Pope, Adrian IV, that proclaimed him "lord of Ireland." The competing British invaders kept mostly to Ireland's south and east, leaving the north and west in Irish hands. The Normans, whose people had left France less than a century earlier, assimilated themselves to Irish life, learning the language and identifying with local interests. Henry's troops, and the settlers who came in their wake, largely remained within the Pale, preserving their political and cultural identity, and exercising limited power through a local, or Irish, Parliament. This division grew more fateful in 1534, when Henry VIII officially broke with Rome. Ireland's "Old English" mainly followed their compatriots and the king, becoming Protestant; the Irish and the gaelicized Normans remained Catholic.

In an age that identified church and state, such a split roused fears that the Catholic Irish would ally themselves with England's enemies, Catholic Spain or France. The English became more determined to repress the native Irish, but the Irish had even more reason to resist. In the sixteenth century, the English fought the Irish nobles who still ruled in Ulster and Connacht. In 1603, after nine years of war, Tyrone's Hugh O'Neill and Tyrconnell's Hugh O'Donnell surrendered; O'Donnell fled to Spain. Initially pardoned, O'Neill fled to the Continent a few years later with about 100 other Gaelic chieftains. This "Flight of the Earls" signaled the end of Catholic political power in Ireland for 300 years. In 1610, James I seized the O'Donnell and O'Neill lands and began bringing in Scottish Protestants to settle them; by 1641 only one-seventh of Ulster remained Catholic.[28] The outbreak of the English Civil War that year destabilized Ireland, and angry Irish tenants took revenge on the Protestants for their lost land.

In 1649, after victory in the English Civil War, Oliver Cromwell and his Puritan forces invaded Ireland. In a brutal campaign, the British massacred civilians as well as soldiers, most famously at the Drogheda garrison, where at least 1,000 civilians died along with 2,500 soldiers. In justification, Cromwell pointed to the Protestants murdered in 1641 and the need to terrify other Irish strongholds into surrender. In 1650, he returned triumphant to England, obtaining an act of Parliament to "settle Ireland," that is, to confiscate Catholic-owned land and distribute it to army officers and other loyal Protestants. Catholic landowners were sent to "hell or Connacht," executed or deported west. For the rest of the century, Ireland's fate remained tied to Great Britain's. The reign of the Catholic King James II (1685–1688) briefly restored some Catholic power, but Parliament soon invited the Protestant William of Orange to replace James, whom he defeated in 1690 at the Battle of the Boyne. Having reasserted control, the British passed a series of "penal laws" designed to stamp out Catholicism. Although parish priests were allowed to remain, no new priests were allowed to enter the country; Catholic bishops were exiled and Catholic schools closed. Catholics were forbidden to own land, join the military, practice law, teach, hold public office, or serve on juries. Widespread passive resistance on the part of Catholics and Britain's selective enforcement kept the church alive; some Catholics even prospered in business and industry. Most, however, were impoverished and humiliated, identifying English law with injustice for Ireland.

By the eighteenth century, then, most of the themes of modern Irish history were in place. The country had its dispossessed Catholic majority and its English ruling elite, the Anglo-Irish, or the Ascendancy. In Ulster, Protestants descended from the Scottish and English working-classes constituted a third class, loyal to Britain but culturally estranged from the Ascendancy. Many of them, no happier about being taxed to support the Anglican Church of Ireland than their Catholic neighbors, were already immigrating to America. Those who stayed derived a distinctive identity from their conservative evangelical religion and the touchstones of their history: persecution in 1641 and victory under the Orange "King Billy" and at the Siege of Derry. Most Catholics developed an equally intransigent identity and an equal obsession with the defining moments and myths of their own history: Drogheda and Cromwell, the priest with a price on his head, saying mass in a pasture with only a rock for an altar.[29]

RESISTANCE

Representatives of all three ethnic groups formed the United Irishmen in 1791. Seeking universal male suffrage and an independent Republic, the movement claimed 300,000 members in 1798. Its most famous leader, Wolfe Tone, visited the United States and then moved to revolutionary France, returning to Ireland with a contingent of Dutch and French troops. Briefly successful, the rebellion was crushed and Tone committed suicide while awaiting execution; after a second rebellion, led by Robert Emmet, failed in 1803, the cause collapsed. In their time, the United Irishmen threatened to spread revolution from the United States and France to English soil. But they are remembered by moderates today for articulating the ideal of a unified, nonsectarian Irish democracy. Tone's stated goal, substituting "the common name of Irishman, in the place of the denominations of Protestant, Catholic, and Dissenter," still remains elusive.[30]

The United Irishmen proved that even Protestant Irishmen posed a danger to English rule. The government therefore proposed making Ireland part of the United Kingdom, abolishing its Parliament and in turn giving Irish voters the right to elect members to the House of Commons. In 1802, the Irish Parliament consented to this Act of Union, perhaps an ignoble response to bribes and deals, as Anglo-Irish tradition has it, or perhaps because its failure to allow Catholics to serve as members cost it their support. After all, although Catholics could not be elected to Parliament either in Dublin or Westminster, many of the penal laws had been abolished, and the expanding Catholic middle class had been able to vote since 1793. Daniel O'Connell, a successful lawyer, worked for full equality, or Catholic Emancipation. From 1824, his well-organized Catholic Association conducted a series of mass rallies, or "monster meetings." In 1828, O'Connell stood for election to the House of Commons, the first Irish Catholic to do so since the seventeenth century. Announcing that if elected he would refuse to take the customary oath abjuring Catholic beliefs as "idolatrous," he won two-thirds of the vote. The next year, King and Parliament recognized that O'Connell had made Catholic Emancipation inevitable.

THE POTATO FAMINE

Throughout the eighteenth century, the Irish diet was changing. Historians cannot provide exact figures, but the potato, first mentioned as growing in Ireland in 1606, gradually spread from the garden to the field and by the early nineteenth century had become the staple food of the rural poor.[31] A cheap food, potatoes are well adapted to wet, temperate climates, produce abundantly with limited cultivation, and require no processing. Seldom supplemented with more than herring or milk, the 10 to 14 pounds of potatoes adults consumed daily constituted a reasonably healthful diet, at least for the nondiabetic. As a result, the population increased dramatically, from an estimated 2 million in 1750 to more than 8 million in 1841.[32] All the same, periods of hunger were taken for granted; by early summer, the previous fall's harvest was depleted or unusable. Famines were as much a recurrent feature of medieval and early modern European life as they are of African life today, and scholars estimate that Ireland endured at least 30 major famines between 1200 and 1750. The famine of 1740–1741, although largely forgotten today, may have been Ireland's largest ever, killing well over a million people.[33]

In 1845, with Irish population at its record high, a blight that had decimated Belgian potato crops reached Ireland. Elsewhere it caused hardship; in Ireland, it caused disaster. The famine raged for four years; a third of the crop was lost the first year and three-fourths the second; in the third, little was sown; by the fourth, 1848, production was still only two-thirds of normal. The vast majority had no alternative food. Irish farmers grew other crops and raised livestock, but they had to sell them to pay rent; if they did not, they were evicted. The prospect of feeding and clothing as many as 6 million people, many sick and homeless, was overwhelming. A few landlords fed their tenants. In County Galway, the Gore-Booth family mortgaged its estate, assuming a debt that took almost 100 years to pay. Many gifts came from abroad, and groups such as the Quakers organized projects to make food and work available to the destitute. But many did nothing, and much that was done was useless. A civic committee might insist on selling low-cost food to the poor, for example, without considering that most had no money at all. American corn, a staple relief item, kept many people alive but was initially distributed in a coarse meal that caused indigestion, even stomach perforations. Make-work construction projects robbed starving workers of their last reserves of energy and paid too little to keep their families alive. Soups distributed at charity kitchens offered little nutrition. Workhouses crowded the desperate into comfortless barracks where diseases such as typhus reached epidemic proportions.

By the Famine's end, at least 1 million people were dead; at least as many others had migrated to England, North America, and Australia. By 1900, Ireland's population was half of what it had been in 1841. Even today, it is 3 million fewer than before the famine. The famine was the defining event of the century and shadowed political developments for generations. If, in the eighteenth century, many victims still regarded famine as a natural and inevitable catastrophe, by the nineteenth century the Irish saw it as a direct result of colonialism. The potato blight was an act of God, but human beings created the agricultural economy that kept bread, oatmeal, and vegetables out of the Irish diet. Moreover, they blamed the failures of relief on British contempt for the Irish and official reluctance to intervene in the free market. Some Britons expressed outrage at the massive suffering so close to home, but too many others lectured the Irish about the value of hard work and the dangers of welfare dependency. The satirical magazine *Punch* ran a series of cartoons mocking the victims, pointing up cruel stereotypes of the Irish as dirty, shiftless, and whining. British economists noted that Irish agriculture would produce higher profits when its tenant farmers and their crops were replaced by grazing sheep, and the *Times* of London was widely quoted as expressing satisfaction at the prospect that soon as few Irish would be found on the banks of the Shannon as there were Indians in Manhattan.[34] Depopulated, post-famine Ireland was a breeding group for revolutionaries and a ready-made justification for an isolationist, "Ireland-for-the-Irish" nationalism.

INSURRECTION

The survivors' rage could be channeled into violence. Today's Irish Republican Army (IRA) has its origins in the Fenians, or Irish Republican Brotherhood, a secret society simultaneously launched in Ireland and New York in 1858. Although the British government survived the Fenians' early activities, which included an 1866 invasion of Canada by some 24,000 Civil War veterans and an armed uprising in Dublin, they posed an ongoing threat. When three of their members were hanged in 1867 for having killed a police officer while attempting to free two Fenian prisoners, the men became posthumous heroes, the "Manchester Martyrs," in their homeland. A rabid offshoot of the Fenians, the Invincibles, outraged British public opinion in 1882 by murdering the newly appointed Irish chief secretary and his under-secretary in Phoenix Park. Later in the decade, the Fenians bombed the House of Commons and Big Ben in London. Relations between the United States and England became strained because people the British saw as terrorists were relying heavily on American money and their ability to promote violence in American newspapers.

Another revolt began in the nonviolent tradition of Daniel O'Connell. In 1879, after a series of bad harvests, Michael Davitt founded a Land League to lower rents and end evictions; its long-term goal was enabling small farmers to own the land they worked. Davitt had been jailed for Fenian activities, and to broaden the League's support base, he invited the Protestant Member of Parliament (MP), Charles Stuart Parnell, to serve as president. Parnell urged workers to shun anyone who refused to follow the League's principles, a nonviolent tactic soon known by the name of an early target, Charles C. Boycott.

All the same, violence accompanied many Land League protests; 1,000 British troops were required to protect the Ulster Orangemen Captain Boycott hired when his neighbors refused to work for him. In the fall of 1881, the level of violence led British Prime Minister William Gladstone to put Parnell in Dublin's Kilmainham jail. In return for his release, Parnell promised to support Gladstone's Land Act, a series of reforms that gradually turned the long-suffering Irish tenant into a small landowner.

WORKING IN THE SYSTEM: PARLIAMENTARY REFORM

By now enormously popular, Parnell turned his attention to securing greater independence; by 1886, he had convinced Gladstone to draft a Home Rule bill. Home Rule had been discussed for 15 years; there was general agreement that Ireland would remain in the United Kingdom but have its own Irish Parliament for domestic policy. Because Irish voters would continue to elect members to the British Parliament, there were questions about such matters as the influence of Irish MPs on England's internal affairs. Such issues helped to defeat Gladstone's first Home Rule bill, but the overriding obstacle was growing opposition in Protestant Ulster. The old anti-Catholicism, the fears of another massacre of Protestants such as the one that occurred in 1641, made any prospect of majority rule unacceptable: "Home Rule is Rome Rule." A second bill was defeated in 1893, and from 1912 to 1914 opposition to a third led Ulster to the verge of civil war. Vowing armed resistance, 100,000 men joined the Ulster Volunteer Force; in March 1914, 60 British cavalry officers resigned their commissions at Curragh rather than face being deployed to enforce Home Rule. In April, as customs officials and the army stood by, the Germans shipped 25,000 illegal rifles and 3 million rounds of ammunition to Unionists. In September 1914, the British prime minister declared Home Rule the law but suspended its implementation until the end of World War I, which had just broken out.

CULTURAL INDEPENDENCE

Parnell's successes leached support for violent methods, and the Fenian movement fell into disrepair. His political career effectively ended, however, in 1889, by a divorce suit brought by the husband of the woman, Katherine O'Shea, with whom he had a long-term affair. Parnell's fall entered the Irish nationalist myth, to be blamed on his betrayal by the Catholic bishops, the Catholic public, and the pusillanimous English liberals. With both strands of the independence movement weakened, the1890s began as the dark time captured in writer James Joyce's pictures of a lower-middle class Catholic proletariat condemned to the backwaters of history in Dublin, "the center of paralysis." The drive for independence, however, soon became channeled into culture. Douglas Hyde founded the Gaelic League in 1893, leading a movement for reviving the Irish language and "de-anglicizing" Ireland. Gaelic League members believed that the authentic original Ireland survived in the West, so that traveling to Connemara or the Aran Islands became a form of time travel, a spiritual quest. Led by Lady August Gregory and poet W. B. Yeats, writers and artists of the Irish Renaissance saw in the ancient Celtic world a distinctive and valuable outlook that the invaders had stifled and were eager to revive the old heroes, the spirit of an undefeated past. The Abbey Theatre, founded in 1899, produced John Synge's *Playboy of the Western World,* Yeats and Gregory's *Cathleen ni Houlihan,* and other plays that celebrated the vitality of Irish speech and wit, or retold Celtic myths with the suggestion that an Ireland without English rulers offered a model worth imitating. The Gaelic Athletic Association promoted its distinctive sports, Gaelic football and hurling, and refused membership to those who played "foreign" sports such as soccer and rugby.

BACK TO REVOLUTION: SINN FEIN, THE IRISH CITIZEN'S ARMY, AND THE IRA

Although the Gaelic League was not a political organization, it created a climate in which nationalist politics could flourish. In 1905, a disparate group of people, some pacifists or feminists, some veterans of Parnell's parliamentary party or the Irish Republican Brotherhood, formed a new organization called Sinn Fein, "ourselves alone." This new nationalist party promoted economic independence and urged passive resistance to British institutions, advising MPs to shun Parliament and all citizens to refuse to recognize the British courts. In the same period, James Connolly was organizing the Irish Socialist Republican Party, the Irish Transport and General Workers' Union (ITGWU), and the Irish Textile Workers' Union. Connolly led a successful dock workers' strike in Belfast in 1911, and by 1913 major Dublin employers were frightened enough to order workers to leave the ITGWU or be dismissed. The union called for other workers to go on strike, thus turning the Dublin lockout into a major crisis that left 20,000 workers idle, Connolly and other leaders in jail, and police and strikers battling each other. To protect workers, the union organized the Irish Citizen's Army (ICA), and although the lockout ended in defeat for the union, the ICA survived as a small but well-organized force disposed to favor Irish independence.

Overshadowed for years, the Irish Republican Brotherhood and its Fenian tradition revived in 1907, when Tom Clarke, who had spent 15 years in prison for taking part in the Fenian bombings of the 1880s, moved back to Dublin. Clarke's shop became a meeting place for militants, and in 1910 his newspaper, *Irish Freedom*, became a voice for revolt. But Ulster's gun-running volunteers also emboldened Republicans who founded the Irish Volunteers in 1914. That an article calling on nationalists to emulate the Ulster Volunteers first appeared in the Gaelic League's newspaper, *An Claidheamh Soluis,* indicates the extent to which the cultural and political movements had become identified. Like their Ulster counterparts, the Volunteers went to Germany for arms, smuggling in some 1500 rifles. But when World War I broke out, most of the Irish Volunteers' 160,000 members, like the Ulster Volunteers, supported the British war effort.[35]

THE EASTER RISING

Although public opinion in Ireland echoed this support, the elements of successful rebellion were in place: real political grievances, a poor economy, a newly asserted sense of cultural identity, a well-organized nationalist political party, and several small but disciplined paramilitaries with access to weapons. By 1916, the Irish Volunteers, reduced to perhaps 2,000–3,000 in 1914, had grown to15,000 members. Key Volunteers formed a military council with James Connolly of the Irish Citizen's Army and the Irish Republican Brotherhood's Tom Clarke to plan an uprising. Despite the scuttling of a German ship bringing arms and a last-minute counter-order from the Volunteers' commander-in-chief, on Easter Monday, April 24, 1916, 1,200 rebels seized the General Post Office in central Dublin and proclaimed an Irish Republic. The Easter Rising was suppressed five days later, leaving 132 British soldiers, 64 rebels, and 230 civilians dead.[36] Crowds heckled surviving rebels as they were led off to Kilmainham jail; most of the Irish public seemed to share the government's view that the Easter Rising was treasonous, a stab in the back when Britain was suffering terrible casualties in France.

Yet what seemed a humiliating defeat in 1916 turned into a full-fledged and widely supported war for independence three years later. It may be that in retrospect, the ability of 1,200 Volunteers to inflict meaningful casualties encouraged the view that a more widely based insurrection could be successful. Although by the standards of wartime, executing 15 rebel leaders seemed to many British people a proportionate and just response, it mobilized the Irish community both at home and in the United States. In addition to Tom Clarke and James Connolly, the dead rebels included two poets, a schoolteacher, and the husband of Maud Gonne, a strikingly beautiful actress well known for her support of radical causes. One of the best-known poems of William B. Yeats, "Easter 1916," meditates on the transformation of the rebels by their courage

Portrait of Padraic Pearse, one of the leaders of the Easter Rising executed in 1916 by the British.

and violent deaths: "a terrible beauty is born." Sinn Fein, which had advocated nonviolent methods, elected a veteran of the Easter Rising, Eamon de Valera, as its president. In the general elections of 1918, Sinn Fein won 73 of 105 Irish seats in Parliament. Declaring loyalty to the republic proclaimed in 1916, Sinn Fein MPs refused to take their seats in Westminster and established their own legislature, the Dail Eireann, in 1919. They adopted a constitution, established a system of courts, and once more de Valera was elected president.

THE ANGLO-IRISH WAR

The British declared Sinn Fein illegal, and violence increased on both sides. Led by Michael Collins, the Irish Republic's army, the IRA, conducted

National Army troops shell the occupied Four Courts in the early days of the Irish Civil War.

a campaign of ambushes, bombings, arson, and assassination. When the Royal Irish Constabulary was overwhelmed, the British called in the army and created a new auxiliary police, soon nicknamed for the color of their uniforms. "Black and Tan" house raids and reprisals became a byword for brutality among civilians, strengthening resistance, and by mid-1921 the British began negotiations with the self-proclaimed Republic. Although the Anglo-Irish Treaty, which the Dail ratified in 1922, may well have represented the best compromise available, it left bitter divisions in Ireland. "Die-hard" IRA, refusing to accept the loyalty oath to the English Crown that the Treaty required, plunged the new Free State into a civil war, which it won, but only after wide-scale internment and other repressive measures had provided new resentments that would bedevil it for two generations. And although the Free State made no effort to annex Northern Ireland, it claimed the right to govern the whole island until 1998.

IRELAND DIVIDED: NORTHERN IRELAND

Partition was always unpopular with Catholics, and the subsequent conduct of Northern Ireland's government only exacerbated religious divisions.

Gerrymandering and a property requirement created a one-party "Protestant Parliament and a Protestant State," as James Craig, Northern Ireland's "architect" and first Prime Minister, proudly declared.[37] The police and civil service were largely closed to Catholics; discrimination in private employment and housing went unchecked, and the Catholic poverty rate remained higher than the Protestant. The divergence of Northern Ireland and the Free State seemed all the more marked during 1939–1945, when the Free State remained neutral and the North followed the rest of the United Kingdom into World War II. More than 1,000 people died in the German bombing in Belfast; the British military presence included new military airfields, as well as servicemen and women; and, by the end of the war, 300,000 U.S. military had also been stationed in Northern Ireland. Britain did acknowledge political realities by refusing to introduce the draft in Northern Ireland. In the end, 38,000 men and women from Northern Ireland enlisted. They were joined by 43,000 men and women from the Free State who also served in the British military.[38]

THE FREE STATE

Although the Free State was always a democracy, with proportional representation, an elected parliament, and freedom to exercise one's own religion, it became more Catholic and conservative as time passed. By 1937, when de Valera's revised Constitution was adopted, the "special position" of the Catholic Church was explicitly evoked, and Catholic doctrine on such matters as divorce, birth control, and censorship were matters of law. As Taoiseach, or prime minister, from 1932 to 1948, de Valera shaped a vision of the Free State as Gaelic, independent, and rural. As the Gaelic League had done earlier, he fostered the identification of the authentically Irish with the poor and the rural; unlike the Gaelic League, he also identified it with Catholicism. De Valera's Ireland shunned communism and cut-throat capitalism equally, offering "frugal comfort" to "a people living the life that men should live."[39] De Valera's vision discouraged modernization, innovation, and collaboration with outsiders, thus alienating many 1916–1922 revolutionaries. Although de Valera's Ireland remained a poor country, conditions improved for many people and income levels were closer to equality than they were in 2005.

Independence became isolationism when de Valera's Ireland opted for neutrality in 1939. Not only did the English see war against fascism as a moral imperative, but its furious prime minister, Winston Churchill, believed he had a right to Irish support. Ireland's chief naval ports had remained under British control until 1938, and their loss multiplied British sea and air casualties; the danger of Germans using the defenseless Free State as a staging area for invasion was real enough. On the other hand, unwillingness to risk draft riots in the North suggests that Churchill realized that an Allied Free State would be at best undependable, and in the end the Free State may have been more helpful as a friendly neutral. However willing to turn a blind eye to British intelligence agents, the Irish government publicly practiced strict neutrality, even limiting news coverage so as to avoid appearing biased toward either side. Stories of bright lights and abundant butter made Dublin idyllic in Londoners' eyes, but neutrality brought hardships, if not the sufferings of the blitz. As prewar coal and petroleum were exhausted, automobiles became useless and the few trains ran at a snail's pace. With turf virtually the only fuel, homes and offices were often cold. At one low point, the tea ration was reduced to an ounce a week and even butter was down to six ounces.[40]

POSTWAR IRELAND: THE END OF ISOLATION

Wartime neutrality kept the nation isolated for a time; when Ireland proposed joining the United Nations in 1946, the Soviet Union vetoed her membership, which was delayed until 1955. In 1949, citing a desire for "national self-respect," a newly elected coalition government officially withdrew the state from the British Commonwealth, renaming it the Republic of Ireland.[41] The postwar Irish government sent significant economic aid to war-torn Europe but refused to participate in the North Atlantic Treaty Organization. Nor were politics progressive at home. In 1951, the minister of Health, Noel Browne, proposed free medical care for mothers and children. The Catholic Church, arguing that the family, not the state, should provide for children, defeated the scheme, an incident still frequently cited as the embodiment of the Irish Republic's deference to Rome. The economy was equally stagnant, and by 1961, with 400,000 of the Republic's citizens living abroad, only 3 million remained at home.[42] In 1958, the deputy head of government, Sean Lemass, announced a plan for economic expansion. Ireland would increase jobs by modernizing its industry, developing expertise in science and technology, and encouraging foreign trade and investment.

Under Lemass's leadership as Taoiseach (1959–1966), De Valera's isolationist Ireland developed a more internationalist outlook. In 1960–1964, the Republic sent its Defense Forces troops on a UN peacekeeping mission to the Congo, where a member of the Department of Foreign Affairs, Conor Cruise O'Brien, was serving as the UN Secretary General's representative. The Republic's admission to the European Economic Community (since 1992 the European Union) in 1973 similarly brought increased cultural and political ties to the outside world. Membership also, of course, increased European investment; the EU also provided loans to help the country develop its infrastructure. Modernizing roads, for example, had direct economic benefits, but it also created a more mobile society. By 1997, when a recent president of the Republic, Mary Robinson, became United Nations Commissioner for Human Rights, the Irish were respected for humanitarian activities around the globe.

PROSPERITY AND CHANGE

European Union members elect representatives to the European Parliament, which is responsible for making EU laws that the European Court of Justice adjudicates. Some of these policies are strictly economic, such as the legislation that created the euro, which the Republic adopted in 1999. Others, such as legislation on workers' rights, move into issues of social justice. Since its inception, the EU has subscribed to the UN's 1948 Universal Declaration of Human Rights. Its European Court of Human Rights has jurisdiction over questions of whether member nations are in compliance with this document. After 1973, the EU became a major player in Irish law, and as the European norm was almost always more liberal than the local standard, EU pressure created social change. Equal pay for women, gay rights, and contraception were all issues on which the Irish acted more rapidly because of European pressure. In some cases, such as capital punishment, change was uncontroversial. Although the Republic retained the death penalty until 1990, it had not executed anyone since 1954. On other issues, the Republic resisted change; an EU exemption permits Ireland to ban abortion, although the Court of Human Rights ruled that women must be free to travel to countries where abortion is available.

THE 1990S

The massive changes of the past two decades have called for dynamic leadership, which has sometimes been found. Northern Ireland's Troubles threatened repercussions in the Republic for more than 30 years. For example, Loyalist bombs killed 25 people in Dublin and Monaghan in the early 1970s. The government generally tried to advocate for Northern Ireland's Catholics, whom it still technically regarded as part of its constituency, without appearing to sanction IRA violence. Most citizens of the Republic sympathized with Catholics in the North but had no desire to be drawn into a war. Thus, although the British public regarded the Republic as a safe haven for terrorists, the government's cooperation with the British in hunting down fugitive IRA members led some nationalists to accuse it of betraying its revolutionary heritage. Successive Irish governments played a key role in negotiations that led to the Belfast Agreement, which commits the Republic and Northern

Ireland to establishing "north-south institutions," to promote cross-border cooperation on issues such as the environment.

Ireland's astonishing economic successes in the late 1990s owe much to government planning, and to the recognition that the right tax incentives and a well-educated English speaking work force would prove irresistible to high-tech companies. Fintan O'Toole, in his *Ex-Isle of Erin* (1996), portrays the new global Ireland as a liberated society, freed of its insularity, its repressive religious tradition, and its obsession with past suffering. And surely no outsider could begrudge contemporary Ireland its elements of hopefulness, its accomplishments, its transformation from days when its chief export, as the Irish used to say, was its own children. Yet many others believe that rapid economic and social change have caused, not just accompanied, equally rapid economic polarization and increasing crime and drug abuse. With all its limitations, de Valera's Ireland offered its citizens a shared identity, a sense of common purpose, that is now lost. Will future generations of Irish people be virtually indistinguishable from Americans or New Zealanders? In the recent book, *Reinventing Ireland: Culture, Society, and the Global Economy* (2002), Peadar Kirby, Luke Gibbons, and Michael Cronin speculate about "re-inventing Ireland," noting the need for Irish people to hold onto the best impulses of the past. In particular, they note that de Valera's vision of "frugal comfort" suggests a welcome alternative to unchecked consumerism, and that remembering the famine might lead to Mary Robinson's passion for human rights rather than the long cherishing of an inherited grievance. In this view, the recent growth of Irish-only schools outside the traditional Gaeltacht, or the enthusiasm young Irish people show for Gaelic football, suggests that an imaginative and creative re-envisioning of cultural identity might well take place.

THE TROUBLES

Whether Northern Ireland can re-imagine itself is an even greater question. "The Protestant state for a Protestant People" spent 30 years at war. Whether today's relative peace can endure depends on the ability of the new government established by the 1998 Belfast Agreement to persuade its diverse population to identity with it. Changes began when Britain's post-war Labour government brought socialized medicine and free university education to Northern Ireland, allowing more Catholics to join the middle class. Discrimination in voting, housing, and employment continued, however, and Catholics were no more ready to identify with the government and dominant culture than they had been in 1922. Most regarded the police, the Royal Ulster Constabulary (RUC), as hostile enforcers of Protestant rule. In 1970,

90 percent were Protestant, as were all members of the B-specials, a police auxiliary dating from Black and Tan days. Catholic students, encouraged by the success of the U.S. Civil Rights movement, organized a similar peaceful campaign for equal rights; and the prime minister, Terence O'Neill, offered limited reform. Hard-line Unionists, however, forced him to resign in April 1969. Protests drew increasing violence from Protestant extremists, with the B-specials and even the RUC joining in. In August, a terrible week of rioting, arson, and murder raged through the undefended Catholic community in Belfast, whose residents mocked the divided and largely paralyzed IRA as the "I ran away." The British responded by sending in the army, which the community welcomed as protectors. The IRA, shocked into action, recruited hundreds of new members, who quickly began assassinations, bombings, and kidnappings. The "Troubles" had begun in earnest.

In August 1971, the prime minister, Brian Faulkner, introduced internment without trial for suspected terrorists. Poor intelligence left most of the leadership free while subjecting the marginal and even the innocent to what the European Court of Human Rights later called "inhuman and degrading treatment."[43] The Troubles had killed 30 people before August; another 143 were added by the end of the year. In January, 1972, on Bloody Sunday, British paratroopers fired on unarmed civil rights marchers in Derry, leaving 14 protestors dead. In March, when Faulkner refused to cede the British control of security, the British government suspended Stormont, Northern Ireland's Parliament, and imposed direct rule. By that point the IRA campaign was at its height, and Protestant paramilitaries, the Ulster Defense Association, the Ulster Freedom Fighters, and the Ulster Volunteer Force, were added to the conflict. That year, the worst of the Troubles, 467 people died; 25 years later, the toll had risen to 3,200.

Under Britain's direct rule, the remaining legal disabilities of Northern Ireland's Catholics ended, but the Troubles did not. Ulster Unionists were adamant about remaining in the United Kingdom. Republicans campaigned for a unified Ireland. The British government spent billions maintaining its army in Northern Ireland, supporting the North's troubled economy, and protecting itself from lethal IRA bombing campaigns at home. In 1973, the British invited the Republic to join negotiations about the North's future, and approved a "power-sharing" executive to include moderate Protestants and Catholics. Cooperation with the Republic, however, enraged many Protestants, who responded with a massive strike that shut down this fledgling effort to restore some local autonomy. In 1985, however, the British Prime Minister, Margaret Thatcher, signed an agreement with the Taoiseach, Garret FitzGerald, for ongoing formal talks. This time, Unionist protest proved futile. In 1993, the two governments outlined a framework for the peace process similar to the 1973 power-sharing

Belfast's Peace Line, where barbed wire and steel separate working-class Protestant and Catholic neighborhoods. © CAIN, http://cain.ulst.ac.uk/ photographs, 2000.

executive. Although the move was repugnant to Unionists, this time Sinn Fein was included, a pragmatic recognition of its importance to a large minority of the Catholic community and its increasingly peaceful platform.

Another change was that the new U.S. President, Bill Clinton, stepped up U.S. support for the peace talks, sending the respected former senator, George Mitchell, as a negotiator. After false starts and setbacks, including a 1994 cease-fire broken by the IRA bombing of London's Canary Wharf in 1996, serious talks began with a second cease-fire, in July 1997. On April 10, 1998, the parties announced the Good Friday, or Belfast, Agreement. Northern Ireland would remain in the United Kingdom until the majority of its citizens voted to leave; the Irish government would renounce its traditional claims to the six Ulster counties; and a new Northern Ireland Assembly would have significant local, or "devolved" power, although Britain would reassert direct rule by suspending the Assembly if it proved unable to function. The Agreement was ratified by voters on both sides of the border, with 94 percent approval in the Republic and 71 percent in the North. A period of euphoria followed, with enhanced foreign investment, tourism, and new prosperity. Although these hopeful trends continue, the major terrorist organizations have kept up brutal "punishment beatings" in their own communities, and splinter groups have committed such atrocities as the 1998 bombing in Omagh that killed 29 people.

Northern Ireland's new government is also beleaguered by the old ethnic divisions. David Trimble, who had led the Unionist Party in the peace talks, became First Minister in the new government, but came under pressure from hard-liners in his own party. In October 2002, the British suspended Northern Ireland's First Assembly for the second time in its short life, and in 2004, with suspension still in effect, voters were asked to selected members for a future Assembly. Results showed extremists making gains in both communities. The fire-breathing Ian Paisley's Democratic Unionist Party overwhelmed Trimble's Unionists, and Sinn Fein outnumbered the moderate Socialist Democratic Labor Party. In July 2005, with its leadership polarized, the Assembly remains closed. Once more, as a British prime minister and an Irish Taoiseach try to broker a workable government for Northern Ireland, the citizens of this prosperous and technologically advanced society realize that they have not yet escaped the shadow of what, as long ago as 1922, Winston Churchill labeled their nation's "ancient quarrel."

NOTES

1. Terry Eagleton, *The Truth about the Irish* (New York: St. Martin's, 2000), 41. Ireland is ranked 18 and the United States 20 in a list of "income inequality"; Japan, Taiwan, and Korea ranked higher, as did most northern European countries. The study measures the ratio of the income of the top 20 percent to the income of the bottom 20 percent. Peadar Kirby, "Inequality and Poverty in Ireland: Clarifying Social Objectives," in *Rich and Poor: Perspectives on Tackling Inequality in Ireland*, ed. Sara Cantillon et al. (Dublin: Oak Tree, 2001), 1–35.

2. Statistics from Sandra Gowran, *Counted Out: Challenging Poverty and Social Exclusion*, City of Dublin Curriculum Development Unit (Dublin: Folens, 2002), 3.

3. John H. Johnson, *The Human Geography of Ireland* (New York: John Wiley, 1994), 24.

4. Johnson, 19.

5. Gordon L. Herries Davies, "The Concept of Ireland," in *The Shaping of Ireland: The Geographical Perspective,* ed. William Nolan (Dublin: Mercier, 1986), 13–27. The geological information in the paragraph that follows comes from Davies.

6. Information on bogs can be found at http://www.irelandstory.com.

7. See Desmond Gillmor, "Land, Work and Recreation," in *The Irish Country-side: Landscape, Wildlife, History, People,* ed. Desmond Gillmor (Dublin: Wolfhound, 1989), 161–195.

8. The information on Northern Ireland that follows comes from Derek Polley, *Home Ground: A Geography of Northern Ireland* (Newtownards, NI: Colour Books, 1999).

9. Http://www.bbc.co.uk/history/timelines/ni/econ_changes.html.

10. Figures come from the Northern Ireland Tourist Board's Web site at http://www.nitb.com.

11. Eagleton, 41.

12. Department of Agriculture and Food, Republic of Ireland, http://www.agriculture.gov.ie

13. Sharon Pagatchnik, "Irish Church Attendance Down." AP 25 September 2003. http://www.phillyburbs.com.

14. Brian Lalor, ed., *The Encyclopedia of Ireland* (New Haven: Yale University Press, 2003), 786.

15. The statistic on video game ownership comes from Eagleton, 37. All other statistics come from the 2002 census or from an official Web site established in 2004, when Ireland was serving a six-month term in the "presidency" of the European Union. See http://www.eu2004.ie.

16. Tony White, *Investing in People: Higher Education in Ireland from 1960 to 2000* (Dublin: Institute of Public Administration, 2001), 1.

17. White, 248.

18. Jim MacLaughlin, *Travellers and Ireland: Whose Country? Whose History?* (Cork: Cork University Press, 1995), 42–43; Yale [encyclopedia, p. 1071–1072].

19. MacLaughlin, 54–55.

20. Martin Collins "Travellers: Culture and Identity," 70 in *Emerging Irish Identities,* Proceedings of a seminar held at Trinity College Dublin, 27 November 1999, ed. Ronit Lentin, 2000.

21. Suzanne Smith and Fidèle Mutwarasibo, African Cultural Project, Dublin http://africansmagazine.com/africanseire.html.

22. Brian Fanning, *Racism and Social Change in the Republic of Ireland* Manchester: Manchester University Press, 2002), 1.

23. Paul Cullen, *Refugees and Asylum Seekers in Ireland* (Cork: Cork University Press, 2000), 49–50.

24. "Spotlight on Immigration," BBC News (15 May 2002). http://news.bbc.co.uk/2/hi/europe/1986739.stm.

25. Edna Longley and Declan Kiberd. *Multi-Culturalism: The View from the Two Irelands* (Cork: Cork University Press, 2001), 49–50.

26. Ronit Lentin, "Racializing the Other," in *Emerging Irish Identities*, ed. Ronit Lentin.

27. Bill Rolston and Michael Shannon. *Encounters: How Racism Came to Ireland* (Belfast: Beyond the Pale, 2002), 1, 2.

28. Richard B. Finnegan, and Edward T. McCarron, *Ireland: Historical Echoes, Contemporary Politics* (Boulder, Col.: Westview, 2000), 10.

29. "Mass rocks" associated with penal times recur in Irish legend and literature, and are frequently pointed out to visitors. Although open air masses were sometimes celebrated in poor parishes, the penal laws did not "prohibit ordinary parochial worship"; churches remained open, and "if they have any basis" rock masses must have been said in the "repression of the Cromwellian era." S. J. Connolly, *The Oxford Companion to Irish History,* 2nd ed. (Oxford: Oxford University Press, 2002), 368.

30. James Lydon, *The Making of Ireland: From Ancient Times to the Present* (London: Routledge, 1998), 271.

31. Connolly, *Oxford Companion,* 480.

32. Connolly, *Oxford Companion,* 478.

33. Connolly, *Oxford Companion,* 194.

34. Quoted in, for example, Seumas MacManus, *The Story of the Irish Race,* rev. ed. (Old Greenwich, Conn.: Devin-Adair, 1921), 610, but without a page and date citation. Although the tenor of this remark is consistent with one school of British thinking about the famine, I have not been able to locate it in the *Times.*

35. Connolly, *Oxford Companion,* 282.

36. Connolly, *Oxford Companion,* 514.

37. Lydon, 393.

38. Connolly, *Oxford Companion,* 533.

39. From de Valera's St. Patrick's Day radio address to the nation, 1943. Searc's Web Guide to Twentieth-Century Ireland. http://www.searcs-web.com/dev.html.

40. Ian S. Wood, *Ireland During the Second World War* (London: Caxton Editions, 2002), 78.

41. Lydon, 385.

42. Lydon, 391.

43. Connolly, *Oxford Companion,* 273.

2

Religion and Thought

WHEN THE BRITISH LEFT THE IRISH Free State in 1922, they left behind a country literally divided by religion. The Ulster Protestants who fought to keep themselves from becoming a minority in a newly independent Ireland saw their religion as a defining feature of Northern Ireland. James Craig, its first prime minister, famously described his legislature as a "Protestant Parliament for a Protestant people," a characterization that excluded the Catholic third of Northern Ireland's population. Gerrymandering, a property requirement for voters, and overt job and housing discrimination all worked to keep political power in Protestant hands. Catholics were free to practice their religion, but the new statelet made sure that overall they remained relatively poor and alienated. It was hard for Catholics to feel at home in a country whose major civic holiday, the Twelfth of July, celebrated the Protestant victory over their ancestors at the Battle of the Boyne.

In the new Free State, Catholics were an even more overwhelming majority; always more than 91 percent of the population, with their numbers increasing as British officials and members of the old Anglo-Irish Ascendancy left. Protestants, Jews, and others were free to practice their religion, but the ethos of the new nation became increasingly Gaelic and Catholic. The Constitution acknowledged the "special position" of the Catholic Church as the religion of the majority, and Catholic views on divorce, contraception, and censorship became enshrined in civic law. Many of the state's institutions—hospitals, orphanages, schools, homes for unwed mothers—were entrusted to Catholic religious orders that operated without effective state supervision. Although the nation's small religious minorities were relatively affluent, it was hard for people who were not Catholic to feel at home in a state whose prime minister, on assuming office, sent a message to the Pope, expressing "a desire to . . . strive for the attainment of a social order in Ireland based on Christian principles."[1]

Thus, although neither part of Ireland had an official, tax-supported religion, in practice the border divided two "confessional states," where religion mingled freely with politics and law. In both cases, the dominant tone was conservative, at times reactionary. Protestant and Catholic Ireland, in their zeal to defend against each other, seemed compelled to assume the most distinctive, even extreme versions of their practice and theology. When Northern Ireland's Catholics organized to demand their civil rights, Protestant Loyalists responded violently. In the next few years, the British government granted all of the protesters' basic demands: equal voting rights, equal access to housing and jobs; but Northern Ireland was already plunged into guerilla war. Talk of "Catholic terrorists" and "Protestant violence" suggested that the North was reliving the Hundred Years' War at a time when most European countries were secularizing. Some, like Martin Dillon, author of *God and the Gun* (1998), blamed the churches for the fighting; others, like the activist Bernadette Devlin McAliskey, argued that the real issues were economic. Whatever the case, for a long time religious questions have had an urgency for Irish life, both North and South, that they do not have for the English or the French. To understand Irish culture, the depth and complexity of a religious heritage that produces such intense passions must be understood.

CATHOLIC IRELAND

In the Middle Ages, the Irish Church was occasionally put at odds with Rome; the Celtic refusal to follow the Roman lead in setting the date for Easter exercised the Venerable Bede when he wrote the first English history in the eighth century. Early medieval Irish stories and poems give us a glimpse of monastic life as rich, satisfying, and fully human: a monk struggling to pay attention in church, or writing poetry in companionable silence with his cat: "hunting mice is his delight/hunting words I sit all night."[2] Married priests were commonplace in Ireland until the twelfth century, a practice that evoked papal condemnation. Well into the nineteenth century, Irish Catholicism retained a degree of separation from Rome. Only formidable Archbishop Paul Cullen, in the post-famine years, could impose Roman discipline on the Irish church. The distinctive Roman collar, which marked priests for more than a century, was a small but telling innovation. Mass attendance increased, the Church dominated education, and Irish Catholicism became synonymous with a preoccupation with heaven and hell, chastity, and discipline.

Theologically, of course, the Irish Catholic Church was linked to the universal Roman Catholic church headed by the pope. The central beliefs stated in the creed, the Latin liturgy of the Mass, and the body of scripture considered binding on believers, was the same everywhere; so were the seven sacraments. Throughout the world, the Eucharist, the ritual consecration of the bread and wine into the body and blood of Christ, was the Church's central rite, and Catholics insisted that Jesus Christ was really present in this sacrament. The church's hierarchical organization, its orders of celibate nuns, priests, and monks, was replicated everywhere it went. Some of its devotional practices, such as saying the rosary, went with them. Yet national and regional differences also emerged as Catholicism adapted to local customs. National heroes became venerated saints, as did some local gods and goddesses. Pagan practices, such as lighting a yule log at the winter solstice, became Christmas customs. Theologians trained at one national seminary might be more preoccupied with the forbidding side of Catholicism, its emphasis on obedience to authority or the sinfulness of human nature; theologians at another might lay more stress on compassion, forgiveness, and the need to relieve poverty and suffering.

Thus, although the Catholic Church appears the model of a top-down global organization whose members subscribe to a unified belief system, Irish Catholicism has always been culturally distinctive. As seen, the identification of the Catholic Church with nationalism strengthened its appeal. While many Europeans slipped into a nominal Catholicism, acknowledged only on special occasions such as baptisms and weddings, religion permeated daily life in the Republic. Even the poorest homes contained an image of the Sacred Heart or the Blessed Virgin, a statue of the Infant Jesus of Prague or of St. Martin de Pores. A central Celtic cross dominated many villages; shrines appeared at many roadsides. When Heinrich Böll, the German Catholic author, visited Limerick one October day in the 1950s, he was puzzled to find the shops closed. He discovered that the whole town was celebrating the Feast of the Holy Rosary, a day that even then passed unmarked in most of the Catholic world. At the annual All-Ireland Football Finals, athletes and spectators joined in the national anthem *and* the hymn "Faith of Our Fathers"; the Archbishop of Cashel, patron of the Gaelic Athletic Association, threw out the first ball; "both practices ceased in 1979."[3] Attendance at Mass was the highest in the world; in 1985, close to 90 percent of the Irish reported going to church at least once a week.[4]

Almost every well-known writer who grew up in this Ireland emphasizes its strong streak of Jansenism, a particularly scrupulous, even puritanical, movement that flourished in seventeenth-century France. Those who favor theological explanations note that during penal times many Irish priests were

trained in French seminaries, where they imbibed Jansenist views of humanity's wickedness and God's wrath. Those who favor economic explanations
point to the need to postpone marriage, even keep some of the population
from marrying at all, that rose from economic stagnation and the desire to
pass the family farm intact to the oldest son. Whatever the reason, Irish society developed a reputation for sexual repressiveness and inhibition. Many
remember the times with great bitterness; Irish novelist Edna O'Brien told
American novelist Philip Roth that "in a lot of ways I feel a cripple. The
body was as sacred as a tabernacle and everything a potential occasion of
sin." Tony Flannery, a contemporary priest, still active in his church, reports
a similar experience of childhood in a home where "sex was never mentioned
or discussed." Strict censorship kept references to sex out of newspapers and
films, and he grew up profoundly ignorant of basic facts. Yet, "a great many
of my attitudes to sex were associated with guilt." After all, "Catholic moral
theology ... asserted that even the slightest sexual thought, as long as it was
'entertained' or 'indulged in' deliberately, was enough to condemn a person
to Hell."[5]

POPULAR CATHOLICISM

Catholic life in Ireland includes many popular customs, some variations on
widespread practices, such as going on pilgrimage, and others more unusual.
Such customs are not necessarily endorsed or advocated by the official church;
they continue because people find them satisfying. As elsewhere in the Catholic
world, visions of the Blessed Virgin are a staple. As elsewhere, they embarrass the hierarchy. Although the Vatican has certified a handful of "authentic
apparitions," usually years later, no Catholic is required to believe in any of
them.[6] The most celebrated Irish apparition was the appearance of Mary,
St. Joseph, and St. John, on the gable of the parish church at Knock, County
Mayo, in 1879. Fifteen villagers stood in the rain saying the Rosary for two
hours until the vision vanished. As the story spread, thousands flocked to the
site and miraculous healings were reported. In 1936, an official church investigation gave Our Lady of Knock qualified approval. Without certifying the
apparition as authentic, they noted that the witnesses were credible and that
"there was nothing contrary to faith" in the story.[7]

It might be expected that such a cult would prosper among poorly educated
people and wane in contemporary times. In 1976, however, the Irish Tourist Board developed Knock as a tourist site, because some three-quarters of
a million people had already visited it. Pope John Paul II's centenary visit in
1979 brought 400,000 people in a single day and boosted the site's popularity
afterward. Today there is an international airport at Knock; the shrine's Web

page lists 48 facilities, ranging from a basilica and folk museum to hotels and camping grounds, with a special hostel and a care center for disabled visitors. During the April–October pilgrimage season, guided tours are offered twice daily, and visitors may watch films in the Prayer Guidance Center. Advocates claim a million visitors annually; and even if that figure is exaggerated, it suggests how successfully the Irish Church has updated the pilgrimage, preserving its Chaucerian mix of tourism and spiritual quest.[8] Participation in the more rigorous penitential pilgrimages to Lough Derg in remote Donegal, which require three days of fasting and a sleepless night spent in prayer, declined by about half during the 1990s, but in 2001 there were still 11,079 pilgrims.[9] Each of these pilgrims performs nine "stations," walking barefoot around the rocky saints' "beds" (perhaps ruins of cells in an ancient monastery) while praying.

Similar ritual circular walks, called "patterns," are associated with numerous other holy sites, including wells. It is thought that holy wells predate Christianity, going back to a time when Celts believed that springs flowed up the earth from the "other world" where the gods lived. At the four turning points of the Celtic year (roughly February 1, May 1, August 1, and November 1), whole communities went to the wells to drink the water, bathe in it, and participate in the patterns. Catholic communities simply changed

Barefoot with his arms extended in the form of a cross, a contemporary pilgrim prays in a ritual prescribed for generations, Lough Derg, 2002. © *Irish Times*.

the associations of the local well, often giving it the name of a saint.[10] A certain pagan mischievousness survived for centuries. In 1660, the bishop of Tuam warned against "dancing, flute-playing, bands of music, riotous revels and other abuses in visiting wells and other holy places"[11] The wells were thought to have healing powers, and one rubbed the affected part of an invalid's body with a strip of cloth, a "clootie," and tied it to the branch of a nearby holy tree in hopes that the illness would leave the person's body and remain in the clootie. A contemporary group called Living Water has mapped the location of approximately 1,350 holy wells in an effort to preserve them. But the practice of tying clooties or praying at holy wells has by no means died out. Donegal's Doon Well continues to draw visitors, who slip off their shoes to repeat a prescribed prayer and carry its water home in plastic jugs. In 2004, its holy tree is not only festooned with rosaries, but with T-shirts and CDs.

Nor is it simply a matter of clinging to tradition; more recent times have produced their own popular manifestations. Most remarkable was 1985's moving statue of Ballinspittle. Throughout an unusually wet and cold summer, tens of thousands of visitors flocked to a statue of Mary fixed in concrete, her head surrounded by a halo of electric lights. Thousands of eyewitnesses reported seeing the figure move; many thought the face changed back and forth from that of the virgin to that of a young rabbi. At peak times, as many

At Doon Well, the traditional clooties and rosaries are joined by CDs and T-shirts that belong to the sick, 2004. Courtesy of Linda Sichenze.

as 40,000 visitors arrived daily, forcing the village to put in a one-way street system to cope with traffic. The noted writer Colm Toibin compiled a collection of essays, *Seeing Is Believing: Moving Statues in Ireland* (1985), which demonstrates the nation's preoccupation with Ballinspittle. Peter Prendergast, the government press spokesman, announced that "three-quarters of the country is laughing heartily"; the other quarter, presumably, were making pilgrimages or going there to write sociological studies.[12] The intellectual and artistic elite weighed in. The novelist Francis Stuart, for example, pointed out that only in a deeply materialistic age would the "derangement of solid objects" be taken for "proof of the existence of the supernatural."[13] The feminist Nell McCafferty, never one to mince words, wrote a dismissive piece called "Virgin on the Rocks" (1985) in which, among other things, she accused the pope of elevating Kevin McNamara to the archbishopric of Dublin as a reward for leading the successful drive for an antiabortion amendment to the constitution. Other commentators agreed with her in seeing the Ballinspittle miracle as part of a backlash against feminism and change; "Those who benefitted from economic change may have become more conservative, all the better to hold that which they have. The future may be full of promise but the past is ... where people knew what to believe in."[14]

VATICAN II AND CHURCH RENEWAL

In 1962, a new Pope, John XXIII, convened a council of bishops to review and revitalize Catholic doctrine and practice. For the outside world, perhaps the two most important changes of Vatican II were allowing the Mass to be said in the local language, rather than Latin, and the jettisoning of saints, most notably the popular St. Christopher, whose historical existence could not be confirmed. But for Catholics the changes went deeper; Vatican II suggested a radically revised view of authority and the institutional church. *Lumen Gentium* (*Light of the Nations*), a document on the nature and purpose of the church , emphasized the laity. It talked less about the church as a hierarchical institution than as the "people of God," a "pilgrim" living in the world—not perfect, like Christ, but in constant need, as all people are, of forgiveness and renewal.[15] In successive documents, Vatican II envisioned a socially active church, fully present in a contemporary world, willing to trust ordinary people's moral and spiritual discernment. The legalistic model, the emphasis on hellfire, dogma, and obeying rules, was to be replaced with the vision of a loving Christ ministering to a suffering humanity. Altars were moved to the center of the church, so that the priest faced the people; nuns modernized their dress, or abandoned distinctive clothing; and all these large and small changes produced expectations of further relaxation and modernization.

The theological or philosophical underpinnings of Vatican II were familiar to many European Catholics, but in Ireland they had only begun to be addressed by two relatively liberal Catholic journals. The redoubtable John McQuaid, archbishop of Dublin, went to Rome to argue for keeping the Latin Mass; returning, he reassured his people that "No change will worry the tranquillity of your Christian lives."[16] But he was mistaken. For a young priest like Tony Flannery, the late 1960s and early 1970s was a period of excitement, "activity and vitality."[17] Face-to-face confession required new counseling skills, a rigid and segregated life was being transformed by encouragement to "read the signs of the times," follow news of political events, explore contemporary music, make friends among the laity, even women.[18] And although the Irish had not clamored for these changes, they were widely accepted. A newly media-savvy generation of priests became familiar figures on television, among them Father Michael Cleary, whose fame spread after an energetic performance leading the huge audience gathered at the Ballybrit racecourse in Galway for a papal mass in choruses of "He's got the whole world in his hands." In this one respect, like John Paul II, Cleary combined enthusiasm for the new media with a highly conservative theology. In a nationally circulated newspaper column and daily radio program, he "constantly irritated" the liberal Father Tony Flannery by acting as a "vehement proponent of the official line on contraception."[19]

Contraception was indeed the issue of the day. In Ireland, as in the United States, a substantial number of Catholics were still guided by the traditional ban on "artificial" birth control. Because the sale or prescription of contraceptives was also against the law in Ireland, people had to cross the border to obtain them. The new modernizing spirit suggested that the Council would relax the old rule, particularly as one could argue that the new contraceptive pill, which regulated hormones that naturally occur in women's bodies, was not really "artificial." When Pope Paul's encyclical *De Humanae Vitae (Of Human Life),* issued in 1968, reaffirmed the traditional teaching, it sent shock waves across the Catholic world. It was not just feminists who were outraged; liberal clergy were equally unhappy. Father James Good, a moral theologian at University College Cork, called the decision a "major tragedy" and predicted that "the majority of Catholic theologians and . . . lay people" would reject it.[20] The French bishops issued a statement saying that married people caught in a "conflict of obligations" would have to decide themselves whether birth control was the lesser of two evils. The Irish bishops, however, publicly supported the pope, and discouraged theologians who followed the French in finding flexibility in the text.

Irish legislation is discussed more in the next chapter. For now it suffices to say that bills to legalize the sale of contraceptives in the Republic were regularly proposed in the Dail from 1974 onward; a bill authorizing their sale to married couples passed in 1979. The increasing birth rate of the late 1960s suggests that some people tried to follow official teaching, but births were soon on their way down again.[21] The Irish, by and large, continued to attend mass, but *De Humanae Vitae* marked a watershed: for the first time, an overwhelming majority chose to disregard a central teaching. Moreover, many clergy were encouraging them; Tony Flannery recounted his attempts to persuade people that they could judge their circumstances for themselves. In 1973, the Irish bishops issued a statement noting that the church's declaring a behavior wrong did not mean that the state needed to make it illegal. This remarkable concession was followed by two decades of increasing secularization in the Irish state. In 1972, nearly 85 percent of voters approved a referendum to remove the reference to the Catholic's church's "special status" from the constitution. By 2004, only the ban on abortion remained to mark the church's influence on civic law, and because many of Ulster's Protestants are equally opposed to abortion, the ban is less divisive than it might be elsewhere.

SCANDAL AND ITS AFTERMATH

It could be expected that rapid modernization and globalization, along with affluence, would change the way Irish Catholics respond to their church. Even before the disastrous encyclical on birth control, the numbers of "vocations," or people who felt called to become priests, nuns, or monks had begun to decline. Afterward, the trend was serious: in 1970, the total number of vocations was 750; only five years previously, it had been 1,375.[22] Fewer vocations meant more lay teachers in schools, more lay nurses and administrators in hospitals, and more lay people running parish councils. Although many admired John Paul II personally, his intransigence on doctrine, coupled with the decreasing numbers of clergy and religious in schools, widened the gap between what the Catholic church taught officially and what actual Irish Catholics believed. A 1998 survey revealed that only 19 percent agreed with the church's position on birth control; 21 percent agreed that celibacy should be compulsory for priests, and 23 percent agreed that only men should be ordained.[23] Earlier Catholics had continued to attend mass even though they dissented from key teachings, but after 1985, mass attendance declined precipitously, at a rate of almost "two per cent a year."[24] By 2002, the latest date for which figures are available, it had fallen to 48 percent, making mass attendance in the Republic a minority practice for the first time since the famine. In June 2004, only one priest was ordained in the archdiocese of Dublin. No ordinations were anticipated there in 2005, and only 13 young men enrolled at the seminary in Maynooth plan to be ordained for Dublin.[25]

Modernization accounts for some of these changes, but it is impossible to ignore the role of church scandal. As seen in Chapter 3, allegations about physical and sexual abuse in Ireland's church-run industrial schools made headlines throughout the 1990s. Accusations of clerical abuse of children will seem familiar to anyone who has followed similar stories about American priests. In Ireland, however, the decade 1992–2002 also brought the downfall of a Taoiseach, two well-known bishops, and the media-savvy Michael Cleary. After his death in 1993, Phyllis Hamilton revealed that she had been in a sexual relationship with Father Cleary since she was 17 years old; they had two sons. Cleary's inflexible public line on sexual morality heightened dismay. The story unfolded as Hamilton's psychiatrist, Ivor Browne, revealed that he had known about the affair for years. Once, when Hamilton was threatening to go to Archbishop McQuaid, Browne persuaded her to talk instead to the Bishop Eamonn Casey. But by the time the story of Casey's failed intervention in Father Cleary's affair became public, he was no longer a bishop.

In 1992, an American woman published a book revealing that she and Casey had a son born in 1974, when he was Bishop of Kerry. Soon after the scandal broke, Casey left for Ecuador, amid serious suspicions that he had used diocesan funds to support the woman and their son. Casey, who had also hewed to the conservative line, was a substantial figure, much admired as one of the founders of Trocaire, an Irish relief agency. His ignominious departure, leaving his fellow bishops to "pick up the pieces," was a major embarrassment.[26] In comparison with these scandals, the revelation in 1995 of another highly visible bishop, Brendan Comiskey, that he had sought treatment for alcoholism in the United States, seemed refreshingly honest. But by 2002, he, too, was gone amid accusations about negligence in dealing with one of his priests, Father Sean Fortune, who committed suicide in 1999 after being arraigned on 29 of 66 sexual abuse charges forwarded by a district court. Questions were raised about why Bishop Comiskey had not done more to investigate allegations dating back to 1984, and Comiskey, after several years of saying that he had done all he could, apologized to the victims and resigned.

Even the highest political officer holder in the land was not immune. In 1991, a priest named Brendan Smyth was arrested in Northern Ireland on charges of pedophilia; released on bail, he fled to the Republic. When it emerged in October 1994 that warrants asking for Smyth's extradition had not been acted on, the Labour Party withdrew its support from the government. As a result, the Fianna Fail-Labour coalition government collapsed, and Albert Reynolds was no longer Taoiseach. What seemed even worse to Fintan O'Toole was that by late October even wilder rumors were acquiring credibility, so that Cardinal Cahal Daly was forced to go on television to denounce as "absurd" a story that he had tried to interfere with Smyth's prosecution. Clearly, "one of the most conservative and deferential societies in Europe" had become one in which "the public was ... so alienated from those in authority that it was prepared to believe almost anything."[27]

The Irish Church has been forced to abandon the confident tone of the 1950s, when it pronounced on morals and doctrine to a docile Republic. Not all change is for the worse. Lay people's influence is stronger; for some, public humiliation has given new depth to Vatican II's description of the church in this world as a penitent pilgrim. Even while seminaries close, a vital popular culture reveals how strong the hold of Catholic spirituality is on the imaginations of ordinary people. Through agencies such as Trocaire, the Irish Church continues to support victims of the famine, poverty, and violence that are still living memories in Ireland. Perhaps there is still a role for a more open and welcoming Catholicism in Ireland, as Tony Flannery believes:

> For me the Catholic Church is always a community that has its door open to any type of person who wants to come in. Its great strength is that it can embrace totally different sections of society, the rich and the poor, intellectual and non-intellectual, people of radically different ideas. And most of all it is a great Church for sinners.[28]

PROTESTANT IRELAND: THE CHURCH OF IRELAND

The Reformation came to Ireland when Henry VIII broke with the Pope and established the Church of England. As seen, persecution of Catholics was at its most violent under Oliver Cromwell, but full equality came only with Catholic Emancipation in 1829. Known as the Church of Ireland, the Anglican Church in Ireland, although numerically outnumbered by Catholics and Presbyterians, was tax-supported until 1871. Once disestablished, it ceased to be under the nominal leadership of the English monarch and, although affiliated with other Anglican churches throughout the world, was no longer subject to the Archbishop of Canterbury. Today a General Synod, made up of bishops, clergy, and lay people, governs the church throughout Ireland. In the 2002 Census, 115,600 people in the Republic, or slightly less than 3 percent of the population, listed themselves as members of the Church of Ireland. In Northern Ireland, the 2001 Census identified 257,788 members, a little more than 15 percent of the population. These figures represent a major decline from 1926, when there were 338,000 members in the North.

Like other Anglican churches, the Church of Ireland claims to be both Catholic and Protestant; that is, the rupture with Rome primarily meant rejecting the Pope's authority. Anglicans rejected medieval practices and doctrines—the celibacy of priests, the practice of praying to saints, the belief in purgatory—that evolved under papal authority. Like other Protestants, they wished to restore the beliefs and practices of the early church. But they retained the liturgical calendar of the Catholic Church, observing its fasts and feasts and stressing the centrality of the Eucharist, or Communion Service, to worship. The Book of Common Prayer replaced the Catholic missal but similarly provided forms for worship and written prayers to be used throughout the year. Anglican orders of monks and nuns take vows of chastity, poverty, and obedience. Although only communion and baptism are considered sacraments, the five other Catholic sacraments are retained as "sacramentals": confirmation, matrimony, ordination, confession, and healing.

Yet these theological points do not tell the whole story. Throughout the world, Anglican churches tend to be divided into "high" and "low." The term "high church" dates to the mid-nineteenth century, when an influential group at Oxford University advocated restoring the Catholic elements in the Anglican heritage to promote spiritual growth and counter doctrinal laxness. Some members of the Oxford Movement, notably the poet Gerard Manley Hopkins and the poet and essayist John Henry Newman, eventually converted to Roman Catholicism; those who remained considered themselves Anglo-Catholics. A "high" church, for example, will offer parishioners the option of confessing individually to a priest. In a "low" church confession will be "general," made with the rest of the congregation at worship. As widely used, however, "high" refers as much to matters of style as belief. A "high" church service may include incense, a sung Eucharist, a clergyman wearing traditional Catholic vestments. An Anglo-Catholic church will usually look like a Roman Catholic church, with a prominent altar, a crucifix, stained glass windows, and statuary.

Although Dublin's beautiful Christ Church Cathedral provides a good example of the "high" Church of Ireland, the tradition, especially in the North, is "low" church, with members inclined to emphasize their Protestant identity. Harold Clarke, former CEO of Eason's (Ireland's dominant bookseller), recollects the church of his childhood as "without ornamentation" other than memorial tablets; "the altar, always referred to as the communion table, was covered in a drab wine-colored frontal, which must be the only color that has no place in the liturgical rota. Then, as now, I could not understand the appeal of this variety of low-Church Anglicanism which ... is still encountered in some parts of the Republic and in many parishes in Northern Ireland."[29] When Hilary Wakeman moved from England in 1996 to serve as priest in the Republic, parishioners criticized her for wearing a cassock and making the sign of the cross. "When asked why I mustn't do these and other things, the answer was always, 'because *they* do that. . . ' it is a matter of retaining tribal identity."[30] In the Republic, such attitudes may reflect a desire to avoid being absorbed into the Catholic majority. In the North, however, they suggest the influence of more militantly anti-Catholic attitudes associated with Calvinists and fundamentalist Christians. Especially in its affiliations with Orange Order, the behavior of some Northern churches has been an irritant to their sister churches in the Republic, which generally share the progressive politics of Anglicans elsewhere.

PRESBYTERIANISM

Presbyterians make up about half of one percent of the Republic's population, but in 2001 they were the largest Protestant denomination in the North, with some 350,000 members, about 21 percent of the population.[31] In addition to the Presbyterian Church in Ireland, there are several smaller breakaway denominations, ranging from the liberal Non-Subscribing Presbyterian Church to several conservative and fundamentalist groups: Ian Paisley's Free Presbyterians, the Evangelical Presbyterians, and the Reformed Presbyterians, or Covenanters. All of these trace their roots back to the Reformation, in particular to the teachings of the sixteenth-century French theologian John Calvin. Like Martin Luther, Calvin believed in the "priesthood of all believers" and the primacy of the Bible over tradition and authority. For Calvin, Catholic practices such as confession with absolution by a priest violated the individual's need for a direct, personal relationship with God. A hierarchical bureaucracy impeded that relationship and violated the spirit of the Gospels. Calvinist congregations were governed by a "presbytery," a board of elders affiliated to a larger organization called a synod. Although Calvin did not go quite so far as later evangelicals in rejecting all printed prayers, he emphasized the need to purify worship services of ritual and ceremony; statues, images, and even stained-glass windows were rejected as "graven images." Each person's salvation depended on faith. To Calvin, the Catholic emphasis on penances and charity heretically suggested that good works might be enough. In its original form, Calvinism painted a dark picture of human nature, irretrievably flawed and doomed to follow its own natural impulses into sin until redeemed by faith in Christ. Calvin's most distinctive doctrine was predestination, the belief that from the beginning of time God ordained that an "elect" group will be saved, while the rest of humanity, including many right-living churchgoers confident of salvation, is headed to hell. Pleasures such as dancing and card-playing, which cater to the weaknesses of human nature, were forbidden the elect.

As Dissenters, Calvinists were persecuted by the established churches; Catholic France killed some 20,000 of them in the St. Bartholomew's Massacre of 1572, touching off a religious war that lasted until 1598. Surviving French Calvinists moved to Switzerland, Holland, and Scotland; a small Huguenot cemetery in Dublin testifies that some even fled to Ireland. But the main source of Presbyterianism in Ireland was the Plantation, or immigration, of Scots in the seventeenth century. The dissenting Scots fared well in comparison with Irish Catholics, but like them were taxed to support an alien church, were prohibited from holding public office until 1828 and, until the religious test was abolished in 1873, ineligible to attend Trinity College Dublin. Their rejection of religious pomp and circumstance, their disdain for hierarchies and the authority of tradition, and their emphasis on the individual's direct relation to God all set them at odds with monarchy and made them sympathetic to plain-speaking self-governance. Thus one tradition within Presbyterianism was revolutionary; Henry Joy McCracken, the most famous example, led United Irishmen against the British in 1798 and was hanged as a rebel. James Connolly, the Scots-born Marxist who was executed with the Easter Rebels, won support in early twentieth-century Belfast when he argued that working-class Protestants needed to forge alliances with Catholics.

This revolutionary Presbyterianism, however, never developed in Ireland as it did in the United States, and Ulster Presbyterianism remains substantially more conservative than its mainstream American counterpart. A nineteenth-century minister named Henry Cooke did much to consolidate conservative Presbyterianism in the North, persuading the Synod of Ulster to expel all congregations that refused to subscribe to the strictly Calvinist Westminister Confession. Under his leadership, Ulster Presbyterianism not only became identified with the grimmest views of human nature, "wholly inclined to all evil," and the most rigid observances of the Sabbath, but became allied with the Orange Order and political anti-Catholicism.[32] The Orangeman's belief that Catholics were theologically wrong became inseparable from a political conviction that an enfranchised Catholic majority would destroy the freedom and culture of Protestant Ireland.

Today, Cooke's strain of Presbyterianism continues unadulterated in what may be the best-known Protestant Church in Northern Ireland, Ian Paisley's Free Presbyterians. In spite of its leader's notoriety, the church is relatively small, with just under 12,000 adherents listed in the 2001 census. Paisley, son of a Baptist minister, graduated from a tiny Reformed Presbyterian school of theology in 1946; he soon began preaching revivals. In early 1951, Paisley supporters planned a revival at a church hall owned by Lissara Presbyterian Church in County Down, but the presbytery voted to refuse permission. Paisley and his supporter picketed Sunday services at the church. shortly thereafter, on St. Patrick's Day, five former Lissara elders and Paisley announced that they were forming a new church. Secession was necessary, Paisley claimed, because the Presbyterian Church in Ireland had forsaken Protestant doctrine and extended "a welcoming hand to Rome."[33]

Separatism is a hallmark of Free Presbyterianism. Indeed, as over the years Paisley has added virtually every other Protestant Church in Ireland to his lists of apostates, he has come close to implying that his denomination is the only godly one. In some respects, the Free Presbyterians resemble other fundamentalists: they read the Bible literally, rejecting all but the King James version. Their services feature Bible reading, hymn-singing, and fire-and-brimstone sermons. They are socially conservative, denying ordination to women and requiring them to cover their heads in church. They believe in evangelization and support missionaries. They differ from many fundamentalists in rejecting not only the Catholic liturgical year, but such Christian seasons as Advent, Lent, and Pentecost. They do not observe Good Friday or Easter and reject Christmas because the Bible does not authorize its celebration or provide a birth date for Jesus. What really sets them apart, however, is the intensity of their anti-Catholicism.

Although the Protestant reformers rejected papal authority and many Catholic doctrines, they always regarded the Catholic Church as essentially Christian. Paisley, however, insists that Catholics are not really Christians at all but part of a "system of satanic deception" whose head, the Pope, is the anti-Christ.[34] Ecumenical Protestants betray the Reformation by moving their denominations closer to Rome. Catholicism, in Paisley's view, is a good deal like the Communist menace of the 1950s: a subtle and many-headed enemy whose machinations can be discerned in many signs, chief among which are Northern Ireland's Troubles. Moreover, Paisley is not a "turn-the-other-cheek" Christian. He believes that Christians must hate sinners as well as their sins. In 1987, when a man whose daughter died in an Irish Republican Army (IRA) bombing announced that he had forgiven her killers, Paisley thundered from the pulpit that it was impossible: "There is absolutely no forgiveness, none whatsoever without repentance."[35]

Over a long career, Paisley's belligerent rhetoric and implacable anti-Catholicism have been played out against the Catholic Civil Rights movement, the Troubles, and the peace negotiations that finally led to the Belfast Agreement. In 1966, when Prime Minister Terence O'Neill attempted modest reforms, Paisley preached on the heroism of the Ulster gun-runners of 1914: "It is men of Lord Carson's stamp that are needed today."[36] In 1968, his own Protestant Unionist Party ran him against O'Neill in the parliamentary elections; Paisley lost, but won the seat in a by-election in 1970. By 1974, Paisley and his party, rechristened the Democratic Unionist Party (DUP), could take much of the credit for the collapse of Brian Faulkner's power-sharing executive, which included nationalists as well as the unionists who had governed Northern Ireland since 1922. Paisley maintained an ambivalent relationship with Protestant paramilitaries, sometimes offering verbal support and sometimes backing away. Ulster Defense Association and Ulster Volunteer Force figures such as John McKeague, David Payne, Tommy Herron, and Ken Gibson all attended Paisley's Martyrs' Memorial Church. He criticized the Peace People scathingly; even British Prime Minister Margaret Thatcher, whose refusal to compromise during the hunger strikes permanently alienated most nationalists, did not escape his wrath. In 1985, after she signed the Anglo-Irish Agreement giving the Republic an official role in negotiations over Northern Ireland, he prayed for God to hand her over to the Devil: "O God in wrath take vengeance upon this wicked, treacherous, lying woman."[37] The DUP opposed the Belfast Agreement in 1998 and continues to agitate for its renegotiation. In the spring elections of 2005, it won more seats in the Northern Ireland Assembly than any other party, defeating the moderate Ulster Unionist Party decisively. This mainstream success of Paisley's party, which he continued to lead in 2005 at the age of 79, suggests how forcefully he expresses the perception of many Protestants that the peace settlement was a defeat, that their culture and traditions are dying.

POPULAR PROTESTANTISM: THE ORANGE ORDER

Every Twelfth of July, in towns across Northern Ireland, the Orange Order goes on parade to celebrate the Protestant victory at the Battle of the Boyne. A fraternal organization founded by members of the Church of Ireland in 1795, the Order currently claims 80,000 to 100,000 members in Northern Ireland, with a few branches in the Republic, South Africa, Canada, and elsewhere. The colorful parades, silk banners, orange sashes, bowler hats, high-pitched flutes, and banging goatskin, or "Lambeg" drums are the most visible and controversial manifestation of Protestant popular culture in the North. The Orange Order continues to insist that it is a religious organization allied to the Reformed tradition. Its current Web site "condemns the paramilitaries, loyalist and republican" and claims that the Order "does not deny to others their civil and religious liberties" and "expects the same tolerance from them."[38] Yet even as it talks of being "a positive force that does not foster resentment or intolerance," the Orange Order takes time in the 2004 edition of its annual July 12th resolution to "deplore" ecumenism, that is, Protestant ministers who "have aligned themselves with the Church of Rome." It speaks of a "crisis" in policing that it attributes to the "weakening," of the Northern Ireland Police force since it adopted a policy of requiring that 50 percent of its recruits come from the Catholic and 50 percent

from the Protestant communities. And it continues to oppose the Parades'
Commission, which mediates between members determined to parade
on any street in Northern Ireland and Catholic communities that wish to
exclude them as manifestations of bigotry that too often bring violence in
their wake.

Members of the Orange Order view the summer parades as an affirmation
of their heritage. The parades not only celebrate the Orange victory at the
Boyne, or the Apprentice Boys' shutting the gates of Derry against Catholic
invaders, but commemorate the Ulster Protestants who died at the Somme
in July 1916. As traditionally portrayed in the *Belfast Telegraph* and in sympathetic accounts such as Ruth Dudley Edwards's *The Faithful Tribe: An*

Orange Parade, Belfast, July 12, 2005. The peaceful
face of a parade that later turned to violence. © *Irish
Times.*

Intimate Portrait of the Loyal Institutions (1999), the parades are a folkloric summer celebration, rather like a Fourth of July picnic in a Disney movie. "At their best," as Edwards points out, participants share "courage, decency and simple faith," and their traditional music, as seen in tunes like "My Father's Sash" and "The Orange Lily-O," is a cultural expression indistinguishable from the singing of "Danny Boy" or "The Rising of the Moon."[39] Undoubtedly many people, especially in rural areas with a Protestant majority, enjoy the parades; many pass without incident. Yet Catholics have grimmer associations with them, dating back to the mid-nineteenth century, when the British banned the parades because they led to "violence, outrage, religious animosities, hatred between classes and, too often, loss of life."[40] Historically, Catholics have seen "the Order as the all-powerful instrument through which they were consigned to second-class citizenship in Northern Ireland."[41] That traditionally Unionist prime ministers, judges, and prominent business owners have belonged to the Order suggested to many Catholics that it was a cabal whose members manipulated the state and the economy to their own advantage.[42]

Most Catholics find it hard to overlook the Orange Order's explicit anti-Catholicism. A 1995 pamphlet called *The Qualifications of an Orangeman* still urges the membership to "strenuously oppose the fatal errors and doctrines of the Church of Rome, and scrupulously avoid countenancing (by his presence or otherwise) any act or ceremony of popish worship."[43] Moreover, the Order not only opposes Catholic theology, but expresses "deep suspicion as to the motives and strategies of this church in the past and present." To Orangemen, neither the Catholic Church nor the Republic of Ireland has changed since 1690 or 1922. They still believe that the Catholic Church "would have the means and the desire within a united Ireland to control individual judgment and political power ... to the detriment of Protestantism."[44] Historic Orange tunes, such as "Billy Boy," with its rousing chorus of "We're up to our neck in Fenian blood/ Surrender or you'll die," strike Catholics as downright offensive; practices of the marching season, such as burning the pope in effigy, seem more menacing than colorful. Moreover, although the Orange Order claims to discourage "all uncharitable words, actions, or sentiments toward Roman Catholics," it allows "blood and thunder" bands, made up of youths who do not belong to the Order, to play in its parades. Such groups often display paramilitary symbols, even pictures of popular paramilitary killers. They also have a reputation for drinking heavily, attacking Catholic bystanders, and vandalizing neighborhoods through which the parades pass. And although the Orange Order does not authorize violence, its detractors believe it should take responsibility for the highly charged atmosphere that surrounds annual confrontations over parade routes.

DRUMCREE

Parade routes are so controversial in Northern Ireland because housing has been segregated along religious lines ever since the Plantation, when landlords created "Irish quarters" for Catholics.[45] After 1922, prosperous areas, such as Belfast's Malone Road, were home to both Catholic and Protestant professionals, but most working-class neighborhoods were divided along religious lines. Segregation only increased with the Troubles, as fire bombings, threats, and vandalism persuaded people to move to neighborhoods where they would be part of a majority. The peace process failed to alleviate the pattern. The 2001 census shows that 66 percent of the population of Belfast lives in areas where residents are either 90 percent Protestant or 90 percent Catholic, up from 63 percent 10 years earlier.[46] Because the distinction between Protestant and Catholic neighborhoods is so often marked and accompanied by distinctions about where people shop and work, a large organized group of outsiders is perceived as an intrusion, even a threat. No one seriously objects to Orangemen marching in Protestant neighborhoods, but when the thundering Lambeg drums come sweeping into Catholic neighborhoods, residents can feel as if a triumphant bully has forced his way in to prove that they cannot stop him. Parades commissions try to work out alternatives, but in the case of the Drumcree parade, no compromise succeeded.

Drumcree is a Church of Ireland parish near Portadown in County Armagh, a few miles from Loughall, where the Orange Order was founded in 1795. The area is the traditional Orange heartland, and the association between the Order and the Church of Ireland there goes back at least 50 years before the building of the present church in 1857. In July 1807, members of the Order marched in formation to the church, which "was bedecked with flags. They were greeted by the rector, a member of [the Order], who conducted a service and preached to them."[47] It was the first Orange service in the parish, and set the precedent for an annual tradition, replicated in many Church of Ireland parishes. Members of the Order attended church together in a body, decked out in their bright orange sashes. The church sported Orange decorations and flags. The sermon recognized and lauded the Order and the Protestant heritage. The service ended with the singing of the British national anthem, and members were dismissed to parade to the local Orange Hall. In a statement included in a highly critical report on the Orange Order adopted by the House of Commons in 1836, a Protestant magistrate described another tradition in full swing: "large bodies ... parading the highways ... firing shots, and using the most opprobrious epithets ... proceeded to Drumcree Church, passing by the Catholic chapel though it was a considerable distance out of their way."[48] At the height of the Troubles in 1972, the Portadown Orange parade was even more provocative, as hundreds of paramilitaries, members of the then legal Ulster Defense Association, joined in, wearing military dress and masks. Moreover, there was a new dimension: Garvaghy Road, on the traditional parade route, had become the site of new housing estates whose residents were almost all Catholic. That summer, eight people were killed in 12 weeks.

Throughout the Troubles, bitterly divided Portadown was the scene of sectarian atrocities—the intrusion of masked gunmen on an Orange meeting in 1975 that left five men dead, repeated IRA bombings of the town center that did damage in the millions, the killing by Loyalist gunmen of four Catholics in a betting shop in 1992. But ironically, it was only in the wake of the cease-fires of the 1990s that the Drumcree Orange parade gained international notoriety as a symbol of religious hatred. As political negotiations advanced, Catholics on the Garvaghy Road formed a Residents' Group to persuade the authorities to reroute the parade. They met with police and repeatedly asked the Order for face-to-face meetings; receiving no response, they decided to greet the 1995 marchers with a counter-demonstration, a residents' march. To prevent this confrontation, police stopped the residents and blocked the Order from entering the Garvaghy Road, but the Orangemen vowed to stand their ground. By the next day, 50,000 Orange supporters had gathered at Drumcree insisting on their historic right to march; both Orange member David Trimble and Ian Paisley spoke. A day later, an agreement was reached that the parade could proceed if it was limited to members of the local lodge and if it took place in silence. Residents were allowed to remain on the roadside in silent protest. But this apparent triumph of reason was quickly marred, as Garvaghy residents watched television coverage of Paisley and Trimble joining hands at the head of the march, and heard Paisley characterize the compromise as one of the "greatest victories . . . for Protestantism in Northern Ireland."[49] When police disavowed promising residents that future Orange marches would not be routed through their neighborhood, they felt betrayed.

For four years, the best efforts of everyone from the police to the Catholic cardinal and Church of Ireland archbishop to British Prime Minister Tony Blair failed to resolve the annual confrontation at Drumcree. In 1996, after initially blocking the parade, the outnumbered police decided that allowing it to proceed was the only way to stop loyalist violence then escalating throughout the province. Scenes of police roughly clearing Garvaghy Road of its residents fueled Catholic resentment. A distinguished panel appointed to make recommendations created the intercommunity Parades Commission, which forbade the Garvaghy route. Loyalist thugs harassed and threatened police. Farther north in Ballymoney, a loyalist crowd kicked a policeman to death. Determined not to be overwhelmed again by sheer numbers, for three consecutive summers the police and army dug moats, laid coils of razor wire, and erected increasingly elaborate barricades; it all cost millions. In 1998, a reporter at Drumcree described how "arc lights swept the fields silhouetting bowler-hatted men against billowing smoke. Helicopters hovered low.... The Orangemen had come to commemorate the Battle of the Somme; at times it seemed they had remained to re-enact it."[50]

Then things grew much worse. Early in the morning of July 12, 1998, two men pitched a Molotov cocktail through the window of a council house in Ballymoney. The blaze it ignited trapped three brothers, ranging in ages from 8 to 10, in their bedroom. As family and neighbors listened to the brothers' screams, heat and flames beat back their attempts at rescue. Within minutes, firefighters arrived and removed three small charred bodies. It was a classic sectarian story, repeating scenes that had been acted out since 1969, but which most people thought the Belfast Agreement had consigned to the past. The housing estate was Protestant; the family had only recently moved in. The children, products of a "mixed marriage," had been brought up with no religion but were ethnic Catholics in the eyes of the loyalists who threw the bomb. Although the Orange Order quickly condemned the attack, most people connected the highly charged atmosphere of Drumcree, with its talk of last stands and implacable resistance, to this act of savage bigotry. Preaching in Drumcree Church, the Reverend William Bingham concluded that "a fifteen-minute walk down Garvaghy Road by the Orange Order would be a very hollow victory because it would be in the shadow of three coffins."[51] For his part, Archbishop Eames of the Church of Ireland, who had been under pressure from members of his church south of the border, declared that it was time that the Orangemen went home: "what is happening at Drumcree is wrong. What is being done in the name of Protestantism is wrong."[52]

THE CHURCHES AND PEACE

Undoubtedly twentieth-century Irish history, on either side of the border, provides object lessons in the injustice and mayhem that follow a fervent belief that God takes sides in political conflicts. Churches also play a role in negotiating disputes and advocating both peace and justice; some leaders have also taken a long hard look at their own traditions. Earl Storey's *Traditional Roots: Towards an Appropriate Relationship between the Church of Ireland and the Orange Order* (2002) thoughtfully questions how Anglicanism, which claims to be Catholic as well as Protestant, became entangled with this belligerently anti-Catholic organization, and how it can separate itself without further inflaming passions that derive in part from Protestant "insecurity." "Trapped and ... used at Drumcree" as the Church of Ireland is, Storey counsels against allowing a "pristine theology" to dictate a "sudden and total break" that "might fuel the more extreme elements of Orangeism in a way that greatly increases ... sectarianism."[53]

Although IRA members often had been practicing Catholics, the official church repeatedly denounced the organization. Cahal Daly, later cardinal, expressed the view that it was "sinful" for Catholics to belong to the illegal organization in 1972.[54] Some observers even believe that his intransigence led him to seem unsympathetic to the real grievances of the community to which the IRA appealed. A priest of a very different stamp, Alec Reid is often credited with leading Sinn Fein and its leader Gerry Adams into the peace process. Reid, who ministered for years in the working-class Falls district of Belfast, was famously photographed as he knelt over two British corporals shot dead by the IRA after they drove through a funeral cortege for victims of loyalist gunmen. This image of Christian conviction and active presence in the violence-torn community gave him credibility with both sides. In 1988 Reid brought John Hume of the peaceful Northern Ireland's Social Democratic and Labour Party into secret talks with Adams and then acted as their "contact person" in talks with the Republic of Ireland. Even in the discouraging climate of 2004, with the Northern Ireland Assembly suspended and the more radical parties in power, he continued to believe that progress was possible and that people needed to focus "on a vision of the peace we want to create."[55]

Other religious groups also worked for peace. Since 1978, the Protestant Irish Council of Churches and the Catholic Commission on Peace and Justice have cooperated in a Peace Education program that provides teacher training and material for schools on both sides of the border. The tiny Irish Society of Friends, remembered for its nineteenth-century efforts to relieve the famine, currently sponsors an intercommunity day-care center for low-income children in Belfast and a support service for relatives of prisoners. Some 31 reconciliation groups have formed, of which the largest is Corrymeela, founded in 1964 by Ray Davey, a Protestant chaplain at Queens University. As a prisoner of the Germans, Davey had survived the Royal Air Force bombing of Dresden in 1945. The group purchased a holiday home named Corrymeela ("hill of harmony") and started sponsoring intercommunity conferences on topics such as housing, education, and mixed marriages. With the outbreak of the Troubles, Corrymeela offered temporary homes to people displaced by bombs and intimidation; by 1978, it could house more than 100 people at any one time. By the mid-1990s, its membership grew to approximately 170, most (88%) identifying themselves as Christian, but representing a wide range of beliefs and backgrounds.[56] Corrymeela's efforts to create conditions in which peace can thrive now include interdenominational summer camps and a school. One of their projects is the Seed Group, which brings young people between the ages of 18 and 25 years old together for six weekends over a six-month period; a similar program, Close Encounters, focuses on 15 to 17 year olds. The membership offers its practical expertise in conflict resolution to other organizations, including the police. Above all, even in its recreational and cultural activities, it aims to be a "sign and symbol that Protestants and Catholics can share together in a common witness and ministry of reconciliation."[57]

BEYOND THE GREEN AND THE ORANGE: MINORITY RELIGIONS

The Protestant-Catholic binary is so deeply enshrined in Ireland that it is easy to forget that Christians share the island with other religious groups. As of the 2001 census, there were 1,943 Muslims, 878 Hindus, and perhaps 50 practicing Buddhists in Northern Ireland. The Republic's 2002 census identified 19,100 Muslims, 3,894 Buddhists, and 3,099 Hindus. Muslims in the Republic have established seven mosques in locations that include Dublin, Galway, Limerick, Cork, and the small Mayo town of Ballyhaunis. Dublin's Islamic Cultural Centre, completed in 1996, houses a library, a shop, a restaurant, and meeting rooms. It sponsors educational programs to increase Irish understanding of Islam. In 2003, the Centre announced plans, supported by a grant from Northern Ireland, to translate the Quran, Islam's holy book, into Irish.[58] The Republic contributes to the support of two Islamic primary schools. As is the case with other schools, the state sets academic requirements that include the Irish language but gives the denomination control over the religious curriculum. Dublin's Chester Beatty Library, which houses a collection of Asian and Islamic art and books, offers a multicultural program in which the Muslim national school participates, along with two Catholic primary schools. A 2002 headline such as "Noah's Ark Captures the Imagination of Children from the Muslim N.S. and boys from Star of the Sea" offers a cheerful contrast to occasional racist incidents, such as the attempting firebombing of the Centre in 2000. The news from the North is characteristically grimmer. In October 2003, a local Muslim leader (*imam*) and his family left Craigavon, near troubled Portadown, after eight men wielding baseball bats smashed up their home. Although the community had received planning permission to build the province's first mosque, its leaders decided to delay the project indefinitely.[59]

Muslims, Buddhists, and Hindus began arriving in Northern Ireland after World War II, but they are mostly much more recent immigrants in the Republic. Jewish people, however, have a much longer history in Ireland.

Oliver Cromwell, seeking allies against Catholics, actually encouraged Jews to immigrate to Ireland. Although numbers remained small, there were approximately 400 well-assimilated and reasonably prosperous Irish Jews, mostly living in Dublin, by Victorian times. The Czarist pogroms, which sent so many Jews from Central Europe and Russia to New York's Lower East Side after 1881, were also responsible for a smaller stream of mostly Lithuanian Jews into Dublin. Most intended to go to New York, but they ended up in Ireland because they ran out of money or were duped by unscrupulous ship captains who realized that their desperate passengers could not tell one English-speaking seaport from another. Although the community numbered no more than 5,500 in its peak years just after World War II, turn-of-the-century immigrants, mostly poverty-stricken, Yiddish-speaking, and wearing traditional Orthodox dress and hair styles, were highly visible outsiders. Some of Dublin's older Jewish families feared that their presence would unleash anti-Semitism, and certainly there were some outbursts. In 1904, after a series of anti-Semitic sermons preached in Limerick by Father John Creagh, Jewish homes and shops were vandalized, and Jewish people were assaulted in the streets. The "Limerick Pogrom" was accompanied by a boycott of Jewish businesses that lasted several months, or long enough to bankrupt shop owners and decimate a community that had included only 32 families in the first place.[60]

Yet compared with the Czarist pogroms, which killed thousands, Irish anti-Semitism struck many Jewish people as minimal. Many families preserve stories illustrating great kindness to the new arrivals. Ninety-year-old Abe Benson describes how his mother arrived with only a name and address. When the Dubliner who was trying to help realized that it was too far for her children to walk, he paid for a cab that took them to their relatives. Many immigrants clustered around Clanbrassil Street, where they soon had a small synagogue and school; kosher butcher shops, bakeries, wineries, and grocery stores; and other businesses, such as tailor's shops and watchmakers. Nick Harris's memoir, *Dublin's Little Jerusalem* (2002), tells the story of this neighborhood, where he grew up in the 1920s and 1930s. Many of his stories might have been set on the Lower East Side, but occasional anecdotes evoke the Irish context. During World War II, when shipping was disrupted, the community found itself facing a Passover without matzos. Lacking the facilities to make them, they enlisted the help of Spratt's, a local manufacturer of dog biscuits. Under careful supervision, the company cleaned its ovens to meet the high standards for Passover baking, but the resultant matzos resembled the company's canine treat in thickness and hardness. "Spratts," concludes Harris, "deserved our gratitude" even though the matzo they produced "had to be soaked in water for two days before you could attempt to eat it."[61]

Although only two Irish citizens, Ettie Steinberg and her young son Leon, lost their lives in the Holocaust, the extended families of "Little Jerusalem" were killed by the thousands. Before declaring neutrality in 1939, the Irish government maintained polite, even cordial, relations with the Nazi government. Its ambassador to Germany from 1993 to 1939, Charles Bewley, a notorious anti-Semite, echoed Nazi rhetoric in his dispatches home. The Nuremberg Laws, which stripped Jews of all civil rights, were in Bewley's view only "inconveniences": Jews "were the chief supporters of communism," practiced "usury and fraud," and had either "caused or exploited Germany's appalling degradation before 1933." Because Jews were a "form of corruption" that caused "grave moral scandals" wherever they went, it was "beyond any degree of reason that they could be treated like ordinary citizens."[62] Although nonrefugee Jews, such as persons coming into the country to marry a citizen, were admitted, the Irish government obdurately refused to admit refugees, protesting that the country was too poor to support them. When the *Anschluss* made "120,000 Austrian Jews stateless, the government made entry into Ireland for holders of German and Austrian passports dependent on a valid visa—available only to applicants 'not of Jewish or partly Jewish origin' and without 'non-Aryan' affiliations."[63] Nor did the situation improve dramatically after the war. In 1946, Irish-born Chaim Herzog, later president of Israel, and an old friend of Eamon de Valera, had to intercede personally to persuade the government to admit 100 Jewish children, Holocaust survivors, so that they could be cared for in a Westmeath castle owned by an Englishman. The visas were granted for one year.

In recent years, the Irish government has apologized repeatedly for this policy of exclusion, which Minister for Justice Michael McDowell characterized as a "betrayal of the Constitution" at a 2003 Holocaust commemoration.[64] How deeply alienated were Irish Jews by their government's policy, which contrasted so sharply with the tolerance and general goodwill most of them seemed to experience in daily life? It is clear that the Jewish population of Ireland, which peaked at about 5,500 in 1946, declined precipitously afterward—by "16.7 per cent from 1946 to 1961, 19.1 per cent in the ten years to 1971, 19.2 per cent in the ten years to 1981, and 25.7 per cent in the ten years to 1991."[65] By 2002, the census reported fewer than 1,800 Jews remaining in Ireland. Some argue that Irish Jews, like Irish Christians, emigrated because of economic stagnation at home; certainly many went to newly independent Israel. As recently as 1998, a Jewish publication reported that it "seems unlikely that there will ever be enough Jews in Ireland again to prevent the virtual disappearance of the community within a few decades."[66] By 2003, slightly more optimism could be felt: there were new immigrants from South Africa and Israel, a new Chief Rabbi from the United States, and a dynamic Lubavitcher rabbi for the largest remaining Orthodox synagogue. Thanks to their efforts, Clanbrassil's old Bretzel bakery was restored to kosher status; a local Safeway supermarket was importing kosher groceries, and a ritual butcher (*shochtim*) traveled to Ireland every two weeks to supervise the slaughter of lambs and cattle. Stratford National School and College, once an entirely Jewish institution, continues to operate on a multidenominational basis. Although most of its students are now Christian, the school prides itself on maintaining a "Jewish ethos," with courses in Jewish studies and Hebrew as well as, of course, the mandatory Irish. With these important elements of the "infrastructure of Jewish life intact," the community is actively recruiting new immigrants from Central Europe and Argentina.[67]

BEYOND THE GREEN AND THE ORANGE: SECULARIZING IRELAND

The excesses of both Catholicism and Protestantism in Ireland lead many people to welcome its increasing secularization. As the title of his 1997 *The Ex-Isle of Erin* suggests, Fintan O'Toole argues that globalization has made most Irish people indistinguishable from the English-speaking populations of Canada, Australia, and New Zealand. Most Irish people are prosperous; they watch American and British films and television; they read books that are best-sellers around the world; they use the Internet and worry about whether they can afford a second Japanese car or whether Grand Theft Auto video games will make their children hyperactive. The old pathologies are dying out; in fact, some see that it is high time that Irish people understand that they are neither victims of the British or of Rome, but players on the world stage who must take responsibility for any damage the global economy inflicts on poor nations: "For so long have we been accustomed to describing ourselves and the Irish experience in the language of grievance, we seem unable to come to terms with the notion that we ourselves are capable of inflicting oppression on others."[68]

But the benefits of secularization remain unclear. By 1998 only 34 percent of Protestants in the North reported themselves as weekly churchgoers, yet Protestant paramilitary activity persists and housing segregation, as we saw earlier, has actually increased in Belfast. Throughout the North, religious labels have remarkable persistence even as religious practices wanes. State census figures diverge from figures provided by churches because "people use religious terms to describe their cultural, national and political allegiance even when they do not practice any religion."[69] One example of how religion is racialized comes out of sociologist Frank Burton's experiences living in a Belfast neighborhood in the 1970s. Burton was fascinated by the community's practice of "telling" the differences between Catholics and Protestants at a glance; facial features were cited as often as names and addresses.[70] An analyst may note fewer scriptural references in wall paintings as Protestant paramilitaries know less and less about the Bible, but their ferocity has not diminished accordingly. If anything, people who practice no religion may miss out on the peace education that almost every church other than the Free Presbyterian has been providing for the past 25 years.

Nor is it clear that a more secular Republic is a less troubled place. O'Toole's optimism disturbs some critics, who argue that the Celtic Tiger's enthusiasts are turning recent history into a "bogeyman": "Either you accept the deregulated ruthlessness of the market or you will be cast back into the eternal night of emigration and high unemployment. Better dead than Dev."[71] The notion that Ireland's ills are all residues of the past, or that replacing a Gaelic Catholic identity with some global "common culture" is an unmixed good, strikes such people as naive. Let's not be too quick, they say, to celebrate "police-canteen culture, sexual-psychopath culture."[72] They urge people to remember that DeValera's vision of Ireland imagined "frugal comfort" as everyone's right, whereas unregulated capitalism has introduced enormous income gaps. The tradition, both revolutionary and Catholic, offered reasons for resisting materialism, for criticizing mainstream middleclass values. To accept the view that the authoritarian and repressive side of the Catholic Church, as revealed in recent scandals, is the whole Church, some believe, is to slip into a home-grown variation on the old British anti-Catholicism. It has been noted that thinkers like O'Toole, "entirely secular in his own beliefs, and with no bridge over to progressive forces among the believers," have cut themselves off from too many other Irish people and from rich "traditions of resistance or progressive thinking within Irish history and experience."[73] Whether that tradition can be revitalized, whether a newer Catholicism will energize a generation that knows only a humbled church in a flashy consumer culture, remains to be seen.

NOTES

1. Louise Fuller, *Irish Catholicism since 1950: The Undoing of a Culture* (Dublin: Gill and Macmillan, 2002), 8. Message of the Taoiseach, John Costello, to Pius XII on taking office in 1948.

2. "The Scholar and His Cat," 9th century, http://ccat.sas.upenn.edu/jod/pangur.html.

3. Fuller, 10.

4. Michael O'Connell, *Changed Utterly: Ireland and the New Irish Psyche* (Dublin: Liffey, 2001), 64. The figure comes from the EU's "Eurobarometer" surveys.

5. Tony Flannery, *From the Inside: A Priest's View of the Catholic Church* (Cork: Mercier, 1999), 59.

6. On this point, see Kenneth Samples, "Apparitions of the Virgin Mary: A Protestant Look at a Catholic Phenomenon," *Christian Research Journal* (Winter 1991), http://www.iclnet.org/pub/resources/text/cri/cri-jrnl/web/crj0078a.html. Although millions of pilgrims have flocked to Medjugorje since Mary made her first appearance there in 1981, the local bishop has "denounced the cult . . . and dismissed the alleged visionaries as 'sick in the head.'" Eamonn McCann, *Dear God: The Price of Religion in Ireland* (London: Bookmarks, 1999), 176.

7. Paul Duggan, "Lessons from Our Lady of Knock," *Catholic Culture,* http://www.catholicculture.org/docs/doc_view.cfm?recnum=1204.

8. Bridget Haggerty, "The Annual Novena of Our Lady of Knock," in *Irish Culture and Customs,* http://www.irishcultureandcustoms.com/ACalend/NovenaKnock.html.

9. Based on records kept by the Prior, St. Patrick's Purgatory, Lough Derg; Fuller, 278.

10. For an alternative scholarly view see Michael Carroll, *Irish Pilgrimages: Holy Wells and Popular Devotion* (Baltimore, Md.: Johns Hopkins University Press, 1999). Carroll argues that the practices associated with holy wells are of much more recent origin.

11. Bridget Haggerty, "Pattern Day in Old Ireland," in *Irish Culture and Customs,* http://www.irishcultureandcustoms.com/ACustom/PatternDay.html.

12. Mary Holland, "Ballinspittle and the Bishops' Dilemma," in *Seeing Is Believing: Moving Statues in Ireland,* ed. Colm Toibin (Dublin: Pilgrim Press, 1985), 45.

13. Stuart Francis, "Man Does Not Live by Bread Alone," in Toibin, 49.

14. Toibin, "Introduction," 8.

15. *Lumen Gentium: Dogmatic Constitution of the Church,* 21 November 1964, Catholic Information Network, http://www.cin.org/v2church.html.

16. Quoted in Fuller, 112.

17. Flannery, 57.

18. The phrase "signs of the times" comes from a passage in Luke's Gospel in which Christ asks his disciples why they do not know how to "read the signs of the times." As used in the context of Vatican II, it refers to the obligation to heed contemporary reality. In Flannery's seminary days, students were forbidden to read newspapers or listen to the radio. See *Gaudiam et Spes: The Constitution of the Church in the Modern World,* 7 December 1965, Catholic Information Network.

19. Flannery, 181.

20. Fuller, 199. Good was later banned from teaching theology, but history proved his opinion correct.

21. The birthrate for 1960 was 21.5 per thousand; in 1970 it was 21.9 per thousand; in 1980 it was 9.8; in 2003, it was 7.2 Figures are from the Republic's Central Statistics Office; http://www.cso.ie/principalstats/pristat2.html#figure11.

22. Fuller, 168.

23. Fuller, 267.

24. O'Connell, 64. His source is again the EU's Eurobarometer. Similar surveys in the United States produce similar results. O'Connell also makes the point about pre-famine mass attendance cited in the next sentence.

25. *Irish Times,* 14 June 2004.

26. Fuller, 253.

27 Fintan O'Toole, *The Ex-Isle of Erin: Images of a Global Ireland* (Dublin: New Island, 1997), 202.

28. Flannery, 135.

29. Colin Murphy and Lynne Adair, *Untold Stories: Protestants in the Republic of Ireland: 1922–2002* (Dublin: Liffey, 2003), 50.

30. Murphy and Adair, 205.

31. Figures provided by The Irish Council of Churches, http://www.irishchurches.org.

32. "Westminster Confession of Faith." Chapter Six, "Of the Fall of Man, of Sin, and the Punishment Thereof." Center for Reformed Theology and Apologetics. http://www.reformed.org/documents/wcf_with_proofs/indexf.html.

33. Dennis Cooke, *Persecuting Zeal: A Portrait of Ian Paisley* (Dingle, Co. Kerry, Ireland: Brandon, 1996), 108.

34. Cooke, 42.

35. Cooke, 97.

36. Cooke, 146.

37. Cooke, 1. The information about paramilitary leaders who attended Martyrs' Memorial comes from Cooke, 184.

38. The Grand Orange Lodge of Ireland, "The Religious Basis of the Order," http://www.grandorange.org.uk/parades/religious_basis.html.

39. Ruth Dudley Edwards, *The Faithful Tribe: An Intimate Portrait of the Loyal Institutions* (London: HarperCollins, 1999), 345.

40. The Party Processions Act banned Orange parades between 1839 and 1872, although with limited effect. Jacqueline Dana, "A Brief History of Orangeism in Ireland," 1998, http://larkspirit.com/general/orangehist.html.

41. Chris Ryder and Vincent Kearney, *Drumcree: The Orange Order's Last Stand* (London: Methuen, 2001), 1.

42. "138 of the 149 Unionist MPs who sat in Stormont between 1921 and 1968, and all of the prime ministers during that time were members of the Order." Ryder and Kearney, 23.

43. Earl Storey, *Traditional Roots: Towards an Appropriate Relationship between the Church of Ireland and the Orange Order* (Dublin: Columba, 2002), 82.

44. Storey, 83.

45. Ryder and Kearney, 35.

46. "Survey Reveals Irish Peace Process Widens Religious Divide," *Catholic News* 7 January 2002, http://www.cathtelecom.com/news/201.22.php. The research quoted is Peter Shirlow's. See his "Ethno-sectarianism and the Reproduction of Fear in Belfast," *Capital & Class* 80 (Summer 2003): 77–93. Eighty-eight percent of the people interviewed in "interface" neighborhoods in Belfast "would not enter an area dominated by the other community at night time." Only 18 percent reported going to shops and restaurants in the other community on a weekly basis. The youngest people surveyed (16 to 24 years old) were the most fearful. Ninety-five percent of

children attend segregated schools. Anne Cadwallader, "In Northern Ireland, Hate Begins Early," *Christian Science Monitor* 4 (September 2002).

47. Ryder and Kearney, 31.

48. Ryder and Kearney, 11.

49. Ryder and Kearney, 122.

50. Ryder and Kearney, 259.

51. Ryder and Kearney, 274.

52. Ryder and Kearney, 272.

53. Earl Storey, *Traditional Roots: Towards an Appropriate Relationship between the Church of Ireland and the Orange Order* (Dublin: Columba, 2002), 125, 126.

54. Martin Dillon, *God and the Gun: The Church and Irish Terrorism.* (New York: Routledge, 1998), 216.

55. Brendan Mulhall, "Father Alec Reid: Redemptorists in Action," http://www.redemptorists-denver.org/news/ria-aug-03.html. Reid's role in the negotiations is analyzed by Dillon, 215–218.

56. Mervyn T. Love, *Peace Building through Reconciliation in Northern Ireland* (Aldershot, England: Avebury, 1995), 128.

57. Corrymeela Online, "Who We Are," http://www.corrymeela.org.

58. "Quran to be Translated into Irish," *Islamic Voice* (April 2003), http://www.islamicvoice.com/april.2003/news.htm.

59. From the Chester Beatty Library's "Education" page, http://www.cbl.ie/education/projects_set.html. On the Craigavon incident, see "Race Attacks 'Rise' in Northern Ireland," BBC News Online, 13 October 2003, http://www.white.org.uk/bbcni1.html. There is a mosque in Belfast, but the Craigavon mosque would have been the first built for that purpose.

60. Ray Rivlin, *Shalom Ireland: A Social History of Jews in Modern Ireland* (Dublin: Gill and Macmillan, 2003), 32–33.

61. Nick Harris, *Dublin's Little Jerusalem* (Dublin: A&A Farmar, 2002), 61.

62. Rivlin, 35.

63. Rivlin, 35.

64. Rivlin, 38.

65. Rivlin, 238.

66. "Ireland's Jews: A Fading Tribe on the Emerald Isle," in *Jewish Heritage Report* 2.1 (Spring-Summer 1998), http://www.isjm.org/jhr/IInos1–2/ireland.htm.

67. Rifkin, 246.

68. Ronit Lentin, ed., *Emerging Irish Identities,* proceedings of a Seminar held in Trinity College Dublin, 27 November 1999 (2000): 81. The quotation appeared in *The Irish Times,* 26 November 1999.

69. Irish Council of Churches, http://www.irishchurches.org.

70. Frank Burton, *The Politics of Legitimacy: Struggles in a Belfast Community* (London: Routledge and Kegan Paul, 1978). An outsider, Frank Burton, studied "telling" in Belfast and found that his own skepticism "about the efficacy of signs was shaken when I found myself employing them." Running after a bus without being able to see its number, he correctly concluded that it was the wrong one because all of the people boarding it looked Protestant (69).

71. Peadar Kirby, Luke Gibbons, and Michael Cronin, eds., *Reinventing Ireland: Culture, Society and the Global Economy,* 3rd ed. (London: Pluto, 2002), 7. The phrase "better dead than Dev" translates to "better dead than part of the Republic of Ireland." Dev is the nickname for Eamon DeValera.

72. Kirby, Gibbons, and Cronin, 20.

73. Barry O Seaghdha, "The Celtic Tiger's Media Pundits," in Kirby, Gibbons, and Cronin, 151.

3

Marriage, Gender, Family, and Education

GENDER, FAMILY, AND SEXUALITY IN IRELAND is the story of a country in which church and state were for many years virtually inseparable, and in which chastity was both a religious and patriotic ideal. It is also a story of modernization at an astonishingly rapid pace and, inevitably, of overlapping practices and moral contradictions. Two popular films starkly present the contrast between past and present. The worst excesses of Irish prudishness form the subject matter of Peter Mullan's film *The Magdalene Sisters* (2003). It depicts a group of teenage girls kept prisoners in a convent laundry. Emotionally and otherwise brutalized by hysterical nuns, they are doing years of penance for sexual sins, such as giving birth to a baby out of wedlock. Some are merely guilty of being pretty, or having been victims of rape or incest. Two years earlier, another Irish film, Gerard Stembridge's *About Adam*, depicted a very different world. Praised by the *Irish Times* reviewer for its willingness to depict middle-class, urban Irish life accurately, the film stars Stuart Townsend as an attractive young man who marries a beautiful young woman. This happy ending is achieved only after he has slept with both of her sisters and come perilously close with their teenage brother. The film could be set in the trendier neighborhoods of any large Western city, where it would be viewed as a sexual farce reflecting the liberated mores of the new century.

An outsider might think that these films represent entirely different worlds, as widely separated from each other as the grim church and courtroom of Arthur Miller's *The Crucible* from the fashionable boutiques and clubs of *Sex and the City*. But in Ireland nothing is that simple. The last Magdalen

The rapid pace of change in Ireland can result in the bizarre overlapping of contemporary and traditional life, which is the subject of Seán Hillen's "Cosmonaut Lands in Annalong Harbour (Security Forces Investigate . . .)." Photomontage, 1992. © Seán Hillen.

laundry in Dublin closed its doors only in 1996. The first Irish divorce was granted in 1997; the sale of condoms to teenagers became legal only in 1993, the same year homosexuality was decriminalized. Although the Irish Family Planning Association estimates that more than 80,000 Irish citizens had abortions in the United Kingdom between 1981 and 1998, in 2005 the procedure remains illegal in their homeland.[1] Where issues of gender and sexuality are concerned, the Irish live with sharp contradictions between the permissive present and the repression, even violence, that marked the not-so-distant past. To understand this struggle requires looking backward, at least briefly.

Chastity as Cultural Ideal

Among the many traumas the famine inflicted was an upheaval in the nature of the families and communities in which most people lived. Before 1850, most Irish people lived on small landholdings that were divided among male children when their fathers died. Not only did the system lead to smaller and smaller holdings, but an elaborate system developed, requiring a man to rent strips of land in several places, often miles apart. Farming necessitated and sustained stable communities with strong traditional ties; famine deaths and emigration destroyed these while proving subsistence farming obsolete. As a result, a new land-owning class shifted to the English system, passing farms down from father to oldest son. Perhaps there was also enough money to give one daughter a dowry. Other sons and daughters might enter religious life; if they did not, a weak economy forced most to emigrate. But in a society without social security or pension plans, even the oldest son might remain economically dependent, unable to marry until his father's death.

As one result, the marriage rate fell; before the famine only 10 percent of Irish women remained unmarried at age 45; by 1926, the figure was 25 percent. Before the famine, 20 percent of husbands were more than 10 years older than their brides; by the early twentieth century, one reflection of the pressure on men to delay marriage, the figure was 50 percent. May–December marriages can doubtless be happy, but the figures reveal a society that discouraged spontaneous relationships between young people. In other European countries, most emigrants were male, but the dearth of marital prospects at home was probably a major reason that 50 percent of Irish emigrants were women.[2] As late as 1973, an anthropologist studying a rural Irish community noted that young people who planned to emigrate postponed any expectation of sex until they arrived in their new country, and those who planned to stay at home assumed they were committed to chastity. Even by 1987, 22 percent of Irish males over the age of 45 had never married.[3]

Given the economic deterrents to marriage, it is not surprising that the Free State promoted chastity and "denounced [sex] as a satanic snare, in even what had been its most innocent pre-famine manifestations."[4] Certainly Catholic moral teaching, which condemns all sex outside marriage, played a key role. But why would this teaching be more influential in the 1920s than it had been 100 years earlier? In the distant past, Irish-speaking children were educated at hedge schools, where the schoolmaster was a lay person. The British introduced compulsory schooling in English and taught children to read the Protestant King James Bible. The Free State's special relationship with the Catholic Church essentially made Catholic education the norm. As educational opportunities increased, more children spent more years in gender-segregated schools that promoted chastity. Even outside school, the official church was more visible and present: in 1840, there had been 1 priest to every 3,500 lay people; in 1960 it was 1 to every 600. In 1841, there was 1 nun to every 7,000 Catholics; a century later, there was 1 nun to every 400 lay people.[5]

The picture of sexual shame, repression, and unhappiness that permeates twentieth-century Irish film and literature reflects the influence of hundreds of hours of schooling in chastity. Well into the 1970s, the absence of sexual images from Irish billboards, the silence about sex in newspapers and magazines, and the reticence to speak of sex might have convinced an outsider that sex was unimportant to the Irish. But, it has been argued that

> sex was very real and demanding and it was rigorously inculcated ... in the demands of leading a pure ... life. The achievement was a fear, guilt, and shame about the body, its pleasures and desires.... Sex was constituted as a danger which lurked in every look, thought, act, word and feeling. It had to be guarded against through constant prayer and a strict regulation of bodies. It had to be sought out and extracted from children and adults in an ongoing process of vigilance, supervision, self-examination, and confession.[6]

WOMEN'S RIGHTS

Catholic influence permeated both the law and the individual psyche. Even today the status of women in the Irish constitution reflects conservative Catholic teachings on the family, an outcome that would have appalled a small but active circle of early twentieth-century Irish feminists who blamed the British for introducing sexism. In 1914, they founded the women's auxiliary of Sinn Fein, Cumann na Ban, pledging to reclaim "for the women of Ireland the rights that belonged to them under the old Gaelic civilization, where sex was no bar to citizenship, and where women were free to devote to ... their country every talent and capacity with which they were endowed."[7] Initially, the Free State granted women full political rights, including the right to vote and to be elected to the Parliament (Dail). However, a series of laws passed during the 1920s and 1930s substantially limited these: "In 1924 and 1927, the Cosgrave government brought in legislation to restrict women's right to serve on juries; in 1925, women's right to sit for all examinations in the Civil Service was curtailed; in 1932, compulsory retirement was introduced for married women teachers and eventually applied to the entire Civil Service; in 1935, the government assumed the right to limit the employment of women in any given industry; in 1937, the constitution defined women's role in the State exclusively in terms of the hearth and home."[8]

A marked retreat from feminism after activists gained votes for women shortly after World War I can also be found in England and the United States. In Ireland, however, the special relationship of church to state produced a rhetoric that tied nationalism to domesticity, as well as sexual purity. Church authorities lectured women about a Gaelic ideal that, according to one observer, owed more to papal encyclicals than to ancient Irish folkways. Modesty became a Celtic virtue when women were urged to cover themselves in the heavy native wool, rather than in clingy foreign fabrics. If foreign dances, such as the waltz, required couples to embrace, the native step dance did not, and it had the additional benefit of quickly exhausting the dancers.[9] But none of these authorities wanted women to go back to the authentic life of a pre-famine peasant, whose mud floor never needed washing, whose family never demanded clean sheets for the piles of straw on which they slept, and whose cooking skills were limited to boiling potatoes.[10] As diet, housing, and clothing improved, women's domestic tasks multiplied, creating an additional incentive for retrofitting the Victorian notion of "separate spheres" to the Gaelic past. Whether keeping house for her aged parents, the parish priest, or a husband, a woman was expected to live in a domestic world of her own for which nature had endowed her.

Catholic nuns, girls in First Communion dresses. Female innocence: many Irish women look back on their religious upbringing with great bitterness.

These expectations acquired the force of law in the Irish Constitution adopted in 1937. Article 40, after declaring "all citizens ... equal before the law," gives the State the right to make laws recognizing "differences of capacity, physical and moral, and of social function." Article 41 declares "the family ... indispensable to the welfare of the Nation and the State ... by her life within the home, woman gives to the State a support without which the common good cannot be achieved. The state shall, therefore, endeavor to ensure that mothers shall not be obliged by economic necessity to engage in labor to the neglect of their duties in the home." One may well argue for the good intentions of Article 41; it acknowledges housekeeping and child-rearing as real work. It explicitly rules out welfare-to-work programs that force women to accept low-paying jobs when they believe their children would be better off if they stayed home. But the Free State had neither the means nor the desire to provide adequate incomes for stay-at-home mothers, and so the more benign possibilities of Article 41 remained unrealized even in 2002, when a government survey of women noted that many expressed a desire that "women who are working full time in the home and caring for young children should receive a payment."[11] Instead, by defining women as mothers and allowing the state the right to make legal distinctions on the basis of a citizen's "social function," the Constitution permitted explicit gender discrimination. Custom and law assumed, in the face of all contrary evidence, that a responsible male provider had been issued to every family; women were even ineligible for unemployment benefits.[12]

PUNISHING INSTITUTIONS

Article 41 failed to protect women economically, but it did provide a rationale for organizing society along conservative, patriarchal lines. Declaring families the foundation of the state justified keeping divorce, homosexuality, birth control, and abortion illegal long after they were readily available elsewhere. The Free State, however, did not just extend the half-life of Victorian morality; it recast its institutions to protect an idealized vision of the Irish family. Working hand in hand, church and state turned the Magdalen laundry and the industrial school into powerful social forces, the first policing female sexuality and the second ensuring that children without parents, or with deviant parents, grew up in a strictly Catholic environment. In the late 1990s, Radio Telefis Eireann broadcast exposés of both. *Dear Daughter* (1996), *Sex in a Cold Climate* (1998), and *States of Fear* (1999) harshly criticized these institutions, with whose existence everyone had been at least vaguely familiar, and raised questions that continue to be asked. "Our dark past," wrote Brendan O'Connor in the *Sunday Independent* in May 1999, "has become an original sin that blackens the soul of every man, woman and child in this country."[13] *The Magdalene Sisters* and Pierce Brosnan's *Evelyn* (2002) gained these themes an international audience.

Magdalen asylums, as the name implies, were originally intended as refuges for prostitutes. In the nineteenth century, middle-class women in Britain and Ireland were recruited to venture into red-light districts to urge their fallen sisters to take shelter and learn how to make an honest living. Given the low skills and illiteracy of most prostitutes, and the limited employment options for women generally, the practice of running laundries in conjunction with asylums established itself quickly. In the nineteenth century, it is quite possible that some women welcomed the opportunity to leave the streets for a job in a laundry. But even then, rigid discipline and poor conditions in asylums caused many "penitents" to flee.[14] Whereas in twentieth-century England, the Magdalen asylum went the way of the Dickensian workhouse, the Irish Magdalen laundries prospered under the supervision of Catholic nuns. The state's special relationship with the Catholic church ensured that it would provide little independent review of Catholic institutions that reflected its own views. By 1996, when Dublin's Gloucester Street Refuge closed, they had become a symbol of the culture's most repressive features.

A major problem was that preventing transgressive sexual behavior replaced the originally narrower goal of rescuing women from prostitution. Fallen women were supposed to enter asylums of their own free will, but one study of Irish laundries run by the Good Shepherd Sisters revealed that about 50 percent of their inmates were "brought" in by "priests, relatives, or friends." Just how unwilling they were, or "under what constraint they were kept," will never be known.[15] Relatives could bring in a young woman because she was suspected of engaging in premarital sex or thought to exhibit an alarming interest in sex. Significant numbers were mentally ill or of low intelligence. In some cases a parish priest might recommend that a girl be placed in an asylum for her own protection, perhaps because she had been a victim of incest. Once institutionalized, all of the girls and women were subjected to the same regimen: hard work, long periods of compulsory silence, observance of curfews and restrictions, and quick punishment for disobedience. Penitence and remorse were constantly preached; "an awareness of guilt was obsessively urged."[16] Therapy an incest victim might need, or special education for the retarded, was unavailable; the company of actual prostitutes or the mentally ill imposed its own liabilities and added to the stigma of confinement.

Moreover, in contrast to the original practice of institutionalizing women for short periods, Irish nuns encouraged inmates to remain indefinitely. The laundry might be a convent's major income source, and good workers, possibly the "dull-witted and easily prevailed upon, were a vital part of the system."[17] Mary Connolly, sent to an asylum in New Ross "for protection" in 1871, when she was 12, died there in 1941 at the age of 82; Nora Gallagher, brought to the Limerick Asylum at age 18, "served 62 years of penance" before her death in 1939.[18] Some who left returned because they were so ill-equipped to cope with independent living. Some seem simply not to have known that they had the legal right to leave, or would when they turned 21. The blurry line between state and church perpetuated this confusion; inmates who fled were sometimes returned by the police. A 1970 government report disclosed that 70 girls between the ages of 13 and 19 were then detained by court order in Magdalen institutions, and commented that "the legal validity of this procedure was doubtful."[19]

Another long and unhappy episode in the collaboration of church and state in Ireland ended on May 11, 1999, when the Taoiseach apologized on behalf of the state to victims of abuse in the industrial school system. Like the laundries, the industrial schools were under Catholic supervision; unlike them, they were "established by law, and funded and regulated by the Department of Education."[20] Well into the 1950s, the 52 Irish industrial schools held at least 6,000 children at any one time, although the numbers dropped to 3,000 children in 31 schools by 1969. Although the schools were often referred to as orphanages, most of their residents—nearly 95 percent in 1933—had at least one living parent.[21] The state's policy of paying religious orders to take care of children rather than providing direct support to parents separated many families. Children entered the system after being committed by a judge, often on the recommendation of government inspectors nicknamed "the cruelty police."[22] Some were homeless, or had been found begging in the streets; but others were picked up because they had missed too much school, or because their mothers were not married to the men with whom they lived. Several schools specialized in rescuing children whose "Catholic faith was perceived to be in danger."[23] Only a small percentage—perhaps 1 percent of the girls and 11 percent of the boys—were committed for acts of delinquency.[24] Nonetheless, many people regarded industrial schools for older boys as reformatories.

What was truly remarkable about these schools is how often and how systematically they abused and even starved children, and how slow the courts and the Department of Education were to intervene. One finds detailed documentation in reports filed as far back as the 1940s and 1950s by P. O. Muircheartaigh, Inspector of Industrial and Reformatory Schools, and Anna McCabe, Medical Inspector of the schools. Here were two officials who should have exercised real power, repeatedly speaking of being "appalled by conditions," accusing nuns of keeping children in a state of "semi-starvation ... for which parents would be prosecuted," describing children as "emaciated, cowed, dirty and unhappy."[25] Yet although they succeeded in having a handful of the most abusive administrators removed, the orders defended themselves vigorously and the deference habitually extended to Catholic religious leaders prevented any systematic reform. When Boys Town's Father Flanagan called severe beatings in industrial schools "a disgrace to the nation," the Minister for Justice, Gerry Boland, denounced his "offensive and intemperate language."[26] Violence was frequently accompanied by sexual abuse, a matter of common knowledge among students seldom spoken of in public. David Murray, employed at St. Joseph's in Kilkenny in the 1970s, received a 10-year sentence for "gross sexual abuse" only in 1997, the same year his replacement at St. Joseph's, Myles Brady, was sentenced to a 4-year term for a similar crime.

LEGALIZING DIVORCE

Murray and Brady's imprisonments, along with well-publicized prosecutions of clergy such as Brendan Smyth for sexual abuse, provide an excellent example of the struggle in contemporary Ireland to bring the law and public rhetoric into line with private realities. The movement to legalize divorce provides another example. The constitutional ban did not prevent marriages from breaking down; by 1994, the year before the Divorce Referendum passed, sociologists estimated that approximately one in eight Irish marriages failed.[27] It is probably reasonable to assume that some similar number of marriages had been unhappy in the past, but few couples were granted legal separations. Between 1946 and 1970, only 27 such separations were granted; between 1970 and 1981, there was an average of 5 separations a year. In 1982, when the law changed to allow circuit courts to hear these cases, the numbers increased so that between 1982 and 1990, an average of 50 separations were granted.[28] A referendum to legalize divorce, promoted by the Fine Gael Taoiseach, Garret FitzGerald, and Labour's increasingly visible Mary Robinson failed on June 26, 1985, when 63.48 percent of the voters rejected it.[29] It is true that the Catholic Church opposed the referendum, and that an Episcopal letter reiterating the church's opposition to divorce was read at every Sunday Mass in the land for three weeks before the vote. But not all opposition was narrowly doctrinal; soaring divorce rates in other countries had raised genuine concern, which conservative campaigners exploited, over such issues as the financial hardships of divorced women and their children. Alice Glenn, a Fine Gael TD, summed up this line of argument by declaring that "any woman voting for divorce is like a turkey voting for Christmas."[30]

In the 10 years between the defeat of the first divorce referendum and the passage of the second on November 24, 1995, the government took several measures to improve conditions for separated couples and their children and to acknowledge that in many second families, a parent was still legally bound to a former spouse. The Domicile and Foreign Divorces Act of 1986, for example, recognized divorces obtained abroad if one partner had actually been living in the country that granted the divorce. In 1987, the Status of Children Act abolished the legal category of illegitimacy; the Judicial Separation and Family Law Reform Act of 1989 added "no fault" grounds for separation and provided a process for adjusting property claims. In 1995, the Domestic Violence Act extended to cohabiting couples the same rights previously offered to married couples. The split between the church and state evident during the 1985 referendum widened. In 1992, Bertie Ahern, then Fianna Fail Minister for Finance, spoke publicly of being separated from his wife and living with another woman. The conservative Fianna Fail adopted a prodivorce position in 1994, and eventually all six Irish political parties campaigned for the second referendum. Although the 1995 victory was the first time a "liberal agenda" had won, it did so by the narrowest of margins, 9,114 votes out of 1.63 million cast.

Bertie Ahern with Tony Blair, 2002. © *Irish Times*.

The Family Law (Divorce) Act was passed in 1996 and scheduled to go into effect on February 27, 1997. In a case that speaks volumes about conditions that had developed under the constitutional ban, the Irish High Court made a special exception, granting the first divorce on January 17, 1997 to a terminally ill man in his sixties. He married his long-term companion, with whom he had a daughter, and died two weeks later. The law requires that divorcing couples have been separated for four years, that no possibility of a reconciliation exists, and that "spouses and dependent members of the family" have been provided for. This last provision reflects the prodivorce advocates' realization of how powerful economic arguments against divorce had been in the mid-1980s, and was intended to prevent divorced women from losing their rights to a publicly funded Deserted Wives Benefit. Long familiar to Americans, the economic stresses of supporting a second family are even greater, and accompanied by more uncertainty, in Ireland. Nonetheless, the divorce rate continues to increase; the 2002 census revealed that the number of divorced persons in the Republic had more than tripled between 1996 and 2002, from 9,800 to 35,100.

REPRODUCTIVE FREEDOM

As seen, the Divorce Act, which separates Irish law from Catholic doctrine, gave official recognition to the social reality of broken marriages. The free availability of birth control today in the Republic represents a similar recognition of a reality that an earlier generation tried to proscribe. The Carrigan Committee, which recommended a law banning birth control in 1931, explicitly acknowledged that birth control had "become extremely prevalent ... so common in some place were such articles ... that there was no attempt to conceal the sale of them."[31] The draconian "Criminal Law Amendment Act" of 1935 banned the import, sale, and distribution of contraceptives and in addition prohibited the circulation of birth control information. One result was, as seen, that people continued to marry late; another was that emigration limited family size. The departure of an "astonishing six million" people between the 1840s and the 1960s "etched a deep wound on the Irish psyche."[32] Virtually every family lost some of its members to far-away places from which they seldom returned: the United States, Canada, and Australia. Many were separated for long periods as a husband or child went off to work in England.

Because contraceptives were available in Northern Ireland, the ban created the greatest hardships for poor and uneducated women who lacked the resources to travel. Although rhythm was the only approved method, a Dublin doctor noted that his experience suggested that 40 percent of his patients were using some other, more reliable, form of birth control by 1968.[33] When the Pill became available in the 1960s, the Republic continued to ban it as a contraceptive but allowed doctors to prescribe it as a "cycle regulator." By 1967, 15,000 Irish women were on the Pill, about 75 percent of them for what their doctors called "social reasons."[34] The birth rate fell from 64,072 in 1964 to 61,004 in 1968, even though more people were marrying, and at a younger age.[35] During this time, many Catholics hoped for a relaxation of doctrinal restrictions on contraception, perhaps for approval of the Pill, and Pope Paul VI's *De Humanae Vitae* in 1968 was a bitter disappointment. That the Irish birth rate increased by 12.5 percent from 1968 to 1974 suggests that many Catholics initially complied with the Pope's teaching.

By 1968, however, the sexual revolution was beginning, even in Ireland, and a feminist movement followed quickly. The ambiguously named Fertility Guidance Clinic opened in Dublin on February 25, 1969. On their lawyer's advice, the medical staff gave contraceptives away free, to avoid breaking the law against their sale. To circumvent the law against shipping contraceptives to the Republic, volunteers smuggled them in from the United Kingdom. Starting with 167 clients in 1969, by 1972 the clinic offered 10,158 consultations.[36] In 1970, one of the clinic's founders, Michael Solomons, was invited to lecture on family planning at Trinity College; in 1972, Dublin's Rotunda Hospital opened a family planning clinic of its own. Partly under growing pressure from feminists, but also because of its interest in joining the European Economic Community, the government established a Commission on the Status of Women in 1970. In its first report, in 1972, the Commission argued for allowing parents "to regulate the number and spacing of their family."[37] And finally, in the most spectacular protest, some 50 feminists organized a "contraceptive train" that took a round-trip to Belfast on May 22, 1971 to bring back scores of forbidden condoms and spermicides.[38] When Customs officials made no effort to seize the products and the police made no arrests, the women were in a strong position to argue that the state itself had no serious interest in enforcing the law.

In spite of all this evidence that many Irish people practiced birth control and believed that doing so should be legal, efforts to pass a law embodying this reality started and stalled throughout the 1970s. As Irish Prime Minister (Taoiseach) Charles Haughey put it, what was needed was "an Irish solution to an Irish problem," a way to placate conservative fears that legalizing family planning would open the door to teenage promiscuity.[39] Senator Mary Robinson's many attempts to introduce a "Pill bill" in the Dail were repeatedly blocked. The first official move toward liberalization came from the Supreme Court in December 1973. A woman named Mary McGee, who lived in a mobile home with her husband and four young children, had a history of serious medical problems during pregnancy. Her Irish Family Planning Association doctor recommended a spermicide, which she ordered from England. When it arrived, Customs seized the package. Believing McGee to be an ideal test case, her doctor encouraged her to go to court, claiming that this action contravened her rights under Article 40 of the Irish Constitution, which defines the citizen's personal rights. More remarkably, McGee's lawyer also argued that notorious Article 41, which gives so much weight to the family, ought to be interpreted as protecting husband and wife against the intrusions of the state. The Supreme Court accepted this argument, thus effectively legalizing the importation of contraceptives, although not their sale in the Republic. It took another six years for the Dail to pass a Family Planning Act, a halfway measure that permitted sale of contraceptives to married couples whose doctors gave them a prescription ensuring that they were using them for "bona fide family planning."[40]

In spite of its limitations, the 1979 law, by permitting any sale of contraceptives, was the state's first refusal to "criminalize practices merely because they contravene the moral beliefs" of the Catholic Church.[41] The die had been cast. In 1985, the Dail voted to allow the sale of condoms and spermicides without a prescription and to anyone over 18 years old. In 1993, the age restriction for the sale of condoms was dropped, advertisements for them were permitted, and vending machine distribution became permissible. By the 2002 census, the birth rate in the Republic had decreased to 15.5 per 1,000, close to the 12.6 per 1,000 rate in Northern Ireland. The average number of children per family, 2.2 in the Republic in 1986, was down to 1.6 in 2002.

The issue of abortion, which reflects some of the same conflicts between Catholic belief and Irish behavior, still remains open. In this case, however, the official Catholic position is endorsed by a fervent grassroots movement spearheaded by organizations such as Family Solidarity. In a 1983 referendum, a Pro-Life Amendment Coalition was instrumental in persuading two-thirds of those voting to support an Eighth Amendment to the constitution, which pledged the state to support "the right to life of the unborn with due regard to the equal right of the mother." Abortion remains one of the most painful issues in public life. The X case, which received worldwide coverage in 1992, traumatized many people and sooner or later seems to come into every Irish discussion of the subject.

"X" was a 14-year-old raped by a family friend who was later sentenced to 14 years in prison. X's parents took her to England for an abortion but, before surgery, contacted the garda (police) to see whether a DNA test performed on the fetus would be admissible in court as proof of paternity. The garda informed the Attorney-General, Harry Whelehan, who on February 12,

1992, issued an interim injunction against X and her parents, compelling them return to Ireland. Shortly after they did so, the High Court granted a permanent injunction to prevent X from leaving the country during her pregnancy. In doing so, the judge rejected the argument that the girl was suicidal, on the view that while an abortion would surely kill her baby, it was not at all certain that she would follow through on her intention to kill herself. Given the girl's age and the circumstances of the pregnancy, many people were outraged. Singer Sinead O'Connor, announcing that she had undergone two abortions, called for protest marches. The President, Mary Robinson, stated publicly that women were frustrated and helpless, and that Ireland "must move on to a more compassionate society . . . and make progress in this very difficult area"[42] As protesters marched and the local right-to-life movement denounced Robinson, the world press drew unflattering comparisons between Ireland and the Ayatollah's Iran.

By the end of February, the Supreme Court had lifted the injunction; on March 5, by a 4 to 1 vote, it ruled that abortion could be permitted if there was a real threat to the mother's life. As it had done in McGee's case, the Court interpreted the Constitution liberally. Using the language of the Eighth Amendment itself, the Court argued that the phrase "with due regard to the equal right to life of the mother" obliged it to recognize suicide as "a real and substantial threat."[43] This decision meant that, in some circumstances, abortion was, after all, legal, although exactly what those circumstances might be remained unclear. On the other hand, three of five judges maintained that the state did have the right to prevent a woman from leaving the state to obtain an abortion. In this pronouncement, the Court put Ireland on a collision course with the recently negotiated Maastricht Treaty, which, among others, guaranteed citizens of the European Community (EC) states the right to free movement within the EC. The situation grew murkier when the right-to-life lobby announced that it would campaign against Maastricht, which the Taoiseach was eager to see ratified by public referendum.

Thus in 1993, the Irish voted not only on Maastricht, but on three other referenda stemming from the X case. The first gave citizens the right to travel to another state; the second gave them a right to obtain information about services that were legally available elsewhere. Both of these passed comfortably. However, a third, which would have permitted abortion in cases where the mother's life, "as distinct from . . . health," was in danger, was rejected by 65.4 percent of the voters. Some of those who voted "no" were in favor of legalizing abortion but objected because the law did not go far enough. But the failure to affirm abortion in any circumstances reflects a broader cultural consensus that includes some women with feminist sympathies. Mary Kenny, one of the organizers of the 1972 "contraceptive train," had an abortion in

London in the early 1970s.[44] Still, although she recounted her misery in 1983 over quarrels with friends about the Eighth Amendment, "when all was said and done, I felt obliged in conscience to defend the proposition that the unborn child is a human being whose life we are not entitled to take."[45]

Indeed, even the narrow grounds the Irish Supreme Court set in the X case—abortion in cases where the mother's life is threatened—remain controversial. On March 6, 2002, the Irish voted on a proposed constitutional amendment that would have excluded suicide as a legitimate threat to the mother's life. It was defeated, but only by the narrowest of margins: 50.42 percent "no" versus 49.58 percent "yes." A study of Irishwomen's social attitudes the same year produced some support for legalizing abortion but also deep opposition. Statements such as "abortion is another form of violence against women and is the ultimate violence against the unborn child" contrast sharply with the mainstream feminist consensus that developed around other topics.[46] Nor is abortion an issue that divides Northern Ireland from the Republic. The legalization of abortion in the rest of the United Kingdom in 1967 has never been expanded to the North, where conservative Protestants oppose abortion as adamantly as Catholics do. Thus, Northern Ireland operates under a 1945 law that permits "therapeutic" abortions under ill-defined circumstances, in recent years, to somewhere between 50 and 80 women per year.[47] In 1983, both Ian Paisley and the Grand Master of the Orange Order, Rev. Martin Smyth, were vocal supporters of the Eighth Amendment.[48]

The English oppressed Ireland for centuries, so it is ironic that today Irish people go to Britain in search of personal freedoms unavailable at home. Since 1967, the availability of abortion in England, Wales, and Scotland has been a fact of Irish life. Many would agree with the comment that "going to England for our abortions is self-contradictory. . . . But it works. Its one virtue is that it's functional."[49] Nonetheless, as the Irish Family Planning Association's anthology of narratives by women who went to Britain for abortions, *The Irish Journey,* demonstrates, the actual experience is difficult. Even with Ryanair's cut-rate flights across the Irish Channel, travel expenses burden working-class women. Some must arrange for childcare; some face surgery alone, in a strange place; for many, there is the additional burden of lying, creating a cover story to account for three days abroad. This process is traumatic. One woman observed that "my abortion becoming a secret was damaging, not the act itself."[50] Another said she had "never realized the emotional isolation imposed on . . . people, when something private becomes, out of fear and necessity, something secret. It seems to me that the difference between the two is vital to the structure of a healthy society."[51]

Feminist and activist Medb Ruane deplores financial gains derived from the abortion ban: "the Irish exchequer profits by over 60,000 pounds a year . . . in

transport taxes paid by people traveling for abortion in Britain.... Irish air-
lines and ferries profit by approximately 7,500 pounds a day as a result."[52]
But what Ruane sees as hypocrisy doubtless seems to others the inevitable
price of an Irish solution to an Irish problem. And, of course, it is a Northern
Irish problem as well; Ann Rossiter and Mary Sexton's *The Other Irish Journey* (2001) found that Northern women face the same obstacles. Forty-four
percent of those interviewed stated that they had to borrow money to go to
England. Fear and distrust kept two-thirds from consulting a general prac-
titioner at home.[53] Psychological similarities are telling: one Christian fundamentalist spoke of believing that by terminating her pregnancy she was
"going to commit murder."[54]

WOMEN IN THE WORKFORCE

The 1972 report of the Irish Commission on the Status of Women alluded
to earlier also raised workplace issues. As seen, the Irish Constitution of 1937
sanctioned job discrimination against women, particularly married women.
Many Irish practices, such as requiring female schoolteachers to resign when
they married, were widespread elsewhere during the Depression. World War II
and postwar prosperity, however, allowed these practices to die a natural death
in most Western countries. In Ireland, which had not entered the war, there
was no prosperity and thus no increasing demand for qualified workers. As
a result, while conditions for working women gradually improved in other
English-speaking countries, the Irish were passing laws to prevent any loosen-
ing of Depression-era restrictions. The Civil Service Regulation Act of 1956,
for example, reaffirmed the practice of requiring women in all but the lowest
civil service ranks to give up their positions when they married.

Such laws are only one reason that the proportion of women in the labor
force in the Republic actually declined between 1961 and 1981, while
increasing sharply in the North. During this period, the Republic's economy
gradually improved; but with prosperity, the old practice of delaying marriage declined. Because families in this era were larger than in the North,
working women with families doubtless faced greater practical difficulties in
the Republic. At any rate, "By 1981 over 44.8 percent of married women in
Northern Ireland were in the labor market, more than double the percentage in the Irish Republic."[55] In some areas, however, the demand for workers made it impossible for the state to put into full practice its legal right to
discriminate in favor of male workers. Women, for example, continued to
work in industries; so "the Industrial Development Authority deliberately
set out to promote investment in industries which employed a majority of
male workers, and in the early seventies they largely succeeded in meeting the

government's aim that 75 percent of new jobs in manufacturing industry" be filled with men.[56]

Thus, although the workplace issues that the Commission on the Status of Women identified in 1972 will sound familiar to any feminist—fair hiring practices, equal pay for equal work, protection from dismissal on grounds of marital status or pregnancy, paid maternity leave—the barriers to be overcome were greater, or at any rate more formal, than they were in England or the United States. The women's cause, however, received a major boost from Ireland's decision to enter the European Economic Community in 1973. Once part of the European Community, Ireland was required to bring its laws and practices into compliance with the European Community's substantially more egalitarian regulations. As will be seen when discussing gay rights, threats to sue the Irish state in the European Court led to substantial social changes. The long-preserved "marriage bar" fell in 1973, although it took the Employment Equality Act of 1977 to end all discrimination on the basis of marital status. In 1975, the Anti-Discrimination (Pay) Act became law; a similar equal pay law had applied to Northern Ireland since 1970. The results for working women have been transformative, and the pace of change continues to accelerate. The percentage of women in the labor force, 48.8 percent in 2002, remains relatively low when Ireland is compared with other Economic Union countries; but it has increased dramatically, by 140 percent between 1971 and 2000. For married women, the figures increased from 7.5 percent in 1971 to 46.4 percent in 2000.[57]

Ireland's . . . Reports under the United Nations Convention on the Elimination of . . . Discrimination Against Women (2003) document remarkable progress. The Equal Status Act of 2002 protects Irish citizens from discrimination on the basis of gender, marital status, family status, and sexual orientation as well as age, religion, race, and traveller status. This act covers the defense services, as well as civilian employers, and has been extended to most nonworkplace areas: access to goods, services, travel, banking, and education. Education levels are on the rise for both men and women. In 2003, 23.1 percent of the Irish population had graduated from college or a similar "third level" of education, compared with 17.3 percent in 1999. Remarkably, there are now more women, 321,000, with these credentials than men, 300,000. For women, that is a 47 percent increase in four years. Women are 53.57 percent of all entrants to postsecondary education and outnumber men in all areas except engineering, manufacturing, and construction. The number of women who are lawyers, doctors, and school or college administrators increased substantially between 1996 and 2002. Eighteen weeks of guaranteed maternity leave, with a government benefit, have now been extended to adoptive parents; eight weeks of additional unpaid leave is optional. A separate Parental Leave

Act allows 14 weeks of leave for each parent, which may be taken in shorter spells if desired, with the proviso that the time be used up before the child is five years old.

Naturally there is room for improvement. Although Ireland has had two women presidents, in 2002 only 13.25 percent of Dail and 16.67 percent of Seanad seats were held by women. Although universities are educating large numbers of women, a list of full-time staff at Irish universities shows women outnumbered at every rank. There were 307 male full professors to 23 female full professors in 2002, and even at the lowly level of assistant lecturer there were 187 men for 169 women. The gender pay gap has narrowed but not closed; the government reports that it relies on the 1997 European Household Panel report for the statistic that the gender pay gap is 15.5 percent. Some of that gap can be explained by time off for maternity or the relatively large number of young women in the labor force, but the government believes that a 5 percent pay gap remains that can be ascribed only to discrimination. Long waiting lists for nursery schools and stories of inadequate care will sound familiar to parents in other countries; it is a sign of progress that the government earmarked $211.63 million for a National Childcare Strategy for 2000–2002.

Again as elsewhere, the problem of domestic abuse receives widespread coverage. In 2001, there were 9,983 reported incidents of domestic abuse that resulted in 1,783 charges being filed. As in other countries, such abuse is under-reported, perhaps by a factor of five.[58] There were 1,286 convictions for domestic abuse in 2001; in 2003 there were 15 shelters for abused women and their children and 13 support services designed to assist victims.

WOMEN AND VIOLENCE

One issue that remains important to feminists is the effect on women of the Troubles in Northern Ireland. The violence was at its most acute in the years when the women's movement was gaining its first successes in other English-speaking countries. Although some of the benefits for women, such as equal pay, reached Northern women, the sectarian struggle dominated people's lives in highly politicized working-class areas. Feminism seemed, even to many women, like a distant and frivolous movement, "bra-burning" while people were being shot dead in the streets of Belfast and Derry. Although women joined paramilitary organizations on both sides, they were outnumbered and usually subordinate. Wives of members of the Irish Republican Army (IRA) interned at Long Kesh were kept under scrutiny, lest they prove unfaithful. In the 1970s, terrible news photographs of women with shaved heads chained to lampposts advertised the consequences to working-class Catholic girls of dating British soldiers. Domestic violence blurred into the general violence of time and place. The police were preoccupied with more public crimes and seldom ventured into the most dangerous neighborhoods on domestic complaints. Illegal weapons were close at hand in many homes. It has been argued that "these weapons have often been used against women," a fact that official discussions about decommissioning weapons continue to ignore.[59]

Nonetheless, the Troubles also compelled many women to find a public voice. Wives of prisoners, even if they could not find work, were forced to negotiate with the social services, cope with bills, and find a way to mend fuses or fix a dripping faucet. Many who had lost husbands, children, and close friends to the violence organized neighborhood centers to provide childcare, classes, and other support for women. The most famous organization was "Women for Peace," the forerunner of today's "Peace People." On August 10, 1976, British soldiers were chasing a car driven by a fleeing IRA man; the car spun out of control, killing three of the children of Anne and Jack McGuire. Mairead Corrigan, the children's aunt and a Catholic, joined forces with Betty Williams, a Protestant who had witnessed the deaths, to organize a nonsectarian peace movement. The women's success in defining an alternative to violence and mobilizing interdenominational peace marches led to their receiving the Nobel Peace Prize in 1976. It is also true that by 1980, when Anne McGuire committed suicide and Betty Williams moved to the United States after insisting on keeping her share of the prize money, the movement was in disarray. Nonetheless, Corrigan and Williams helped to set Northern Ireland's still incomplete peace process in motion, and that they were a model for later groups, such as the Northern Ireland Women's Coalition, which played an active role in the talks leading up to 1998's Good Friday Agreement.

GAY RIGHTS

Many feminists were directly involved in the struggle for gay rights, and the burgeoning gay and lesbian movement used many of its strategies. Mary Robinson, who fought for so many women's issues, also supported the gay community. In 1992, as President, in one particularly memorable gesture of solidarity, she invited 35 lesbian and gay activists to join her at the "Irish White House," Aras an Uachtarain.[60] Kieran Rose, a leading activist, chronicled the Irish Gay Rights Movement from its origins in 1974, when the group set up a Gay Center in Dublin's Parnell Square, to the Dail's adoption in 1993 of a bill that in one stroke abolished "any rule of law by virtue of which buggery between persons is an offence."[61] In particular, he noted two crises that faced the gay movement in the 1980s: the international catastrophe of

AIDS and the growth of the pro-life movement, best known for its success in promoting passage of the Eighth Amendment but also militantly opposed to liberalizing the laws on homosexuality.

Many liberals blamed the aggressive "family values" of the period for what they saw as official tolerance of anti-gay violence. In 1983, a gang of young men chased a gay man, Declan Flynn, through a Dublin park and then beat him to death; after their conviction, the judge gave them a suspended sentence. Nor were things better in Ulster, where the 1967 liberalization of British law on homosexuality did not apply. When, in 1975, 23 gay men who had tried to organized a gay rights movement were arrested, they appealed to the European Court of Human Rights. In 1977, the Northern Ireland Human Rights Commission recommended reform of laws on homosexuality and the British government announced that liberalization would be forthcoming. At this news, Ian Paisley launched his infamous "Save Ulster from Sodomy" campaign, gathering 70,000 signatures in favor of keeping homosexual acts criminalized. The British government threw up its hands, claiming that it could not carry out reforms in the face of so much opposition from both Catholics and Protestants.

Gay and lesbian activists responded to hardships with new strategies. In response to the victory march of Flynn's killers, the Dublin Lesbian and Gay Collective organized the largest gay protest march Ireland had ever seen;

Gay Pride parade in Dublin, 2002. © *Irish Times*.

feminists, trade unionists, and others outside gay community joined in. This coalition was to prove highly effective at tapping "real and positive traditional Irish values, arising from the struggle against colonialism and for civil, religious, and economic rights" in other sections of the community.[62] One sign of this strategy's effectiveness is the Irish Congress of Trade Unions' adoption of *Lesbian and Gay Rights in the Workplace: Guidelines for Negotiators* in 1987. The solidarity of the gay community, and its organization skills, also grew as the AIDS crisis worsened. The Department of Health was slow to provide information about AIDS prevention on the view that it might be taken as information about gay sex. A new organization, Gay Health Action, took on the work of providing information itself. An organization called Cairde was formed for those with AIDS or testing HIV-positive. Some measure of the respect these organizations generated can be seen in Charles Haughey's successful proposal to add homosexuals to the list of persons protected under the 1989 Incitement to Hatred bill. One of his main arguments was that the government should take into account the danger that gay people would be blamed for the AIDS epidemic.

The European Court of Human Rights played a key role in changing the laws on homosexuality in both Northern Ireland and the Republic. In 1981, in response to British intransigence over decriminalization in Northern Ireland, the Court ruled that no member nation had a right to make laws imposing a total ban on homosexual activity. The next year, Parliament extended the 1967 British law to Northern Ireland. Meanwhile, back in Dublin, in 1977, David Norris, a gay activist and Trinity College professor, filed a claim with the Irish High Court claiming that Article Fifty of the Irish Constitution, which revokes all previous laws inconsistent with the Constitution, should be interpreted as invalidating the Victorian laws criminalizing homosexuality. Both the High Court and the Supreme Court rejected this claim, in part because Norris had never been prosecuted under any of the laws in question. In 1983, Norris filed a complaint against Ireland with the Human Rights Court, which reiterated its 1981 decision and declared that homosexuals were victimized by the fear and shame Irish law produced. The Irish government said it would ponder the decision and then stalled. In response, gay activists focused their campaign on new legislation. As consensus grew, even the Catholic bishops issued a conciliatory statement, saying that the Church "does not expect that acts which are sinful should, by that very fact, be made criminal offenses."[63] Remarkably, the new liberal law passed in 1993 went beyond the British law, legalizing homosexual acts between consenting adults rather than simply decriminalizing them.

On the whole, the Victorian family values that the Irish Free State rewrote as traditional Gaelic purity have now lost their grip on Irish law and society. As in many other countries, the city is distinctly more liberal than the countryside; but then more people live in cities now—a third of the population of the Republic lives in Dublin. Yet are there any other prosperous modern societies in which nearly half of the voters oppose abortion even in cases where the pregnant woman is suicidal? As has been seen, the recent narratives of Irish women who sought English abortions suggest that years of sexual repression still shadow the national psyche. A more hopeful narrative is found in the career of Mary Robinson, the woman whose name, as senator and president, is linked to so much courageous advocacy for an open and tolerant Ireland.

MARY ROBINSON, PRESIDENT

Although the Irish Presidency is largely ceremonial, Robinson used her visibility in that office from 1990 to 1997 to promote justice and compassion. As president during the 150th anniversary of the famine, she made a point not only of memorializing the Irish victims but of reminding her nation that "the bailiff and the coffin ship have equally terrible equivalents in other countries for other peoples at this very moment." She reminded the Irish that they had been emigrants for 200 years and were morally bound to offer refuge to African and Eastern European refugees. She went on to become United Nations Commissioner for Human Rights for five years and then assumed the directorship of the Ethical Globalization Initiative, a position she continued to hold in 2004, when she joined the faculty of Columbia University. In 2004, her organization focused on a "rights and gender-based approach" to three issues: migration, international trade and development, and the HIV/AIDS crisis in Africa. As most issues of gender and rights reach resolution at home, Robinson remains committed to turning the Irish experience of discrimination and injustice into a force for a more humane world.

NOTES

1. Irish Family Planning Association, *The Irish Journey: Women's Stories of Abortion* (Dublin: IFPA, 2000), 10.

2. Hugh Brody, *Iniskillane* (London: Jill Norman and Hobhouse, 1973): "the young people who anticipate emigration have transferred any expectation of sexual gratification—in or outside marriage—from home and countryside to cities far away from home. Equally, those who have decided to stay at home do so in the full realization that the decisions almost certainly entails a life of chastity" (180).

3. Tom Inglis, *Lessons in Irish Sexuality* (Dublin: UCD Press, 1998), 33.

4. Joseph Lee, *Ireland, 1912–1985: Politics and Society* (Cambridge: Cambridge University Press, 1989), 135.

5. Lee, 135.

6. Michel Peillon, *Contemporary Irish Society: An Introduction* (Dublin: Gill and Macmillan, 1982), 102.

7. Nancy J. Curtin, "'A Nation of Abortive Men': Gendered Citizenship and Early Irish Republicanism," in *Reclaiming Gender: Transgressive Identities in Modern Ireland,* ed. Marilyn Cohen and Nancy J. Curtin (London: Macmillan, 1999), 47.

8. Maryann Valiulis, *Gender and Sexuality in Modern Ireland* (Amherst: University of Massachusetts Press, 1997), 158.

9. Valiulis, 155.

10. Lee, 134.

11. *Aspirations of Women Collected in the Course of the Consultation Process on the National Plan for Women 2002: Towards a National Women's Strategy* (Dublin: Stationery Office, 2002), 9.

12. Yvonne Scannell, "The Constitution and the Role of Women," in *De Valera's Constitution and Ours,* Brian Farrell, ed. (Dublin: RTE and Gill and Macmillan, 1988), 128.

13. Quoted in Mary Kenny, *Goodbye to Catholic Ireland: A Personal, Social, and Cultural History from the Fall of Parnell to the Realm of Mary Robinson* (London: Sinclair-Stevenson, 1997), 314.

14. Frances Finnegan, *Do Penance or Perish: A Study of Magdalen Asylums in Ireland* (Piltown, Co Kerry: Congrave Press, 2001), 37.

15. Finnegan, 45.

16. Finnegan, 43.

17. Finnegan, 35, 42.

18. Finnegan, 40, 43.

19. Finnegan, 46.

20. Mary Raftery and Eoin O'Sullivan, *Suffer the Little Children: The Inside Story of Ireland's Industrial Schools* (New York: Continuum, 2001), 11.

21. Raftery and O'Sullivan, 23

22. Raftery and O'Sullivan, 21.

23. Raftery and O'Sullivan, 25.

24. Raftery and O'Sullivan, 22.

25. Raftery and O'Sullivan, 124–126.

26. Raftery and O'Sullivan, 190.

27. Gabriel Kiely and Valerie Richardson, *Family Policy in Ireland—1993.* Report to European Observatory of National Family Policies (Brussels, Belgium: European Commission, 1994), 37.

28. Chrystel Hug, *The Politics of Sexual Morality in Ireland* (New York: St. Martin's, 1999), 25, 26.

29. Hug, 47.

30. Hug, 43.

31. Hug, 80.

32. Terry Eagleton, *The Truth about the Irish* (Dublin: New Island, 1999).

33. Hug, 87.

34. Hug, 86.

35. Hug, 88.

36. Hug, 91.

37. Hug, 89.

38. Hug, 89.

39. Hug, 111.

40. Hug, 111.

41. Hug, 115.

42. Hug, 167.

43. Hug, 168.

44. Mary Kenny, *Abortion: The Whole Story* (London: Quartet Books, 1986), 4.

45. Kenny, *Goodbye to Catholic Ireland,* 361.

46. *Aspirations*, 121.

47. Ann Rossiter and Mary Sexton, *The Other Irish Journey: A Survey Update of Northern Irish Women Attending British Abortion Clinics, 2000–2001* (London: Marie Stopes International, 2001), 7.

48. Mary Kenny, *Goodbye to Catholic Ireland,* rev. ed. (Dublin: New Island, 2000), 292.

49. Nuala O'Faolain, *My Dream of You* (New York: Riverhead, 2001), 323.

50. Irish Family Planning Association, 42.

51. Irish Family Planning Association, 47.

52. Rossiter and Sexton, 4.

53. Rossiter and Sexton, 7.

54. Rossiter and Sexton, 7.

55. Mary E. Daly, *Women and Work in Ireland: Studies in Irish Economic and Social History* (Dublin: Dundalgan, 1997), 41.

56. Daly, 50.

57. "Jobless Rate below 5 percent for the First Time," *Irish Times,* 8 June 2000.

58. Karina Colgan, *You Have to Scream with Your Mouth Shut: Violence in the Home* (Dublin: Mercier, 1995), 11.

59. Megan Sullivan, *Women in Northern Ireland: Cultural Studies and Material Conditions* (Gainesville: University of Press of Florida, 1999).

60. Kieran Rose, *Diverse Communities: The Evolution of Lesbian and Gay Politics in Ireland* (Cork: Cork University Press, 1994), 36.

61. Rose, 1.

62. Rose, 4.

63. Rose, 57.

4

Cuisine, Holidays, and Leisure Activities

NOTHING REVEALS THE IRISH CHARACTER better than the simple pleasures of daily life: eating, drinking, celebrating holidays, and playing or watching sports. Each of these activities has its distinctive roots in Irish history, and each has changed significantly in the last two decades. Before Oliver Cromwell, the Irish diet was varied and plentiful. The land system the English imposed after 1690 sent meat and grains to the cities or to England; tenant farmers turned to the potato, brought from the New World to Spain by early sixteenth-century conquistadores. After the famine, most people were apparently happy just to get a full, carbohydrate-laden meal. The contemporary Irish interest in food, whether seen in imported supermarket items or gourmet restaurants, is a product of recent prosperity. On the other hand, although drinks and drinking customs have changed in the last 20 years, the heavy drinking traditionally associated with the Irish, and regarded by Irish people as a serious social problem since the mid-nineteenth century, continues. Many of the old Celtic holidays that survived in rural Catholic communities have died out in modern times, but local festivals keep their memories alive, and one, Halloween, has spread across the English-speaking world. Sports remain the most popular leisure activity in Ireland and one of the most distinctive. Irish sports such as Gaelic football and hurling, strongly promoted by nineteenth-century nationalists, remain popular even as Ireland fields internationally competitive teams in soccer and rugby.

CUISINE

Whatever the part played by Sir Walter Raleigh, said to have planted the first potatoes in Ireland on his Cork estate in the 1590s, the wholesale shift of the rural poor from a typical Northern European diet to the potato was a direct consequence of British colonialism. By the early nineteenth century, perhaps a third of the population, or close to 3 million people, had no other staple food.[1] The potato blight features in the ongoing story of Irish cuisine. When the Irish gentry lost their estates, a tradition of feasting died with them. The Anglo-Irish who replaced them brought with them the heavy diet of their homeland, with its roasted meats, its bland and long-boiled vegetables, its thick steamed puddings and fondness for sugary cakes and treacly puddings. After the famine, as some Catholic Irish struggled into middle-class respectability, they adopted the British diet. Readers of James Joyce will recall the Dickensian flavors of the festive dinner in "The Dead," with its "fat brown goose" and "great ham," its "blocks of blancmange and red jam."[2] At the same time, the urban poor adopted the white bread, margarine, and tea of their counterparts in England, a diet notably less nutritious than the pre-famine potato. For at least 100 years after the Famine, hunger and malnutrition of the kind described in Frank McCourt's *Angela's Ashes* (1996) were endemic in poor neighborhoods and even in some church-run schools.[3]

TRADITIONAL IRISH FOOD

Well into the twentieth century, just having enough to eat was a goal for many Irish people, and it is hardly surprising that post-famine Irish cuisine centered on plain, filling dishes, heavy on inexpensive carbohydrates and cheap cuts of meat. Nor, given the continuing close economic ties to England, is it surprising that British staples such as shepherd's pie or fish with chips and vinegar were equally popular in Ireland. Some of the more colorful dishes of the early twentieth century survive largely in specialty shops or folk memory. Few tourists will lament the passing of drisheens, a local version of the British black pudding, concocted of sheep suet, sheep's blood, and milk, all steamed together in sheep's intestines. Nor will they lament the days when tripe and onions in white sauce regularly accompanied drisheens. Nonetheless, there is a story of a contemporary Corkman, an exile in Dublin, who regularly orders 10 pounds of drisheens and 15 pounds of tripe from a butcher in his home town, a practice his wife permits on condition that she does not have to be in the house when he cooks them.[4] Another Cork tradition is "skirts and kidneys," a dish in which the membrane that separates a pig's stomach from its heart and lungs is simmered with pig's kidneys and onions. Pig's feet, cooked with carrot and onion, are called crubeens. Although not normally in high demand, crubeens sold out at Cork's Old English Market during Ireland's successful World Cup run in 1994.[5] "Dublin coddle," a working-class favorite, requires potatoes and onions to be simmered for an hour or so with sausage, bacon, and enough water to cover.

Irish stew and corned beef and cabbage seem to appear less frequently in Irish restaurants than in their Irish-American counterparts. In Ireland the stew contains lamb with onions and potatoes; carrots and turnips may be added. Similar ingredients may be baked into a Kerry pie. The Irish version of corned beef and cabbage is nearly identical to the American version, but a close variant, bacon and cabbage, is "without question Ireland's national dish."[6] To make it in the United States, one would need to use Canadian bacon. The cabbage is cut into thin strips, simmered with the bacon, then drained and buttered. The other national dish, the potato, is often served plain, either boiled or roasted, to be eaten with butter and salt. Still, there are numerous variations: champ is potato mashed with green onions and butter; if cabbage is added, it is called colcannon. Boxty is a pancake containing grated potatoes and flour, celebrated in a rhyme: "Boxty in the griddle/Boxty in the pan;/ If you can't make boxty/You'll never get a man." Sometimes an egg was added to the dough, producing "stampy." A dish made of mashed

Typical English supper, set for six, in a farm kitchen in County Tyrone, 2004. Courtesy of Linda Sichenze.

potatoes, flour, and butter cooked in a griddle, and then cut in quarters, is beloved in the North, where it is called "fadge" or potato "farls."

A generation or two ago, many Irish women baked soda bread every day, creating an unforgettable treat for visitors who quickly wearied of other staples, such as roast mutton and boiled potatoes. Recipes varied, but they usually involved a mix of whole wheat flour or oatmeal with white flour, salt, buttermilk, and a teaspoon or two of baking soda. The bread required little kneading and did not require a loaf pan; one simply shaped it into a round loaf and cut a cross through the top before baking. During the famine, corn meal (the "yalla male") was imported from America. The Irish generally despised it, but in Kerry and West Cork, "yellow buck," a soda bread that incorporates cornmeal, remained part of the local diet for generations. Soda bread is still popular, although in the twenty-first century it is more likely to be bought in the supermarket than baked at home. American recipes for it often call for raisins or caraway seeds, but these are not standard ingredients. At times of year when men were working especially hard in the fields, women used to add extra ingredients, such as sugar, raisins, or an egg, to produce a richer loaf known by such names as "spotted dog," "railway cake," and "currie cake."[7] Barmbrack, a rich yeast bread filled with raisins, currants, and citrus peel and sweetened with sugar, is also available in today's supermarkets. At Halloween the custom used to be to wrap various objects—a wedding ring, a matchstick, a pea, a thimble—in parchment paper and bake them in the barmbrack. The object that appeared in a young girl's slice supposedly determined her future fate from a dismal list of alternatives, not all mutually exclusive: marriage, an abusive husband, poverty, or spinsterhood. Ingredients similar to those in barmbrack—raisins, candied fruit, nutmeg, brown sugar—along with a cupful of Guinness, flavor the porter cake.

There is a rich array of traditional desserts, many featuring the locally grown apple. One familiar cake is made simply from a batter of flour, butter, sugar, and baking power into which a generous quantity of chopped apple has been stirred. In another variation, a dough made of mashed potatoes, flour, and salt is rolled out into a circle and cut into quarters. Sliced apples are placed on two of the quarters, which are then sealed with the remaining two; the resulting cakes are cooked on a griddle until the apples are soft. In the final step, the cook cuts a hole in the top of each to add butter and sugar. Apple pies, sometimes incorporating custard, and apple crumble, with its topping of oatmeal, sugar, flour, and butter, closely resemble their American counterparts. Homemade Christmas cake, heavy on dried fruit, butter, whisky, and eggs, traditionally was made in late October or early November, then sprinkled with more whisky and wrapped up in waxed paper and foil to mature. It was topped off with icing and covered with Christmas decorations. Like

Christmas cake, the meringues, shortbread, and tea cakes found in Ireland seem to have their origins in England. A shell of baked meringue filled with whipped cream and topped with fresh fruit, Pavlova, "the national dessert of New Zealand," is now an Irish favorite.[8]

No Longer an Oxymoron: The Irish Gourmet

With increasing tourism, immigration, and increasing prosperity, the Irish diet has become more varied. A generation ago it was hard to find rice in an Irish grocery store, but today, such once exotic items as sun-dried tomatoes, curry powder, and garlic have become commonplace. Salads and vegetables now appear on the menus of even modest restaurants; an inexpensive café will often offer a choice of quiche or lasagna. At this price range, absolute authenticity is not to be expected; vegetarians might easily rue the day the Irish discovered sweet corn and, apparently vowing never to be without it again, made it an inevitable ingredient in any vaguely foreign food, even stir-fried rice. Today a reasonably sized city can be expected to have Indian, Chinese, and Italian restaurants. Dublin's Temple Bar is filled with high-quality restaurants featuring Afghani, Nepalese, Peruvian, and Japanese food. In the early 1990s, restaurants catering to the gourmand spread across Dublin, a development the novelist John Banville reminisces about fondly. He recalls the unfamiliarity of a mozzarella and tomato salad flavored with extra-virgin olive oil. "'Extra virgin' was a term still new to us, and carried a troubling overtone ... of Mariology [that part of Christian theology dealing with the Virgin Mary]." When he asked the waiter the source of the tomatoes and learned that they had been flown in from the Paris markets only that morning, "a new age dawned for us in Dublin."[9] Expensive French, nouvelle cuisine, Asian fusion, or vaguely described "classic continental" restaurants are now part of the Dublin landscape: at Restaurant Patrick Guilbaud, which boasts two Michelin stars, one can enjoy a world-class tasting menu for about $200 per person.

Perhaps the most interesting trend of the last two decades has been the movement to create a new, world-standard Irish cuisine. Darina Allen, the proprietor of the Ballymaloe Cooking School in County Cork, is the best-known figure. Allen, a graduate of a hotel school in Dublin, founded her school in 1983 after popularizing her version of Irish cuisine at Ballymaloe House, the nation's first country house hotel. Allen describes herself as motivated to ensure the preservation of traditional cooking at a time when frozen and processed foods threatened to replace it. Her careful transcriptions of old recipes for drisheens and yellow buck reflect this mission, as does her revival of largely forgotten ingredients such as dulse, dilisk, sloke, and carrigeen moss—all native seaweeds. It is also seen in her descriptions of seeking out an elderly rural woman who still cooked over an open fire and taught her to bake a cake in the traditional bastible, a cast-iron pot oven with a lid that is covered with hot embers. But it is also seen in her insistence on native, organically grown produce, local dairy products and fish, and eggs from free-range chickens. The school even offers a course called "How to Keep a Few Hens in Your Garden." Thus, when visitors come to dine at Ballymaloe, they will be offered some authentic nineteenth-century dishes, such as roast leg of lamb with Cullohill apple pie. But they will also encounter authentic ingredients adapted into new dishes: Bruschetta of Roast Peppers and Ardsallagh Goat's Cheese with Basil and Olives, Baked Ballycotton Brill with Herbed Hollandaise Sauce and Buttered Cucumbers, or Roast Ballycotton Cod with Ulster Champ.[10]

At its best, today's modern Irish cuisine is innovative, flavorful, and healthful. Margaret Johnson's *The New Irish Cuisine* and Eamonn O'Cathain's *Around Ireland with a Pan* incorporate more international ingredients than the Ballymaloe Cookery School model allows and offer more dishes that will satisfy the weight conscious. Johnson's salmon with land and sea vegetables and haddock in cider, or O'Cathain's steamed fish with chilli-lime sauce and Thai crab and mango salad seem designed for today's prosperous new customer, too conscience-stricken for another authentic scone dripping authentic butter and authentic rhubarb-and-fig jam. But the 50 percent of the adult population who are overweight can take even more drastic measures if they are willing to spend a week at one of the new spas or health farms that have sprung up across rural Ireland. The historical ironies of paying huge sums to slim down on the site of Europe's last peacetime famine are particularly clear at the Delphi Mountain Spa and Resort. In one of the most notorious incidents of 1847, a large delegation of starving people walked 10 miles from Louisbergh in Mayo to the Delphi Lodge. They had intended to petition the Board of Guardians, who were meeting there, but the Board was at lunch and could not receive them; when it did so, it offered no help. A snowstorm came up, and many of the petitioners died before they could return home. They could not have imagined that in 2004, Irish people would be invited to spend $2,400 for a four-day package that includes two nights in Dublin, and two nights in Delphi, with restaurant meals featuring fresh fruit, steamed vegetables, chicken breast, and yoghurt.

THE IRISH CONSUMER

Although the traditional preference for plain, heavy meals makes sense in terms of Ireland's history of hunger and malnutrition, its preservation into the prosperous present poses a public health problem. When questioned for a 1999 survey about diet in the European Union (EU) countries, the Irish ranked third in their confidence about leading a healthy lifestyle, second in their confidence they ate a balanced diet. Yet in fact "daily calorie consumption in Ireland was the highest in Europe after Portugal and Greece," and life expectancy was lower than the EU average.[11] Stories about Irish obesity fill the popular press, many quoting from an April 2003 national health and lifestyle survey that "indicated 32 percent of Irish children are overweight and 10 percent are obese.... Fourteen percent of Irish men and twelve percent of Irish women are obese."[12] Put otherwise, 47 percent are "oversight or obese," with obesity accounting "for at least 2,500 deaths in Ireland" every year.[13] In March 2004, under pressure from the food industry, the minister for health withdrew a proposed tax on junk foods. By November 2004 a less controversial "public information initiative," Get Ireland Moving, urged adults to exercise at least 30 minutes daily. The ultimate bad news came in the same month from researchers who warned at a conference in Killarney that a study to be released in 2005 would show that "Ireland's rates of overweight people and incidence of diabetes are near U.S. levels."[14]

The culprits are the familiar ills of increased prosperity and modernization. It may seem shocking that 45 percent of Irish children are driven to school by their parents, especially when we consider that one-third of these live within 0.6 of a mile of school.[15] But rising crime statistics increase the reluctance of middle-class Irish parents to let their children roam free. For those wishing to blame the ills of society on working mothers, an increasing reliance on British and more recently American convenience foods is easily demonstrated. Like its counterpart in north London or Manchester, an Irish Tesco's or Safeway offers packets of Bird's trifle (custard, pudding, and Jello), frozen fish 'n chips, green peas with or without mint, thick-crusted pizza featuring ingredients such as roast pork and pineapple and, for breakfast, Denny's cereal-stuffed sausages, cornflakes, and Weetabix. The traditional cans of Heinz beans are now supplemented with peanut butter; taco kits and U.S.-made carrot cake mixes are widely stocked. In 2003, Coca-Cola was the best-selling brand in Irish supermarkets, although two Irish-based dairies and the Northern Irish Tayto company, makers of potato crisps, came in directly behind Coke.[16] Nutritionists who compared the diets of people in the United States and 10 European countries found the Irish among the bottom three in the home consumption of fruits and vegetables, but second only to Poland in the consumption of sugar and potatoes.[17] These basic dietary preferences may help to explain why the nation's largest fast-food chain, McDonald's of Ireland, saw sales increase by 5 percent in 2003, to a total of $210 million.[18]

An even more recent phenomenon is the growing disparity between food prices in the Republic and in the North of Ireland. In November 2004, the price of filling a typical grocery basket in the Republic was about 25 percent higher than in the North, "often in branches of the same supermarket."[19] A study released at the same time by Mintel International, a market research group, showed that only about half of respondents from the Republic reported visiting a supermarket once a week, whereas in the North nearly two-thirds did so. It also showed that a higher proportion of people who shop in high-priced convenience stores in the North are from low-income groups, people who presumably lack cars and easy access to the supermarket. But in the Republic, convenience store shoppers are more likely to be middle and upper-middle class, suggesting lack of time for full-scale expeditions to the super-market. "The economic and demographic trends that are pushing people toward convenience stores are accelerating faster than the stores can open.... they can continue to operate at [profit] margins consistently in the region of 20 percent, significantly ahead of European norms."[20] When they do take the time for a shopping expedition, many Dubliners are heading to the border. Hordes of shoppers from the Republic flocked to Newry, Northern Ireland, before Christmas 2004, boasting of bottles of liquor purchased for $13.60 under their cost at home. The Newry branch of Sainsbury's, where cross-border shoppers accounted for approximately 60 percent of the pre-Christmas trade, "sold more tinned confectionary than any other store in the company"; "only two of the stores across the UK have sold more mince pies."[21]

IRISH HOLIDAYS

Many popular Irish holidays follow the Catholic liturgical calendar, although some have roots in pre-Christian tradition. Pagan Celts believed that another world of gods and goddesses lurks behind our own, linked to it through springs of water. At the four turning points of the year (February 1, May 1, August 1, and November 1), the barriers between the Otherworld and ours were thought to be especially thin. Samhain, or "summer's end," November 1, was the most important, marking the end of the harvest and the beginning of a new cycle. Families extinguished their fires, waiting for the ritual lighting of the new fire. People made objects symbolizing their wishes, perhaps in the shape of a body part in need of healing, and tossed them into the new fire. The ceremony over, they returned home with firebrands to relight the hearth. Samhain was a time when the powers of magic and prophecy were at their height, and symbols of the season—fire and foods from the harvest—were used in fortune-telling rituals.

With the coming of Christianity, Samhain became All Saints' Day, or Hallowmas; the day before became Halloween. The traditional fire symbolism remained, with giant bonfires lit on Halloween night in many rural areas well into the twentieth century. Irish emigrants brought the practice of hollowing out a turnip to hold a firebrand to the United States, where the turnip became a pumpkin. In time an orange and Americanized Jack O'Lantern migrated back to Ireland. The traditional plea of Irish children, "Help the Halloween party," is now in danger of being replaced by an equally Americanized "Trick or treat!" The mythic apple tree of the Otherworld, to which one journeyed through water, survives in the custom of bobbing for apples, and the holiday's association with magic and creatures from an invisible spirit world survives in costumed ghosts and witches.

The Celtic harvest festival, Lughnasa, celebrated the year's first crops on August 1, when people cut a swathe of new wheat and buried it in a high place, as an offering to Lugh, a trickster god described as "clever, with superior power or skill ... a dispossessor and annexer of other's good for his followers, a winner of meat and corn."[22] The story was that to feed his people, Lugh had to struggle with Crom Dubh, "the dark crooked one," the miserly owner of a bull and a full granary. In Christian times, Lugh was replaced by a local saint, but the customs of making a pilgrimage to a high place and holding a fair remain. On the Dingle peninsula, that saint was Brendan; and until 1993, when it was stolen, an ancient carving of Crom Dubh was part of a graveyard in Cloghane. Today a revived "Féile Lughnasa" is celebrated there, complete with music, stories, crafts, and a pilgrimage to Mount Brandon. The better-known Puck Fair in Killorgan, County Kerry, attracts as many as 100,000 visitors for three days in August; its most distinctive feature is the crowning of a male goat as King Puck.

Many Irish Christmas customs, such as placing a lighted candle in the window to welcome Mary and Joseph, resemble their American counterparts. The old Irish custom of leaving out milk and bread for Mary and Joseph is now a treat left out for Santa. Holly grows wild in many parts of Ireland, and traditionally homes were decorated with it. The Christmas tree and the wreath are more recent acquisitions. As in England, a plum pudding, made weeks in advance and soaked in whisky, is the traditional Christmas dessert. Gifts are opened on Christmas day, and many attend church. The day after Christmas, St. Stephen's Day, is a public holiday as well; in Ireland's moderate climate it is a favorite time for sporting events, including horse races.

In the United States, St. Patrick's Day is the chief Irish holiday, but in Ireland this feast of the nation's patron saint was traditionally a holy day, an occasion for Mass going. After Irish independence, it became yet another occasion for associating Irishness and Catholicism. Club finals for both

Carnival atmosphere pervades the Saint Stephen's Day parade in Dublin, 2003. © *Irish Times*.

hurling and Gaelic football are always scheduled for March 17 at Dublin's Croke Park. St. Patrick's Day parades go back at least a century, but with the prosperous 1990s, they have assumed a new and American-influenced character. Indeed, events such as the Killarney St. Patrick's Day parade are heavily populated by American tourists. Since 1995, the Dublin St. Patrick's Day Parade has had its own artistic director, who defines it as "an artistic festival showcasing Ireland," as opposed to the New York City model of "representative groups marching behind a banner." The director, Maria Moynihan, told the *Irish Times*, in March 2003, that it was not true, as a Catholic group had charged, that she had banished St. Patrick from the parade. Catholic groups were welcome, provided that they were willing to work with her to develop "the entertainment value" and "artistic feel" of their entries.[23]

IRISH DRINK

One of the few loan words that crossed into English from Irish is whisky, from *uisge beatha*, the "water of life." The Norman-Welsh soldiers who invaded in 1171 reported that the natives had a "drinkable spirit," although actual references to *uisge beatha* do not appear in Irish sources until the fourteenth century.[24] Whisky seems to have been the drink of choice in the Irish countryside, whereas ale was favored in Dublin. Because it was also made in monasteries and was the principal drink of the monks, widespread familiarity with beer and ale can be assumed. In 1780, John Jameson purchased a famous distillery in Dublin; later, Jameson's boasted that a million gallons of whisky were aging in its cellars. Today Jameson's whisky, having joined the Pernod Ricard conglomerate, is made in Midleton, Cork. Two other remaining Irish distilleries are Old Bushmills in County Antrim and Cooley Distillery in Dundalk. Other than whisky, the most famous drink manufactured in Ireland is Guinness Stout, which gets its characteristic dark color from the darkly roasted barley used in its manufacture. Since 1997, Guinness has been part of the British conglomerate Diageo. An aggressive marketing strategy has increased sales in the United States and Africa, making up for stagnant sales at home. Between June 2003 and June 2004, Irish sales of Guinness dropped 6 percent.[25]

Overall alcohol consumption in Ireland has increased steeply, up 41 percent per capita between 1990 and 2000. In that period, sales of spirits increased by 50 percent, sales of cider by 100 percent.[26] The market diversified; a new demand for imported wine followed on the new interest in continental dining. In the 1990s, the adult males who had always visited pubs had more to spend, but the liberalization of Irish society also increased tolerance for drinking by women and teenagers. Niche marketing resulted in new drink combinations, new drink venues, even in "alcopops," a product popular among teenage girls. For years, tourism promotions have been tied to alcohol, with quaint pubs and foaming glasses of Guinness prominently featured. Music, film, arts, and pseudohistorical "festivals," in many cases "culturally shallow, sham occasions created by commercial interests" to attract tourists, have mushroomed, in most cases accompanied by legal exemptions from local laws regulating alcohol sales.[27] On the view that liberalizing access to alcohol might discourage binge drinking, the Intoxicating Liquor Act of 2000 allowed pubs to extend their hours; however, the effect has been to give sales another boost.

THE IRISH PUB

For centuries, social life in Ireland has revolved around the pub. In 1650, when Dublin's population included just "4,000 families there were 1,180 drinking houses."[28] People in other cultures may drink at home, or with meals, but the Irish meet their friends at the local pub. In the years of desperate poverty, attractive Victorian bars with gleaming mahogany fixtures were only one option; illegal and generally filthy "shebeens" operated out of rented rooms while "kips" offered prostitutes as well as strong drink. Traditionally the pub was a male preserve, with women accommodated in a small separate space known as the "snug"; even a generation ago women were often restricted to the mixed-gender "lounge." The incidence of alcoholism among women seems to have surged after 1791, when grocers were permitted to sell up to two quarts of liquor to be consumed off the premises. Such establishments were ill-regulated, and many operated as clandestine pubs for women.[29] The pub itself was a home away from home for men who lived with their families in overcrowded and wretched rooms. Even those in less desperate circumstances sought it as Englishmen once sought their clubs. It was a place where men could talk for hours about sports and politics, where they might laugh uproariously and speak freely. The pub's owner, or publican, of nostalgic memory was a respected figure in his community, dispensing loans, mediating disputes, offering sage advice, even reading and writing letters for illiterate patrons with family overseas.

A publican was conceded the same control of his pub as of his own home. An 1872 licensing law allowed pub owners "an absolute right to refuse service to any customer and bar him at will without having to cite any reason."[30] Most pub-goers have a "local" that they frequent more or less exclusively, and pubs develop their own subcultures, attracting regulars with common interests, tastes, and convictions. The practice of buying rounds, rather than paying for one's own drinks, encouraged excess. Even today, with the custom supposedly on the wane, "it isn't really acceptable to refuse the offer of a drink in Ireland, though you don't have to choose alcohol any more. You must return the favor and buy drinks for those who have treated you. The hospitable Irish frown on anyone who doesn't pull their social weight."[31] In the past, patrons of a pub would take up a collection for the family of a regular when he died, and the publican would supply some free drink to his grieving kin; the continuing custom of marking a death in the pub family is seen in the taping of the deceased person's photo to a mirror behind the bar.

During the civil war and the Troubles, there were IRA pubs (and, in the North, Ulster Defense Association and Ulster Volunteer Force pubs) where the hard men conspired at back tables and others turned a blind eye. In the middle decades of the twentieth century, Dublin was famous for its literary pubs, where men such as Anthony Cronin, Brendan Behan, Patrick Kavanagh, Liam O'Flaherty, J. P. Donleavy, and Brian Nolan (Flann O'Brien) held court. Survivors still reminisce about the excitable Behan and Kavanagh, who "stirred up trouble" and were kept in line by the legendary Paddy O'Brien, head barman at McDaid's, who put them on "probation" once they sobered up. O'Brien lost a chance to buy McDaid's in 1972, when he was outbid by a wealthy London woman who wanted to buy a literary pub. The same day the sale was closed, a friend of O'Brien's bought a pub a few blocks away called Grogan's. He persuaded O'Brien to move there as manager. The entire literary and artistic clientele, which by then included younger figures such as Michael

Hartnett and Benedict Kiely, decided to move to Grogan's with O'Brien. By the late 1990s, Grogan's was the only and "undisputed ... surviving authentic literary pub." Its owner continues to forbid television, radio, and piped music, thus ensuring "a setting conducive to intimate human interaction and thoughtful conversation."[32]

At its best, the Irish pub is a lively social institution that offers participants solace, companionship, and entertainment; for some, it becomes almost a family. Traditionally conversation is an Irish art, honed in the pub where story-telling, fiddle-playing, and singing are the main entertainments, rather than televised sports. Feminism brought women into every pub, but did not diminish its appeal. More recently, the pub largely seems to be weathering the Republic's ban on smoking in public establishments, which took effect in March 2004. True, the Diageo conglomerate reported a 1 percent decline in sales, and a shift of sales from the pub (down by 6%) to the liquor store (up by 7%), but its Irish sales still netted a profit of more than $260 million.[33] The Irish pub has proved to have global appeal. Since 1991, the Irish Pub Company, an affiliate of Guinness Brewing, has set up more than 300 branches in such places as Tokyo, Dubai, and Cuzco, Peru. Although one might wonder how authentic a Peruvian Paddy O'Flaherty's could be, the company arranges to build its pubs of materials exported from Ireland, trains cooks to prepare a hundred Irish recipes, books Irish musicians, and even offers to provide "real Irish staff."[34]

THE DEBATE OVER ALCOHOLISM

Irish tolerance for heavy drinking has always come at a social cost. One can only imagine how much of the abuse, neglect, and malnutrition that fill accounts of Irish childhoods from the pamphlets of Victorian reformers to the novels of Roddy Doyle can be attributed to some lethal intersection of poverty and alcoholism. And although pub culture has many charms for the regulars, its traditional separation of genders, in a society already marked by gender-segregated schools and sexual repression, is widely blamed for perpetuating immature relationships between men and women. In the immediate pre-famine years, a crusading Capuchin friar named Theobald Mathew started an indigenous temperance movement that crystallized around the Pioneer Total Abstinence Association of the Sacred Heart, founded by Father James Cullen in 1898. Without sharing the evangelical Protestant view that alcoholic consumption is always the work of the devil, the Pioneers encouraged their members to pledge lifelong abstinence as a penitential practice. Practiced as "part of a genuinely charitable disposition," total abstinence might effect "the conversion of excessive drinkers."[35]

By the end of the 1950s, Pioneers numbered close to half a million, one mark of a society apparently polarized between extremes of abstinence and alcoholism. Yet even in the early 1990s, when close to a quarter of the population of the Republic were teetotalers, the Irish had one of the highest per capita expenditures on alcohol in Europe: "In 1994, the Irish spent a total of 2.46 billion pounds [$4.7 billion] on alcohol . . . if you exclude the teetotalers and the children from your calculations, Ireland shoots back to the top of the European alcoholic league table."[36] By 2001, with the percentage of abstainers down to 17 percent, the annual sales figure was up to $9.2 billion, up 47 percent in five years.[37] At the opposite pole from abstinence, binge drinking is a greater problem in Ireland than in any other European country. In December 2004, a survey of 35 European countries showed Irish teens with the highest level of binge drinking; 72 percent reported that they had been drunk in the previous 12 months.[38] Among adults, Ireland has the highest incidence of weekly binge drinking: 48 percent for men and 16 percent for women. Evidence abounds that this high association between drinking at all and drinking to get drunk makes Irish drinking especially dangerous. As one example of "alcohol-related harm" in Ireland, researchers cite a recent study that showed 11.5 percent of Irish men reporting that they got into fights after drinking; in Italy the figure was 1.2 percent, and the only country coming close was the United Kingdom, at 7.5 percent.[39] In 2004, alcohol-related accidents, hospitalizations, violence, and absenteeism cost the Republic more than $3.5 billion.[40]

Yet Irish society has been slow to respond and deeply reluctant to impose legal restrictions on the Scandinavian or even American model. Years of warding off the stereotype of drunken Paddy and an intense dislike of the prohibitionist moralizing associated with Protestant evangelicals and one strain in the Pioneers predispose many to deny that alcoholism is an Irish problem. Then, too, alcohol's economic clout is extreme in a country where whisky, stout, and beer are major exports and the nation's largest industry, tourism, is so closely tied to alcohol consumption. In 1994, when the government lowered the legal blood alcohol limit to .08 (80 milligram per 100 milliliters) and added strict penalties that included an automatic two-year suspension of a driver's license for the first conviction, respected public figures such as the *Irish Times* columnists Kevin Myers and Nuala O'Faolain led the backlash. Noted Myers, news that "300 people had failed breath tests last Christmas" might have been "a splendid use of resources in the northern wastes of Sweden. . . . But in this Republic, it was a bizarre and almost immoral squandering of State resources."[41] Two months later, although it retained the .08 standard, the government reduced the penalties markedly. As late as 1996, a *National Alcohol Policy* issued by the Department of Health affirmed that "the drinking of alcohol is an integral part of Irish social life." Yet it went on to argue that "the description of the Irish as particularly alcohol-prone race is a myth. . . . It is doubtful whether Ireland ever occupied a prominent role with regard to alcohol use or misuse."[42]

Since then persistent headlines such as 2004's "December Road Deaths up by 68 percent" and "Suicide Attempts Increase by 7 percent" reflect increasing alarm over the consequences of alcohol abuse.[43] One reads increasingly that the Irish must accept what seems obvious from the statistics, that their culture has distinctive patterns of alcohol use that need addressing. Doing so means not only overcoming denial, but to some extent modifying the widely adopted Alcoholics Anonymous treatment model. To discourage blaming, "she-drove-me-to-drink," AA has always stressed individual responsibility. One of its traditions forbids the organization from taking stands on public issues, such as alcohol advertising. It is also arguable that AA's emphasis on alcoholism as a disease tends to divide the world between the healthy and the diseased, with a consequent downplaying of the problems associated with social drinking or the extent to which any particular person might move from one side of the equation to the other.[44] Some acceptance of social responsibility, the public health model, seems to be growing. In early 2005, banning alcohol advertisements on daytime television, placing warning labels on bottles, and ending ties between alcohol manufacturers and sporting events, such as Guinness's sponsorship of the All-Ireland Hurling Championship, were all considered inevitable developments. But not one of these proposals had been enacted.[45]

SPORTS

As their disproportionate success in international soccer suggests, sports is the dominant leisure activity of the Irish. In 2002, when the Republic of Ireland's soccer team made it into the World Cup competition for the second time in eight years, 11,000 fans flew to Japan and Korea to watch Spain edge out their compatriots in the quarter-finals, 3–2. Ireland also fields an internationally competitive rugby team, and individual athletes excel in swimming, diving, and track. The Republic sent a national team of 48 to the 2004 Olympics in Athens. Sports represented ranged from the men's and women's 5,000-meter races to show jumping and laser sailing. More than two-thirds of Irish adolescent participate in some sport. Among boys, soccer is the favorite activity, followed by Gaelic football and hurling; basketball is the top sport for adolescent girls, followed by (field) hockey and soccer.[46]

The Gaelic Athletic Association (GAA), founded in 1884, played an important role in the nationalist movement that led to independence. In sports as

Since the 1960s, women have played Gaelic football enthusiastically. © *Irish Times.*

elsewhere, nationalists wanted to affirm native traditions. Rather than teaching boys to play "foreign games" such as rugby and soccer, the GAA encouraged them to play Gaelic football, hurling, handball, and rounders. In 1904, Cumann Camogaiochta na nGael was founded to provide Gaelic games for girls, and a game similar to hurling, camogie, became popular. Since the 1960s, "ladies' Gaelic football" has grown in popularity. Closer to soccer than American football, Gaelic football requires teams of 15 players. In addition to kicking the ball, players are allowed to carry it in their hands for a distance of four steps, after which they must pass the ball to another player or "solo" it by dropping the ball onto the foot and kicking it back into the hand. A player scores a point by putting the ball over the crossbar by foot or hand. A three-point goal is scored by putting the ball under the crossbar into a net. Resembling field hockey, hurling is played with a curved stick and a puck-sized ball with raised ridges called a sliothar. It is played on a pitch that resembles a soccer field. The ball may be hit on the ground or in the air. Players are allowed to pick up the ball with the hurley and carry it for up to four steps, after which it must be bounced back to the hand. Being able to run with the ball balanced on the hurley is an important skill. As in Gaelic football, there are 15 players on a team. A ball that goes over the crossbar scores one point, and a ball that goes under the crossbar into the net scores three points.

Hurling: The player is allowed to carry the sliothar (ball) on the hurley for four steps. © *Irish Times*.

Gaelic sports enthusiasts insist that rounders, a bat-and-ball game brought to America by Irish immigrants, was the inspiration for baseball. Handball was traditionally played against an outdoor wall. As elsewhere, it is now played in several variations, including an indoor (five-wall) version in which the ball is bounced against the ceiling. All told, 2,500 Gaelic sports clubs in Ireland support hurling and Gaelic football. County and provincial matches are televised nationally and are the most popular programming on TG4, the Irish-language television channel. Since the GAA dropped the requirement that no one who played "foreign sports" could join, many children in the Republic grow up playing rugby and soccer as well. In Northern Ireland, however, sports are divided, like so much else, along religious lines. Playing Gaelic sports is a nearly certain sign of being Catholic, but then so is wearing a Glasgow Celtics football jersey; Protestants support the Glasgow Rangers. At the height of the Troubles, wearing the wrong football jersey was enough to provoke an attack in the street.

NOTES

1. Cormac O'Grada, "Ireland's Great Famine," EH. Net Encyclopedia. http://eh.net/encyclopedia/?article=ograda.famine.

2. Robert Scholes and A. Walton Litz, eds., *Dubliners: Text, Criticism, and Notes* (Harmondsworth, England: Penguin, 1968), 196.

3. Actual statistics on malnutrition in modern Ireland are hard to come by. But one strongly suspects that poor diet played a role in the fact that, in 1949, 1 of every 16 children born in Ireland died before reaching the age of five; by 1998, the figure was 1 in every 138 children. "Press Statement: Central Statistics Office," http://www.cso.ie/pressreleases/prelspecial.html.

4. Darina Allen, *The Complete Book of Irish Country Cooking* (New York: Penguin, 1995), 135.

5. Allen, 130.

6. Allen, 119.

7. Allen, 228.

8. Margaret M. Johnson, *The Irish Heritage Cookbook* (San Francisco: Chronicle Books, 1999), 272.

9. "John Banville's Restaurant Days: Dining in Dublin in the 1990s," June 2004, *The Dubliner,* 27.

10. Both listed at the cooking school's Web site: http://www.ballymaloe.ie/ballymaloesite/menu.php#hr1.

11. "Irish Say They Have Healthy Lifestyle," *Irish Times,* 10 March 2004.

12. "Martin Considers Fat Tax as Obesity Levels Rise," *Irish Times,* 25 August 2003. The SLAN (Survey of Lifestyles, Attitudes, and Nutrition) study was conducted by the Irish government's Health Promotion Unit, http://www.healthpromotion.ie.

13. "Martin Rules Out Tax on Junk Food," *Irish Times,* 11 March 2004.

14. "Study to Show Ireland's Rate of Obesity and Diabetes near U.S. Levels," *Irish Times,* 15 November 2004.

15. Desmond Broderick and Gerry Shiel, *Diet and Activity Patterns of Children in Primary Schools in Ireland* (Dublin: St. Patrick's College, 2000), v.

16. "Coke Sales Show It's Still the 'Real Thing,'" *Irish Times,* 28 August 2003.

17. C. Byrd-Bredbenner et al., "A Comparison of Household Food Availability in 11 Countries," *Journal of Human Nutrition and Dietetics,* 13 (2000): 199.

18. "McDonald's Trims the Fat to Keep up with Fast-Food Trends," *Irish Times,* 4 June 2004.

19. John McManus, "Time-Poor Public Willing to Pay for Convenience," *Irish Times,* 1 November 2004.

20. Ibid.

21. Roisin Ingles, "Invasion of the Trolley-Fillers," *Irish Times,* 11 December 2004.

22. "Lughnasa: Cloghan and Brandon Celtic Festival," http://www.irishcelticfest.com/history.html.

23. "Festival Executive Denies St. Patrick is Banished," *The Irish Times,* 18 March 2003.

24. Kevin Kearns, *Dublin Pub Life and Lore: An Oral History* (Niwot, Col.: Roberts Rinehart, 1997), 9.

25. Brian Lavery, "Can This Stout Keep Its Clout?" *Time Europe Magazine,* 5 September 2004. http://www.time.com/time/europe.

26. Malcolm Maclachlan and Caroline Smyth, eds., *Binge Drinking and Youth Culture: Alternative Perspectives* (Dublin: Liffey, 2004), 84.

27. Maclachlan and Smyth, 87. The authors cite a "ninefold increase" in the number of exemptions granted between 1967 and 1994.

28. Kearns, 1.

29. Kearns, 15.

30. Kearns, 31.

31. Terry Eagleton, *The Truth about the Irish* (Dublin: New Island, 1999), 14.

32. Kearns tells the story of Paddy O'Brien and the literary pub, 65–69.

33. Cathal Hanley, "Guinness Sales Hit as Drinkers Head for Offy," *Irish Times,* 2 September 2004.

34. A. La Ban, "Lucky Pubs: Uncovering the Secrets of a Successful Irish Pub," New City Chicago, http://www.newcitychicago.com/chicago/food-2000-03-16-194.html.

35. Diarmaid Ferriter, *A Nation of Extremes: The Pioneers in Twentieth-Century Ireland* (Dublin: Irish Academic Press, 1999), 34.

36. Eagleton, 12.

37. "Prosperity Is Blamed for Irish People Topping Drink League," *Irish Times,* 27 May 2002, http://www.ireland.com.

38. John Downes, "Scale of Teen Bing Drinking Problem Revealed," *Irish Times,* 15 December 2004.

39. Maclachlan and Smyth, 10. The figures cited come from a 2004 study by the Irish Department of Health and Children. M. Ramstedt and A. Hope, "The Irish Drinking Culture: Drinking and Drinking-Related Harm: A European Comparison." The statistics on binge drinking by Irish adults come from the same source. Maclachlan considers binge drinking a pattern (of drinking a large amount quickly in order to get drunk) rather than a scientific category to be defined precisely in terms of the number of drinks ingested per hour, see Maclachlan and Smyth, 4.

40. Susan Calnan, "One Pint Too Many Is Taking Its Toll on the State," *Irish Times,* 4 January 2005.

41. Quoted in Ferriter, 94.

42. Quoted in Ferriter, 1.

43. From the *Irish Times,* 30 December 2004 and 17 December 2004, respectively. Forty-three percent of suicides involved alcohol; a study based on deaths in Cavan, Monaghan, and Louth in 2001–2002 showed that 40 percent of fatal car accidents involved alcohol. Carl O'Malley, "40 percent of Fatal Crashes Alcohol-Related, Figures Show," *Irish Times,* 25 November 2004, http://www.ireland.com. For a fuller discussion, see Justin Brophy, "Alcohol, Culture and Suicide in Ireland: Exploring the Connections," in Maclachlan and Smyth, 71–99.

44. For an excellent discussion of this issue in the Irish context, see Ferriter, "Conflicting Paradigms: The Disease Concept and the Public Health Perspective on Alcohol in Ireland 1973–1988," 44–74.

45. Carl O'Brien, "Daytime Television Drink Ads to be Banned," *Irish Times,* 29 December 2004.

46. Sean Connor, *Youth Sport in Ireland: The Sporting, Leisure and Lifestyle Patterns of Irish Adolescents* (Dublin: Liffey, 2003), 96.

5

Literature

FROM THE EPIC EXPLOITS OF PAGAN HEROES such as Fergus, Cuchulain, and Finn MacCool to the sacred and secular poetry of medieval monks, Gaelic Ireland has a rich literary heritage. This oral and manuscript literature slips from sight after Oliver Cromwell's conquest, when British power and printing technology created a new equation of literature with published writing, in English. Throughout the seventeenth, eighteenth, and nineteenth centuries, many writers who were born in Ireland, or spent most of their lives there, were absorbed into English literature largely because they published in its language. Regardless of their political sympathies or subject matter, such writers as Jonathan Swift, Oliver Goldsmith, Richard Brinsley Sheridan, Maria Edgeworth, Oscar Wilde, and George Bernard Shaw were anthologized and taught with Chaucer, Shakespeare, and Dickens. The rare exceptions, such as the Irish-speaking Ulster Protestant William Carleton, who wrote sympathetically about rural Catholic Ireland during the famine, could safely be classified as minor writers of merely historical interest. Only in the last two decades of the nineteenth century did a literary movement, the Irish Renaissance, seek to reclaim and create a distinctively Irish literature. Although Douglas Hyde's Gaelic League aimed to restore Ireland's language as the medium for its culture, the best known writers of the Irish Renaissance, W. B. Yeats, John Synge, and Lady Augusta Gregory, like their contemporary James Joyce, understood that English, already the daily language of most Irish people, would be the language of their modern literature.

The Irish Renaissance

What would make Irish literature Irish? For Yeats, Synge, and Lady Gregory, a revival of the ancient Celtic myths offered one answer. Pre-Christian Ireland's legends and heroes should live again, as they did in Lady Gregory's translations of oral tales collected from the rural poor, or in the high serious drama of Synge's *Deirdre of the Sorrows*, or in Yeats's poems and plays about Cuchulain, the king whose betrayed wife tricked him into killing his own son. As cultural nationalism developed into a renewed drive for political independence, patriotic subjects featured in Yeats's poetry and plays. In a play called *The Rising of the Moon,* he celebrated the 1798 rebellion; in another, called *Cathleen ni Houlihan,* he glorified a youth ready to die for Irish independence. Later, in poems such as "Easter 1916" and "Meditations in a Time of Civil War," Yeats offered more ambivalent, even agonized reflections on political violence. For Synge and Yeats, the poor fishers and farmers of rural Ireland, especially the Irish-speaking West, offered a living connection to heroic Celtic Ireland, and they celebrated their strength, simplicity, and what both saw as the poetry of their daily speech.

Yeats, Synge, and Gregory were all Anglo-Irish, born into Protestant privilege and perhaps owing some of their idealization of the Irish to cultural distance. With the instinctive anti-Catholicism of their class, Yeats and Gregory looked back to the heroic age for a model of Irish people uncontaminated by the Roman Church, whereas Synge joked about papal dispensations and a funeral where the mourners, still suffering the effects of the previous night's wake, "stretched out retching speechless on the holy stones."[1] James Joyce, the towering figure of Irish modernist fiction, was born into a middle-class Catholic family reduced to poverty by his father's incurable alcoholism. Having lived in the Dublin slums, Joyce took its residents and their language as the authentic speech of Ireland. His early fiction reveals an urban, Catholic Ireland populated by spongers, political hacks, and ruthless landladies; one social layer above them is a devout middle class whose respectability masks repression and loneliness. Joyce left Ireland as a young man and spent most of his writing life in Italy, Switzerland, and France. With the publication of *Ulysses* (1922) and his last novel, *Finnegans Wake* (1939), he became a leading figure of literary modernism. In *Finnegans Wake*, experiments in new techniques of representing consciousness culminated in what seems virtually the creation of a new language, full of loan words from ancient and modern European languages, refusing the basic conventions of English syntax and punctuation. In his early work Joyce offered Irish literature the model of an urban realism, ironic about the pretensions and pieties of public life, but deeply lyrical and sympathetic to the pain felt by figures on its margins. In his later career he modeled the Irish writer as expatriate, the censored novelist whose books cannot be published in his native land. Set in Dublin and deeply Irish, Joyce's novels reject political and social Ireland in favor of an alternative aesthetic world.

IRISH FICTION FROM INDEPENDENCE TO 1970

The towering figures of Yeats and Joyce cast a long shadow over the literature of newly independent Ireland. Whether they reject Joyce outright or follow him into modernism and experiment, novelists and short-story writers of the mid-twentieth century struggle with this powerful figure who, after all, defined Irish fiction for most outsiders. Daniel Corkery (1878–1964), novelist, short-story writer, and influential critic, rejected Joyce and other literary exiles, insisting that a genuinely Irish literature remain grounded in observation and experience of daily life. His "Rock of the Mass" exemplifies this Irish realism. In a story set on a prosperous farm, an American son brings his wife and sister-in-law to visit his dying father. The sister-in-law, a young widow, is drawn to the old man and elicits the story of the enormous price paid for his land, not only in labor, but in the lives of his first wife and their children, sacrificed to "the meanness, the overreaching, the unconscious tyranny" of his desire to reclaim a farm the gentry had left in ruins.[2] The old patriarch tells her of his pangs of conscience the night before he moved to the farm from Carrick-an-Afrinn, a stony place named for an ancient rock where, according to tradition, Mass was said in penal times. What none of his children will tell him is that this landmark has recently been blasted away to allow a road to be widened. Although Corkery's insistence on such native realism earned him the scorn of a later generation, who saw him as the "cultural commissar... of de Valera's Ireland," he was very far from idealizing rural Irish life and well aware that the Free State's program of modernization might obliterate the past it claimed to hold sacred.[3]

Corkery's most famous pupil, Frank O'Connor (1903–66) studied Irish with him and went on to fight for independence. Yet although O'Connor softened the rougher edges of his impoverished childhood with an alcoholic father in comic stories like "My Oedipus Complex," he, too, criticized the Free State's pieties. In a famous story, "Guests of the Nation," set during the War for Independence, two Irish Republican Army (IRA) men become attached to a couple of English soldiers they are guarding at an old woman's cottage. Out of common humanity, or working-class solidarity, the men and the old woman quickly become a family, sharing chores, playing cards, and arguing about religion and politics. When an IRA man, Jeremiah Donovan, arrives to tell them that Headquarters has ordered the English soldiers shot in reprisal for the execution of four rebels, the gulf between the simplicities of political rhetoric and the subtleties of his bond with the two men stuns the young narrator. Numbed, he watches Donovan shoot them, helps to bury them in the bog, and senses his moral universe collapsing: "And anything that happened to me afterwards, I never felt the same about it again."[4]

Although one understands why Irish writers chafed under the yoke of Corkery's realism, it remained influential for at least two generations. One can trace it in the Aran stories of Liam O'Flaherty; it slips into Sean O'Faolain's "The Sugawn Chair," which mocks but also evokes a citified couple's nostalgia for rural Limerick. Too poor to buy the old farm they fantasize about, lacking the skill to twist straw into the rope that would repair the beloved rocking chair brought from the old kitchen, they bequeath to their son a not entirely ironic nostalgia for "the tall wildflowers of the mallow...a rank weed that is the mark of ruin in so many Irish villages and...for me the sublime emblem of Limerick's loneliness, loveliness, and decay."[5] Two major contemporary writers who continue this tradition are Eugene McCabe, whose *Heaven Lies about Us,* a collection of stories set in rural Ireland, was published in 2005, and John McGahern. The latter's 1990 novel, *Amongst Women,* won three literary prizes in Ireland and was short-listed for the Booker Prize. In 2002, McGahern

Scenic rural Ireland, central to romantic nationalism, can still be found less than an hour's drive from Dublin, Wicklow, 2004. Courtesy of Linda Sichenze.

won the PEN Award for lifetime achievement, and his *By the Lake* (2002) was a prizewinner in Ireland.[6] In McGahern, however, local realism is tinged not only with irony, but with a lyricism that rivals that of Joyce's *Dubliners.*

McGahern, the son of an Irish policeman, graduated from St. Patrick's Teacher Training College. After taking a job at Scoil Eoin Baiste in Clontarf, he began work on a bachelor's degree from University College Dublin in 1957. His first novel, *The Barracks* (1963), is set in a police barracks similar to the one where he lived with his father after his mother's death, when he was 10 years old. Its central character is a young mother dying, as his own had, of breast cancer. This novel was praised in Ireland, and the year following its publication McGahern won a fellowship to take a one-year sabbatical in England. As soon as his second novel, *The Dark,* came out, however, it was banned in Ireland, and on McGahern's return he was fired from his teaching job. In *The Dark* (1965), McGahern took on a subject that was to scandalize the Irish public when it broke into the headlines 30 years later: a son physically and sexually abused by his father strongly suspects that the boarding school priest who takes such a paternal interest in his spiritual development offers only more of the same. Yet 40 years later, the writer banned for his unwelcome honesty is now admired for offering, in *Amongst Women* (1990) and *By the Lake,* the "swansong of a disappearing civilization"—the rural, Catholic, and patriarchal Ireland of the Free State.[7]

By the Lake is a beautifully written book, set in a vaguely contemporary rural community where almost all of the characters are at least 50 years old. There is Ruttledge, an educated Irishman returned from London with his successful wife, a gentleman farmer befriended but not entirely accepted by the natives: there is Jamesie, the incurable if kindly gossip who links Ruttledge to the community and its history. Telephone poles intrude on the landscape, but the community's characters are softened versions of figures from McGahern's earlier fiction: a charitable priest with no desire to make converts, the damaged but possibly contented survivor of Catholic industrial schools and slavish farm labor, a household tyrant who, having driven one wife to an early grave, has been left by another, and currently seeks a third through a marriage bureau in the holy town of Knock. Some of the past, like Bill Evans's institutional childhood, remains repressed, too painful to tell. Some of it is losing its grip, like the Shah, Ruttledge's rich uncle, who is selling his business to a long-time employee. Toward the end of the novel, one of its saddest characters, Jamesie's brother Johnny, an old bachelor who spent his life working in a Ford plant in England, comes home for a visit and collapses and dies in a pub. Yet McGahern's tone is elegiac, evoking the strength of the community as Ruttledge joins the others in laying out the body and digging the grave in the old cemetery, where Johnny will lie with his head in the west "so that when he wakes he may face the rising sun."[8]

A Joycean fate, to be banned at home and self-exiled abroad, met Edna O'Brien when she first started publishing her *Country Girls* trilogy in 1960.[9] Like her contemporary, McGahern, she was skilled at evoking rural Irish life. Less explicitly than McGahern had done in *The Dark,* she hinted at sexual abuse. She depicts her teenage protagonists, Baba and Cait, as far more knowing about sexuality than the public morality of the times could accept. In their convent school chapel, Baba deliberately drops a holy card on which she has written an obscene suggestion about the relationship between a priest and a nun, knowing that she and Cait will be expelled when it is discovered. In Dublin, both become involved with much older men; Cait's lover is married; Baba's, "about eighty," deliberately chosen because "young men have no bloody money."[10] At the time it may have been the frank discussion of stripping and touching that drew the censor's wrath, but from today's perspective the girls' complicity, their resignation to these skin-crawling relationships, is more troubling. As the author remarks in her semi-autobiographical *Mother Ireland:* "The early mortifications, the visions, endless novenas...the melting glands at the cinema, the combined need for, and dread of, authority had all paved the way and it was in a spirit of expiation and submissiveness that I underwent that metamorphosis from child to bride."[11]

Having lived abroad, mostly in London, since 1959, for years O'Brien set most of her novels, such as *August is a Wicked Month* (1965), *Night* (1972), and *The High Road* (1989) abroad. She also branched out in short fiction, poetry, and drama, including a play about Virginia Woolf. In the dramatically changed climate of the 1990s, O'Brien began returning to Irish subjects. It was easy to criticize *The House of Splendid Isolation* (1994), the story of an IRA man on the lam from the North finding shelter with an aging woman in the South, for its apolitical treatment of the contemporary Troubles and its lack of feeling for the day-to-day realities of Ireland in the 1990s. But the scandals of the decade—the X case, in which a 14-year-old rape victim was denied a passport to go to England for an abortion, revelations of child abuse in Catholic industrial schools, stories about bishops with lovers and children—made headlines of issues at which O'Brien's earliest work had only hinted. *Down by the River* (1996) reprises the X case in an even darker register, making the girl pregnant by her own father and showing her in the pitiless hands of an antiabortion activist, who screams at her "that...you murdered it" when she starts to miscarry.[12] *In the Forest* (2002), which is based on the real story of Brendan O'Donnell, who in 1994 murdered a priest, a young woman and her child in County Clare, returns again to the theme of Irish complicity in child sexual abuse. Generalizations such as the defense attorney's claim about the murderer that "the country itself was on trial, it had failed him," remain unwelcome when they come from an exile. Even the usually progressive Fintan O'Toole scolded O'Brien for intruding on the grief of the family and attributing to O'Donnell's actions a public meaning they did not have.[13]

The Irish realists who descend from Corkery, like the landscape painters of the Free State, saw the farm and fishing village as the purest manifestation of the nation's spirit, even as they evoked the damage that church and poverty, isolation, and immigration had done to many lives. Joyce, of course, offered another model: not just his hero Stephen flying above the nets of family, church, and nation, but modernist experiment and linguistic innovation. The best-known mid-century Irish writer, Samuel Beckett, moved to France, where he worked as a secretary for Joyce and had some unhappy association with Joyce's schizophrenic daughter, Lucia. He fought in the French resistance; wrote most of his plays, novels, and stories in French; and remained in France until his death in 1989. After *More Pricks than Kicks* (1934), a story collection set in Dublin, most of his work seems placeless, evoking the land of his birth only tangentially: in the names of the eponymous protagonists of *Murphy* (1938), *Molloy* (1951), and *Malone Dies* (1951), or in marginal allusions to his rage at its censorship, its banning of birth control and divorce, its backwardness and mediocrity. But then nothing is more Irish than emigration, and on one reading Beckett's rejection of realism and even the English language is something equally Irish, an act of rebellion, as much a refusal to be defined by his literary debts to Joyce as by Gaelic nationalism.[14]

Alternatively, linguistic experiment might be continued by an Irish speaker and writer who remained at home. Flann O'Brien's *At Swim Two-Birds* (1939) mocked but also imitated Joycean modernism. Self-consciously literary, the book is loosely framed by the story of a nameless Dublin student writing a novel about one Dermot Trellis, a novelist taken to court for plagiarizing a great writer named Tracy. His own characters serve as judge and jury. They are surprisingly judgmental, we might think, as all along they have been interrupting the realistic frame with their own stories, with quotations, with parodies and pastiches of Irish writing, both popular and classical. Embedded in the novel, and narrated by a character named Finn MacCool after the legendary Gaelic hero, is a translation of the ancient story of Sweeney, a tribal king cursed by a priest. Sweeney became a bird-man, condemned to fly over the north of Ireland and Scotland, estranged from his own people. In Flynn's version we have all the elements of modernism, even perhaps of postmodernism and magical realism: a world of mirrors, of allusions and quotations from a bewildering mix of high and low texts. O'Brien refuses reason and plausibility in favor of the apparently random and impossible. He refuses to develop coherent characters and to care about politics or social reality and consistently rebuffs the reader's desire to identify with, understand, or master the text.

Joyce, given a copy by a friend, enjoyed it very much; O'Brien, however, claimed to be quite sick of it: "As you know, this AS2B gives me a pain in the neck, even if I've never read it...."[15]

As this survey shows, both realism and experiment characterized twentieth-century fiction, and although plenty of devotional and patriotic writing could be found, serious writers consistently undermined the complacencies of Irish public life. Nonetheless, there is a marked shift in the literature of the last quarter century, both in tone and subject matter, which corresponds to the enormous changes in Irish society. A novel that marks this shift might be John Banville's *Birchwood* (1973). Like *At-Swim Two Birds,* the novel violates most conventions of literary realism. Banville remarked in 1992 that he only realized retrospectively "how much of the early seventies there was in it. When Northern Ireland was beginning to be really bad."[16] As for the world of the novel itself, it is impossible to specify a precise historical date. At the beginning, when the eponymous Big House is equipped with a telephone and the narrator refers to the new State, it might be roughly 1923. However, after the narrator joins a circus, a potato famine strikes. Later, he alludes to the Molly Maguires, the Irish secret society remembered for its role in the Pennsylvania coal mine strikes of the 1870s. The book's time, then, is an Irish anytime in the past two centuries, populated by characters based on the stereotypes of the Anglo-Irish Big House novel, from the mad mother to the menacing peasants. For Toibin, *Birchwood*'s publication was a landmark event that "offered closure, tried to put an end...to certain tropes and themes....it made fun of rebellion and land wars and famine, Irish myths of origin.... Full of dark laughter, *Birchwood* was, more than any historian's work, the most radical text in Irish revisionism"[17]

If Banville tried to liberate Irish literature from a sacramental view of the Irish nation as purified and justified by famine suffering, Joseph O'Connor's *Star of the Sea* (2003), set on a voyage to America in the famine year 1847, offers a re-reading of the past consistent with twenty-first century Irish prosperity. Framed as a limited-edition reprint of a Victorian travel narrative, the novel observes some mid-nineteenth-century conventions, including chapter headings such as "The Visions at Delphi, In which the wretched Husband of Mary Duane, quite undone by the Evil of Want, records his Last and Terrible thoughts."[18] The book's frankness about syphilis introduces a note of anachronism, as do stories assuming a knowledge of later events. Thus a famine victim driven to crime in London tells an English novelist, Charles Dickens, a story about an imaginary Jew's school for child thieves; Dickens swallows it whole, including the name "Fagin," which belongs to the most anti-Semitic Irish priest Pius Mulvey knows. Like Banville, O'Connor also recreates familiar Big House figures: both Mulvey and the Anglo-Irish landlord David Meredith are in love with the peasant colleen, Mary Deane. Incest and assassination loom. Mary is revealed to be Meredith's half-sister, and a secret society has put Mulvey on board to murder him.

O'Connor's realistic descriptions of starvation or life below decks pull no punches. Indeed four quotations that stress British responsibility for the famine and indifference to its victims preface the text, including *Punch*'s infamous characterization of the Irish as the missing link between " the gorilla and the Negro." Similarly, Mulvey's mission to kill Meredith, although fully authorized by romantic mythology, creates agonizing conflict for the intended assassin, whom the revolutionaries are blackmailing. Further acquaintance with Meredith creates sympathy for this imperfect man who once dreamed of becoming a model landlord. Instead, the famine bankrupted him. Although doubtless many of the tenants whose tickets to Canada he paid for will die on the terrible passage, he did what he could for their future. Contemporary Irish readers who enjoy a comfortable middle-class life do not have the luxury of execrating this traditional enemy. Instead the novel challenges them to see in Meredith's relationship to the starving and homeless peasants a reflection of their own relationship to, say, present-day refugees from African famines.

Not only do contemporary Irish novelists rewrite the past, but they turn their attention to new, often violent realities: the still-simmering Troubles of the North, and the urban underclass, with its poverty, crime, alcoholism, and drug abuse. More of the new generation of Irish writers are women, or openly gay or lesbian, and they offer new voices, perspectives, and subject matter. Starting in the 1970s, popular American and English novelists found terrorism and guerilla war congenial subjects for the thriller: Gerald Seymour, Jack Higgins, Jimmy Breslin, Tom Clancy, and Leon Uris reaped enormous sales from books that superficially reproduced the grit and grime of urban Belfast and Derry along with the simplicities of political rhetoric. Uris and Breslin offered a sentimental, although entertaining, version of the Republican myth that serious Irish writers had debunked for two generations. On the other hand, Clancy and Higgins portrayed the Troubles as a war between IRA terrorists and a legitimate British government embodying all the English virtues of rationality and restraint. References to an international terrorist conspiracy funded by Moscow deflected attention from the local context, which few of these writers knew.

The most basic impulse of Irish writers turning to the Troubles was to counteract such narratives. For women writers, Northern Ireland's Troubles seemed the archetypal patriarchal conflict, with women sidelined as spectators and victims. To tell the story from a female perspective was to rewrite it, and feminist themes abound in women's fiction about the Troubles. In the stories of Jennifer Johnston, Deirdre Madden, Anne Devlin, and Fiona Barr, the combatants emerge not as revolutionaries advancing a new order or heroes defending civilization, but as reactionaries bent on punishing the deviance of women from roles originally assigned to them by church and state. As the polarity between terrorist and civilization breaks down, a woman's success in forging her own identity becomes a model for social change. Mary Beckett's *Give Them Stones* (1987) tells the story of a working-class woman radicalized by the violence around her. Martha's family history retraces the history of the Catholic working poor in the North from the creation of the state in 1921 to the 1980s.

Like African American women, poor Catholic women in the North have often been their families' breadwinners; Martha goes them one better by founding a bakery. She cannot bring herself to refuse service to the mostly working-class British soldiers who patrol her neighborhood; nor does she accept the punishment beatings and knee-cappings the IRA dole out to unruly teenagers in their own community. When she defies their order to stop serving the soldiers, the IRA fire bomb her bakery. Yet as the book ends she is preparing to rebuild the bakery, with the help of a British compensation fund. On the ground, where Martha lives, the political rhetoric of both Unionists and Republicans is equally useless, their violence equally destructive. Any hope lies in defiance of both and a will to build and nurture.

A similar impulse animates Robert McLiam Wilson's *Eureka Street: A Novel of Ireland Like No Other* (1996). In Wilson's contemporary Belfast, the occasional bombing and more than occasional punishment beating remind people that the Troubles persist. For most people, times are prosperous and offer many opportunities to exploit the "peace dividend," grant money from the British and sympathetic foreigners available for start-up businesses and dubious cultural projects. The novel is particularly hard on outsiders who refuse to see that things have changed since 1969: Amnesty International researchers who look for police brutality but ignore paramilitary violence, say, or Shague Ghintoss, a lightly disguised national poet along the lines of Seamus Heaney, who stirs up Republican sentiment when he is in Catholic pubs and plays the peacemaker when the international press is watching. Neither nationalism nor Unionism wants to address the real problems of Belfast, which are economic: "The tragedy was that.... Protestants thought themselves like the British.... Catholics thought themselves like Eireans.... The comedy was that any once-strong difference had long melted away and they resembled no one now as much as ... each other."[19] For residents of "Povertyland," the real oppressors are their own militants, exploitative journalists, and the extortionists who run ghetto businesses like the rent-to-own store.

Another contemporary Northern writer, Glenn Patterson, lacks Wilson's wild humor; but novels such as *Burning Your Own* (1988), *The Fat Lad*

(1992), and *Number 5* (2003) provide an equally realistic view of ordinary Protestants who will never join Ian Paisley's church or a paramilitary organization. Nonetheless, *Number 5,* set in a postwar housing development, shows how precarious their hold on middle-class identity remains. No matter how detached and alienated they seem from their roots or, for that matter, from the radical politics of the inner city, they remain vulnerable to sectarian violence. When a woman's husband is killed in his shop, the murder seems an inevitable denouement, although her friends tell her that "this was not something that anyone could have imagined, at least not anyone sane. Murdered for selling urinals."[20]

Urban poverty in the Republic features prominently in the works of Dermot Bolger, Michael Collins, Roddy Doyle, Patrick McCabe, and Ken Bruen. Doyle writes eloquently of Edwardian Dublin's tuberculosis-ridden tenements in *A Star Called Henry* (1999) and of contemporary domestic violence in *The Woman Who Walked into Doors* (1996). In *The Commitments* (1987), *The Snapper* (1990), and *The Van* (1991), the Rabbitte family's struggles with such issues as unemployment and single motherhood are leavened by deep blood ties, resourcefulness, and humor. Even triumph is possible, however briefly, for an inner-city rock band or a family determined to sell burgers and chips in the glorious summer of Ireland's World Soccer Championship. Yet the family always undermines its own successes, and Doyle's detractors point out a family resemblance between Jimmy Rabbitte and the stereotyped, drunken, hapless-even-if-lovable stage Irishman.

An even more brutal world fills the pages of recent Irish *noir* crime fiction. In three recent novels, Ken Bruen's Jack Taylor, disgraced ex-Garda and cocaine addict, stalks murderers through the grim back streets of a Galway that tourists never see. Adrian McKinty's *Dead I Well May Be* (2003) and *Hidden River* (2005) take their heroes from Belfast to a criminal underworld in the New World, which contracts much of its dirty work to illegal Irish aliens. Whether riding the Greyhound bus, hiding out in a Denver slum, or spending six months starving in a Mexican jail, McKinty's heroes are doubly jaded when they discover that even America fails to offer them a fresh start. Perhaps the most eloquent example of Irish *noir* is Dermot Bolger's 1990 *The Journey Home,* the story of Hano, a child of postwar industrial Dublin. A displaced farmer, Hano's father kept his family just above the poverty line by toiling as a mechanic for Pascal Plunkett, brother of the rising politician Patrick Plunkett. When he dies, the boy and his mother become financially dependent on them. Hano becomes witness to the Plunkett corruption, which extends into Irish society through dozens of subsidiary businesses, including illegal drug selling.

When his employer's nephew murders his best friend, Hano stabs Pascal Plunkett and runs off to the countryside. In Irish nationalist mythology, going West signals a return to simplicity and authenticity; however, Hano finds the cellar of the crumbling Anglo-Irish Big House in which he takes shelter an emblem of Irish displacement. The West's new prosperity, driven by tourism and the European Union, belongs to outsiders: "This crumbling house...is our destination....wherever they cannot move us from."[21] In a few years, the Economic Union will shut down the remaining Irish industries to preserve the "last corner of Europe, the green jewel free from the paths of acid rain." In his apocalyptic vision, only a million Irish will remain among all the Germans, French, Dutch, and Italians, a mix of guilty civil servants and "red-haired girls in peasant aprons bringing menus to diners in the converted castles." "We," the real Irish, will hide in the "woods" that "sheltered us for centuries. After each plantation this is where we came, watched the invader renaming our lands, made raids in the night on what had once been our homes."[22]

Recent literature has also spoken with a new frankness about sexuality. Given the repressive censorship that prevailed even a generation ago, openly gay fiction is a new phenomenon. Although Emma Donoghue has turned to historical fiction recently, two of her novels of the 1990s, *Hood* (1996) and *Stir-Fry* (1994), deal with the realities of lesbian life in Dublin. Pen O'Grady, the protagonist of *Hood,* loses her lover of 14 years, Cara, to a car crash. Her terrible shock and grief must be masked, for although she and Cara have a small circle of lesbian friends, her job as a teacher at a Catholic school compels her to keep their relationship closeted. The book blends scenes from the women's past, which began at a convent school, with scenes from a domestic life shared in Cara's father's house, and traces their vividly evoked sexual history and the emotional upsets triggered by Cara's periodic infidelities. The reader is struck not only by the peculiar isolation of Pen's grief, but by the many traits she shares with Irish women encountered in, for example, Edna O'Brien. This treatment of homosexuality, which shows gay and heterosexual lives lived side by side, and gestures toward the gradual conciliation of families with their gay members, is equally poignant in Colm Toibin's *The Blackwater Lightship* (1999).

The central consciousness of Toibin's novel is Helen O'Doherty, happily married, mother of two sons, a school principal in Dublin. Helen lives comfortably with the knowledge that her brother Declan is gay but is nonetheless shocked when one of his friends abruptly reveals that Declan is acutely ill with AIDS. He has never talked about his sexual orientation with their mother and grandmother, but now he wants Helen to accompany him to their grandmother's house, an emotionally loaded setting for both because as children they spent six months there while their mother tended their dying father in Dublin. Neither their mother, Lily, or their grandmother, Dora, told the children the truth about the crisis, and feelings of grief and emotional abandonment have kept Helen estranged from her mother for years. Now it falls on her to pull the family together and explain what Declan could not bring himself to say.

Toibin's depiction of extreme emotional reticence as a family pattern underscores the profound ties binding Declan and the three generations of women. It is assumed that he hides his sexual orientation from the older women because he fears rejection, yet neither responds to the truth with bigotry or expressions of shame. Because Declan himself is too wretchedly ill to recognize how his silence hurt the older women, or to associate it with their silence about his father's dying, this recognition must work its way through Helen's consciousness. The novel ends inconclusively; Declan is back in the hospital, perhaps to recover; perhaps even, in this undated narrative, to survive into the era of protease inhibitors. Helen and Lily share a cup of tea and tentatively plan to reconnect. What is most certain is that Declan is fully realized, not as a gay martyr persecuted by Catholic women, or as a victim sacrificed to reconcile heterosexual relatives, but as a member of an Irish family, deeply embedded in its history, its failings, and its love.

IRISH POETRY AFTER YEATS

The idealizations of rural Ireland that are found in Yeats's poetry, in the landscapes of Paul Henry and Sean Keating, and in the political rhetoric of de Valera's Free State, suggest no close acquaintance with the harsh realities of farm labor. When Patrick Kavanagh, a farmer in County Monaghan, published *Ploughman and Other Poems* in 1936, he spoke of familiar subjects in a fresh voice. *The Great Hunger* (1942) evokes not the nineteenth-century famine but the sexual frustration, economic hardship, and cultural poverty of an intelligent young man trapped into supporting his widowed mother on the family farm. From its first words, "Clay is the word and clay is the flesh," the poem images a spirit mired in the earth, men bending down mechanically to pick up potatoes.[23] Against Yeatsian visions of "little lyrical fields" Kavanagh sets the sterile reality of a farmer tied to his mother's womb "like a goat to a tree." For such a man, death and burial in a damp churchyard will hardly be distinguishable from life.

Kavanagh lived in Dublin, often wretchedly, from 1939 until his death in 1967. A fierce critic of his contemporaries, in "The Paddiad" he paints a dark but recognizable portrait of "Paddy Celtic Mist" slavishly imitating Yeats while "Chestertonian Paddy Frog" reconciles his muse with Church and censor. As writers drown their sorrows at the local pub, the Devil, disguised as a genial critic, praises the dead, the only poets he admires.[24] An even fiercer

Although this photo looks posed, Patrick Kavanagh was indeed a farmer.

denunciation of "Celtic mist" and a sentimental nationalism associated with Yeats animates Louis MacNeice's *Autumn Journal* (1939). Calling Cathleen ni Houlihan "a bore and a bitch," MacNeice ridicules the Irish revival,[25] while asserting his disdain for the materialistic Protestants of his native North.

But the Irish revival might also be re-imagined. Thomas Kinsella, a poet born in 1928, published a translation of the Gaelic epic, *The Tain,* in 1969. His own poems show the influence of such texts; "Finistère" and "The Oldest Place," for example, evoke images from "The Book of the Conquest of Ireland," a medieval compilation that harmonized pre-Christian Irish myths with a Biblical time scheme. Partly because they are cast as first-person narratives, the poems suggest a continuity between the emotions of the first Celts to reach Ireland and the nation's contemporary inhabitants. The speaker in

"Finistère" is an explorer whose half-understood desires compel him "further than anyone had ever been." In a quite modern way, he fears his own impulses as much as external danger.[26] Kinsella's lines assimilate the smell and sights of a prehistoric passage tomb to a much later image of the mind as labyrinth. As they do so, they prevent the contemporary reader from imagining the Celts as a separate and superior race of heroes. More significantly, they prevent the Celtic mist that conjures up a warrior tradition to justify a violent contemporary politics.

SEAMUS HEANEY

Kavanagh's unsentimental farms and Kinsella's ear for what Seamus Heaney calls "the nutrient original deposits of early Irish...legendary matter" nourish the imagination of Ireland's first Nobel Prizewinning poet since Yeats.[27] Heaney is part of an extraordinary generation of Irish poets, many born in the North, who began writing in the 1960s. His first collection, *Death of a Naturalist* (1966), demonstrated his considerable skill as an observer of nature. In the title poem, a farm boy fetches "jampotfuls" of "the warm thick slobber/ Of frogspawn" from a nearby flax-dam, and watches as tadpoles swim out of it.[28] In such poems, close observation seems to disclose a further layer of meaning, like the straw token the speaker in "Harvest Bow" strokes, "gleaning the unsaid off the palpable."[29]

The oldest of nine children who grew up on a 40-acre farm, Heaney was a beneficiary of postwar Northern Ireland's free secondary and university education. As he began his teaching career at Queen's University in Belfast, however, the campaign for Catholic civil rights erupted into the full-fledged Troubles. In 1972, after Bloody Sunday, Heaney moved to County Wicklow. For 20 years afterward, Heaney's poems brooded over the question of a poet's responsibilities in violent times and suggest a guilty sense of deserting the victims at home. In "Singing School," the speaker stands among dripping alders in his garden, declaring himself "an inner émigré" who has escaped "the massacre."[30] In "Station Island," he goes on the rigorous pilgrimage to Lough Derg and confronts apparitions: among them, a second cousin murdered by a Protestant, who scorns the elegy he wrote for him. But after the three-day ordeal, the poet is welcomed ashore by a blind man who tells him to write "for the joy of it."[31]

The metaphor of echo-sounding is especially apt for Heaney's bog poems, which contemplate the lives of ancient people whose remarkably preserved bodies and belongings are occasionally disinterred from peat fields. Perhaps the best known of these, "Tollund Man," evokes a Danish site where workers discovered an apparent victim of human sacrifice, a rope still twisted about his neck. The poem's speaker imagines declaring the Danish grave holy ground and petitioning the ancient victim to "make germinate" the bodies of Irish laborers laid out in the farmyard where paramilitaries gunned them down. The juxtaposition of a long-abandoned belief system with the contemporary practice of political murder shocks, as does his declaration that he would feel at home in Jutland, "in the old man-killing parishes."[32] Similarly, in "Punishment" a speaker contemplates the recovered body of a young woman, weighted down with stones, her head shaven, the noose still twisted about her neck. Her prehistoric punishment for adultery brings to mind news photos of Catholic girls in Belfast, their heads also shaven, their bodies tarred and chained to fences because they have gone out with British soldiers.

Heaney's enormous success—his professorships at Harvard and Oxford, his celebrity in England and the United States, his popularity as a reader and lecturer, even his Whitbread-Award winning translation of *Beowulf* (2000), still on the bestseller lists five years after its publication—have made him a visible target.[33] Complaints abound, for example, that poems such as "The Tollund Man" locate Northern Ireland's Troubles in the realm of some inexpugnable hereditary shame rather than in contemporary politics where solutions, however difficult to achieve, are at least thinkable. The Irish poet Hugh Maxton, a contemporary of Heaney's, went so far as to write "An Urgent Letter," complaining of Heaney's indifference, imagining him in the midst of the Troubles cheerfully strumming a guitar for admiring young women.[34] Yet Heaney's struggles to reconcile his poetic vocation with harsh political realities, let alone accommodate other people's political opinions, differ little from those of his contemporaries. Like Heaney, Michael Longley, Derek Mahon, and James Simmons began writing several years before the Troubles broke out. Yet no matter how much they might wish otherwise, outsiders perennially see their work in its local historical context; as Heaney himself notes guiltily, "We cannot be unaware . . . of the link between the politic glamour of the place (Ulster), the sex-appeal of violence, and the prominence accorded to the poets."[35]

Thus, a reader of Michael Longley will note his precise, domestic poems. "An Amish Rug," for example, describes a patchwork quilt given to his wife. In a similarly apolitical poem, Seamus Deane conjures up the paradoxes of modern travel: a speaker rushed through a wet landscape by a speeding train, barely able to believe that he is home again, yet simultaneously recognizing that he has never left it, for his identity is there "like sound implicit in a bell."[36] Derek Mahon's poem about the owner of the *Titanic* recalls the "Belfast of ship-making and a man forever humiliated by his survival."[37] Like these older poets, Paul Muldoon has a wide range. One of his most frequently anthologized poems evokes a family word for hot-water bottle, "quoof," which he has shared with many lovers.[38]

Yet few readers can resist the impulse to turn to poetry for insight, consolation, or even healing in the face of terrorism and war, issues that were urgently present in Northern Ireland long before the Oklahoma City bombing and the attacks on New York and Washington brought them home to the United States. And much of the poetry about terrorism is compelling. Michael Longley, a Protestant with an English father, has written hauntingly of the disastrous first day at the Battle of the Somme, July 1, 1916, when the Ulster Division lost 5,600 men. This brutal episode burned itself into the consciousness of Ulster Loyalists, who continue to evoke it in songs, wall paintings, and even Web pages, but has largely been forgotten by outsiders, including most Irish Catholics. Longley's father was wounded there, and one of his most powerful poems invoke its horrors, including the callousness of a chaplain who walked "over a landscape of dead buttocks" with his swagger-stick.[39] In the poem's second stanza Longley turns from his father's grave to the recent death of a family man killed by a terrorist. The brute factuality of the poem's images, its unblinking insistence on moments in which young men kill or die horribly, strips away the rhetoric, whether Loyalist or Republican, that often romanticizes political violence.

The poetry of Tom Paulin, also a Northerner of Protestant birth, denounces the Loyalist ethos, repeatedly making the direct political statements Maxton's "Urgent Letter" seems to advocate. "Settlers" recapitulates the illegal gun-running of 1913, when British authorities winked at Loyalists stockpiling weapons against the prospect of Home Rule. "Under the Eyes" begins with a straightforward attack on the Protestant working class.[40] Such verbal attacks, of course, leave Paulin open to the charges of inciting hatred. Comparing Loyalist Protestantism with militant Islam, as he does in "Desertmartin," may be emotionally satisfying, but it offers no real alternative to the simplicities of public rhetoric.

The poems of Ciaran Carson, born in Belfast in 1948, provide a different, perhaps initially confusing, perspective. If, like "Dresden," they offer a narrative—a World War II rear gunner recalls a mission that broke his heart—it will be intercepted and interrupted by others, stories about the IRA in the 1920s and in the 1970s. If they produce two of Carson's favorite images, the map and the ethnic neighborhood, these will be shown literally exploding, fragmenting, and therefore changing almost beyond recognition. Often, as in the title poem of *Belfast Confetti* (1989), map and city street, the abstract representation and actual place, suffer the same fate. After a bombing, the sky rains "exclamation marks" as well as metal parts."[41] This deliberate blurring of the word/representation with a real act of violence embodies the problematic relationship between poet and violence. Those who complain that mythicizing violence allows Heaney to evade its real consequences, or that savaging Loyalists leads Paulin to endorse ethnic hatred, can find Carson's "Belfast Confetti" a liberating alternative. Reduced to their most basic elements, words and action become "two distinct but mutually affecting variables." The poem expresses the impact of violence but also engages with the possibility that language itself promotes violence.[42] The image of an exploding "fount of broken type" makes no judgments about whether a printing press churns out pacifist tracts or terrorist propaganda. The press may be an image of civilized discourse destroyed by violence, but bits of type, like nails, become lethal shrapnel when propelled by the force of an exploding bomb.

WOMEN AND POETRY

The generation of poets who emerged in the 1960s includes numerous women, a group previously notable for its absence. The feminist poet Eavan Boland, who teaches at Trinity College Dublin, has argued that the tradition of imagining Ireland as a woman—beautiful Cathleen ni Houlihan, dark Rosaleen, the old woman of Beare—paradoxically helped to keep women silent during the Irish Renaissance. The lyric poet, like the patriotic soldier, was defined as "a specially endowed male" who reclaims a female body invaded and occupied by foreign males.[43] Once that female speaks, neither Irish poetry nor politics can ever be the same again. Some of Boland's early poems address this issue directly, compelling the reader to revise the image of woman as sacrificial victim. "The Oral Tradition" evokes the actions and heroism of a woman giving birth to her son in an open field.[44]

"Anna Liffey," taking its title from "Anna Livia Plurabelle," the mythic river woman of Joyce's *Finnegans Wake,* carefully teases out the distinctions between nature and the female body, that a river is not a woman and a woman is not a river. The poem's speaker nonetheless struggles to imagine a relationship to Dublin's landscape, including the River Liffey. By the poem's end, she concludes that her own gender will not matter. Having chosen and articulated her relationship to the Liffey, the speaker concludes that this achievement is the essence of her identity, so that when everything else is gone people will remember that "I was a voice."[45]

An equally distinctive voice belongs to Medbh McGuckian, a Northern Irish poet who studied with Seamus Heaney at Queen's. Her poetry is more difficult than Heaney's and Boland's. It is much less likely to have a readily accessible narrative or a recognizable scene at its center. McGuckian is also much less likely to identify herself in such straightforward statements as Boland's "I am a voice" or Heaney's "I am an internal émigré." Her poems proceed more by association than by logic or chronology. Their settings and motifs, domestic and natural, are so often imaged in terms of the human body as to leave some confusion about whether the poem refers to, say, a kitchen or a woman. The first line of "A Conversation Set to Flowers" exemplifies McGuckian at her most surreal: the poet evokes "fine china we conceived in spring" and says it has blown the "crumbs out of the book I was reading." Substitute "baby" for china or "wind" for "china," and the line is conventional; leave the language as it is and the metaphor resists interpretation. Yet a reader who gives into the poem, who does not insist on finding a message to take away, may revel in a succession of images, a lace dress, a woman's hands, a dream in which lovers change into apples.[46] Asked "But what does it all mean?" Ciaran Carson replied that one might as well ask what Charlie Parker 'means.' He means music. McGuckian means poetry."[47]

A somewhat younger generation of women poets includes Rita Ann Higgins, Paula Meehan, Moya Cannon, Mary O'Malley, and Kerry Hardie. Several of O'Malley's poems revisit the Irish myths and Western landscapes of early Yeats. Among them is "The Price of Silk is Paid in Stone," which begins with a conventionally picturesque landscape. But then the poet declares that there is "no romance in Connemara," evoking the harsh realities of a world in which Sunday's chicken must be killed. Yet still she recognizes its beauty and feels torn between "the price of leaving" and "the cost of coming home."[48] Rita Ann Higgins, on the other hand, addresses working-class resentment and poverty. "Some People" provides a catalogue of the humiliations that face poor women and their children, from waiting years for dental care to lying to the bill collector.[49] Paula Meehan conjures up images of the past, a mother staying up all night to make over an old dress for a daughter starting school, a grandmother who asked, "Would you jump into my grave as quick?" when her grandchildren take her favorite chair. But she also writes about harsh contemporary realities: a jailed woman addicted to heroin, an abandoned woman who has not eaten for days suffering "the cold sweats."[50]

POETRY IN IRISH

Although Irish is often called a dying language, it remains a vital medium for poetry. More than 80 years of compulsory Irish in the Republic's schools have failed to produce a nation of Irish speakers, but they have produced three generations of bilingual poets and an audience for their work. Most of Ireland's best-known poets have published translations from their Irish language contemporaries, such as Nuala Ní Dhomhnaill, Michael Davitt, and Cathal Ó Searcaigh. Irish words, references to the Irish language, and imitations of Irish poetic forms appear even in English-language poems. Aidan Carl Mathews's three-line lament, "The Death of Irish" evokes this loss by noting that Irish has 32 words for seaweed.[51] A similar sense of loss penetrates Michael Hartnett's "Death of an Irishwoman." The belated recognition of the fifteenth line, "I loved her from the day she died," says volumes about the language's appeal to poets.[52]

Hartnett is an interesting example of bilingualism. Having begun writing in his first language, he published a celebrated poem bidding "Farewell to English" in 1975.[53] For Hartnett, his second language offered new aesthetic challenges, and for 10 years he continued to publish exclusively in Irish. He did, however, eventually relent: "my English dam bursts," he wrote in a 1985 poem, "and out stroll all my bastards."[54] Hartnett is one of a list of distinguished poets. Others are John Montague, Heaney, Muldoon, Carson, McGuckian, and Derek Mahon, who have translated the Irish language poet best known outside her country, Nuala Ní Dhomhnaill. Bilingual since early childhood—she was born in England in 1952 and grew up in the Kerry Gaeltacht—Ní Dhomhnaill writes a thoroughly contemporary poetry that refers to refrigerators with freezing compartments, chain saws, and rock music celebrities. "Do thánig bean an leasa/ le *Black & Decker,*" begins a poem called "An Crann," which Paul Muldoon has translated "As for the Quince." A lovely young woman with a Black and Decker saw cuts down a wife's quince-tree; when the wife tells her husband, he loses his temper and wonders why she did not stop the vandalism. The next day the young woman returns to inquire about the husband's reaction. The wife collapses, but the quince "hold[s] its ground."[55] The suggestion of Celtic myth—mysterious visitor, precious tree, a wife's disproportionate response, as though to a spell cast—mixes agreeably with the latest in do-it-yourself technology and the breezy speech of a contemporary household. The resilient tree might be an image of Irish culture itself, miraculously surviving into a foreign language and a new century.

NOTES

1. John Synge, "The Playboy of the Western World," in *The Complete Plays of John Synge* (New York: Vintage, 1960), 67.

2. "Rock-of-the-Mass," [1929], in *Modern Irish Short Stories*, ed. Ben Forkner (Middlesex, England: Penguin, 1980), 104.

3. Paul Delaney, "Becoming National: Daniel Corkery and the Reterritorialized Subject," in *Critical Ireland: New Essays in Literature and Culture*, ed. Aaron Kelly and Alan A. Gillis (Dublin: Four Courts, 2001), 41–42.

4. Frank O'Connor, "Guests of the Nation," in *Stories by Frank O'Connor* (New York: Vintage, 1956), 16.

5. Sean O'Faolain, "The Sugawn Chair," in *The Oxford Book of Irish Short Stories*, ed. William Trevor (Oxford: Oxford University Press, 1989), 340.

6. Published in London by Faber and Faber as *That They May Face the Rising Sun.*

7. Eamon Maher, *John McGahern: From the Local to the Universal* (Dublin: Liffey, 2003), 99.

8. John McGahern, *By the Lake* (New York: Knopf, 2002), 318.

9. Followed by *The Lonely Girls* (1962) and *Girls in Their Married Bliss* (1964). These were republished in 1986 with a new epilogue as *The Country Girls: Trilogy and Epilogue.*

10. Edna O'Brien, *The Country Girls* (New York: Knopf, 1960), 154–155.

11. Edna O'Brien, *Mother Ireland* (New York: Harcourt Brace, 1976), 141.

12. Edna O'Brien, *Down by the River* (London: Weidenfeld and Nicolson, 1996), 259.

13. Edna O'Brien, *In the Forest* (London: Weidenfeld and Nicolson, 2002), 201. O'Toole's criticism appeared in "A Fiction Too Far," *Irish Times Weekend Review,* 2 March 2002, p. 1. Amanda Greenwood discusses O'Toole's argument in *Edna O'Brien* (Tavistock, England: Northcote House, 2003), 102–106.

14. This is Neil Corcoran's reading, which he supports by quoting a passage from *Molloy* that puns on Joyce's name, as well as the titles of *Ulysses and Finnegans Wake.* "I who had loved the image of old Geulinex . . . who left me free, on the black boat of Ulysses, to crawl towards the East, along the deck . . . And from the poop, poring upon the wave, a sadly rejoicing slave, I follow with my eyes the proud and futile wake. Which, as it bears me from no fatherland away, bears me onward to no shipwreck." Geulinex was a seventeenth-century Belgian follower of Descartes, hence a model of someone who adopted French. *After Yeats and Joyce: Reading Modern Irish Literature* (Oxford: Oxford University Press, 1997), 31.

15. Sue Asbee, *Flann O'Brien* (Boston: Twayne, 1991), 49. The quotation is from a letter to O'Brien's French translator, Henri Morisot, dated 10 February 1965.

16. Derek Hand, *John Banville: Exploring Fictions* (Dublin: Liffey, 2002), 37.

17. Colm Toibin, *The Penguin Book of Irish Fiction* (New York: Viking, 2000), xxxi.

18. Joseph O'Connor, *Star of the Sea* (New York: Harcourt, 2002), 34.

19. Robert McLiam Wilson, *Eureka Street: A Novel of Ireland Like No Other* (New York: Arcade-Little, Brown, 1997), 163.

20. Glenn Patterson, *Number 5* (London: Penguin, 2003), 306.

21. Dermot Bolger, *The Journey Home* (London: Flamingo-HarperCollins, 2003), 387.

22. Bolger, 388–390.

23. Patrick Kavanagh, "The Great Hunger," in *Collected Poems* (New York: Norton, 1964), 34.

24. Kavanagh, "The Paddiad or The Devil As a Patron of Irish Letters," in *Collected Poems,* 90–95.

25. Frank Ormsby, ed., "Autumn Journal," *Poets from the North of Ireland,* 2nd ed. (Belfast: Blackstaff, 1990), 49–53. Cathleen ni Houlihan is both the name of Yeats's paly and the name given to the idealized Ireland.

26. Thomas Kinsella, "Finistère," in *Soft Day: A Miscellany of Contemporary Irish Writing,* ed. Peter Fallon and Sean Golden (Notre Dame, Ind.: University of Notre Dame Press, 1980), 73–76.

27. Seamus Heaney, "On Thomas Kinsella," in *Finders Keepers: Selected Prose 1971–2001* (New York: Farrar Straus, 2002), 265.

28. Seamus Heaney, "The Death of a Naturalist," in *Opened Ground: Selected Poems 1966–1996* (New York: Farrar Straus, 1998), 5.

29. Heaney, Opened Ground, "Harvest Bow," 175.

30. Heaney, Opened Ground, "Singing School," 136.

31. Heaney, Opened Ground, "Station Island," 245.

32. Heaney, Opened Ground, "Tollund Man," 63.

33. In April 2005, Heaney's *Beowulf* was ranked sixteenth in the list of poetry books sold in the United States. American Booksellers Association. Bookselling This Week. The Book Sense Poetry Bestseller List, April 19, 2005, http://news.bookweb.org/booksense/.

34. Peter Fallon and Derek Mahon, eds., "An Urgent Letter," in *The Penguin Book of Contemporary Irish Poetry* (London: Penguin, 1990), 299. "Jimmy": Seamus is Irish for James.

35. Matthew Campbell, ed., quoted in Fran Brearton, "Poetry of the 1960s," in *The Cambridge Companion to Contemporary Irish Poetry* (Cambridge: Cambridge University Press, 2003), 100.

36. Ormsby, "Return," 156.

37. Ormsby, "Bruce Ismay's Soliloquy," 172.

38. Ormsby, "Quoof," 262.

39. Ormsby, "Wounds," 146–147.

40. Peter Fallon and Derek Mahon, "An Urgent Letter," in *The Penguin Book of Contemporary Irish Poetry* (London: Penguin, 1990), 299.

41. Ormsby, "Belfast Confetti," 197.

42. See Alex Houen, "Re-Placing Terror: Poetic Mappings of Northern Ireland's 'Troubles," in *Terrorism and Modern Literature, from Joseph Conrad to Ciaran Carson* (Oxford: Oxford University Press, 2002), 272.

43. Guinn Batten, "Boland, McGuckian, Ni Chuilleanain and the Body of the Nation," in Campbell, 189.

44. Peggy O'Brien, ed., "The Oral Tradition," in *The Wake Forest Book of Irish Women's Poetry 1967–2000* (Winston-Salem, N.C.: Wake Forest University Press, 1999), 13.

45. O'Brien, "Anna Liffey," 31–36.

46. O'Brien, "A Conversation Set to Flowers," 99.

47. Quoted by Philip Harvey, "In the Country of Comparative Peace," interview with Margaret Coffey. *Encounter,* ABC National Radio, 12 December 2004. McGuckian was a fellow guest on this program.

48. O'Brien, "The Price of Silk Is Paid in Stone," 246.

49. O'Brien, "Some People," 200.

50. O'Brien, "Her Heroin Dream," 222–223; "Laburnum," 226.

51. Fallon, "The Death of Irish," 422.

52. Fallon, "Death of an Irishwoman," 216.

53. Fallon, "Farewell to English," 145.

54. From Michael Hartnett, *Inchicore Haiku* (Dublin: Raven Arts, 1985). Quoted in Frank Sewell, "Between Two Languages: Poetry in Irish, English, and Irish English," in Campbell, 159.

55. O'Brien, "An Crann," 141–142; "As for the Quince," 142–143.

6

Media and Cinema

IRISH MEDIA, FROM THE EARLIEST NEWSPAPERS to the latest Web cast, give outsiders an extraordinary opportunity to observe the Irish representing themselves. Sensitive to the often negative images of themselves in English publications such as the *Times* of London and *Punch,* Irish writers and broadcasters have often seen their media as offering an opportunity to right wrongs. Then, too, Ireland's relatively small and homogeneous population has made it easy for clerics, patriots, and revolutionaries to believe that they might transform Irish reality by remaking the Irish image. For many years, the high value the Irish church placed on chastity and doctrinal conformity led to extraordinary censorship. The goal of cultural and political independence led to special taxes on British newspapers. When BBC television programming threatened the Irish home, the state belatedly set up its own television channel. In the past 20 years, Irish filmmakers have challenged the sentimental Irish-American eyes through which their nation has been seen in films ranging from *The Quiet Man* (1952) to *Ryan's Daughter* (1970). To filmmakers such as Gerard Stembridge and Thaddeus O'Sullivan, depicting the Irish as serial adulterers and drug dealers seems as much a cause as displaying piety and hard work did to their forerunners. Although the Irish-speaking population has been a tiny minority for more than 100 years, the political importance of the language surfaces repeatedly in the history of broadcasting and film. Politicians have seen radio and television as instrumental in preserving Irish, whereas serious filmmakers, like writers, have often turned to Irish as integral to the expression of a unique and threatened identity.

Radio and the Irish state came of age together. In a prescient move, on Monday of Easter Week, 1916, rebels occupied the Irish School of Wireless Telegraphy on O'Connell Street in Dublin.[1] Like the Easter Rising itself, the takeover was of more symbolic than practical significance. Prevented by British fire from setting up an antenna, the rebels moved the transmitter to their headquarters at the General Post Office, where they announced the birth of the new Republic in Morse code. Delayed somewhat by the civil war, the new state opened its first radio station, 2RN, on January 1, 1926. Its first broadcast was a speech by Douglas Hyde, founder of the Gaelic League, urging Irish people to remember how central their own language was to their identity. For most radios, the broadcast range of 2RN was about 25 miles, but by June 1932 a national radio station, soon known as Radio Eireann, had a signal strong enough to be picked up over the whole country. The Republic did not give up its monopoly on broadcasting until 1988, although BBC broadcasts from the British mainland and Northern Ireland were available to people who lived along the border or the eastern seaboard in the 1920s. The diffusion of British and then global media increased with each technological development, from shortwave radio to cable television. Nonetheless, Radio Eireann's dominance contributed to Irish insularity in the first 40 years of the Republic's life.

IRISH-LANGUAGE RADIO AND TELEVISION

Hyde's inaugural broadcast was the opening gambit in a long struggle to harness the new medium to the old, to make radio an instrument for reviving Irish as the spoken language of daily life. Until Easter Sunday 1972, when the all-Irish national station Radio na Gaeltachta began broadcasting, Radio Eireann produced several hours per week (4.2 in 1935, 10.6 in 1945, 8.4 in 1955, and 6 in 1965) of Irish-language programming.[2] Although calls for increasing this programming were more or less constant, several obstacles stood in the way. One was that 95 percent of the Irish population did not understand spoken Irish well enough to follow a radio program; another is that Irish has three distinct dialects. Even native speakers understand each others' dialects only with difficulty. Finally, as Irish was the spoken language of the rural poor, trained announcers, writers, actors, and technicians with fluent Irish were hard to come by, and radios remained a rare luxury in the Gaeltacht until the 1950s. Apparently, most Irish-language programming was unimaginative. A legislator who immersed himself in it before a debate reported that "to listen to the productions night after night was one of the greatest penances I have ever had to impose on myself."[3] In the mid-1950s, the Minister for Posts and Telegraphs commissioned four surveys to determine how many people were actually listening to Irish-language radio. The results were so embarrassing that the Cabinet declined to publish them.[4]

Still, even with these constraints, some Irish-language programs became relatively popular. In the mid-1940s, *Listen and Learn,* a program to teach Irish, had devotees even in France and English. More than 40, 000 copies of a companion text were sold. One might speculate that this program found a natural audience in people who wanted to learn the language, rather than assuming a nonexistent audience of fluent Irish speakers with a keen interest in, for example, Italian opera. But the real transformation in Irish-language radio came in the 1960s, when all but a few diehards had accepted English as the Republic's de facto national language. By then, rural electrification had also linked most of the Gaeltacht to the modern world, and most homes had radios. For the first time, it was possible to think seriously about native Irish speakers as an audience for radio, one as much interested in sports and entertainment as any other. The U.S. Civil Rights movement had inspired a Gaeltacht Civil Rights movement, which in 1970 set up its own pirate radio station, Saor Raidió Chonamara, Radio Free Connemara. Within a few years, the state-sponsored Raidió na Gaeltachta (RnaG) was broadcasting nationally.

Perhaps paradoxically, the notion of an Irish radio station designed to meet the needs of Irish speakers, rather than a government policy, almost immediately resulted in less provincial programming. From the beginning, RnaG attempted to use Irish-speaking correspondents stationed around the globe, and "to show that the Irish language can be used to discuss the modern world."[5] By 2001, a market research study showed that RnaG had 41 percent of the adult radio audience share in the Gaeltacht, in addition to a scattering of people around the world who listened in via satellite and Internet broadcasts.[6] But Irish-language television is an even more intriguing phenomenon. For decades after its first broadcast on New Year's Eve 1961, Radio Telefís Eireann (RTE)'s television programming mirrored its radio programming, English broadcasts dominated, and, with a few exceptions, ratings for Irish-language programs remained low.

Having failed for years to convince RTE to add Irish programs, Gaeltacht activists began investigating the possibility of setting up their own television station. In November 1987, after visiting the Faroe Islands, which were already producing low-cost television programs in the local language, activists aired 18 hours of illegal Irish television from a pirate station in Ros Muc, County Galway. Having proved to themselves that no insuperable economic barrier existed, in 1989 Gaeltacht activists joined with a Dublin-based group to promote a separate Irish TV channel. By the early 1990s, every major political party in the Republic had pledged to support the proposed Teilifís na Gaeltachta (TnaG), which was to be a national channel funded, like

RTE, partly through taxes, partly by licenses fees collected from television owners, and partly by commercial advertising. TnaG began broadcasting on October 31, 1996.

What has proved remarkable about the Irish-language channel, renamed TG4 in 1999, is its unexpected popularity. Doubtless helped along by increased interest in Irish during the 1990s, the channel's success also owes much to the medium's visual cues. After all, Irish has been a compulsory school subject for three generations, so the country is full of people who, while falling short of the near-native proficiency required for understanding a radio discussion, know enough Irish to follow a television program. Even an American who has never studied the language can enjoy a football game or recognize a voice-over slogan when a bottle of Coca-Cola is flashed on the screen. By 2001, TG4 had a "reach" (defined as the number of people who tune in the channel for more than a minute a day) of 700,000. Its September broadcast of the All-Ireland women's football final set a record when it achieved an audience share of 20 percent.[7]

TG4 does relatively little in-house production but does commission special programs. As a result, some of the channel's offerings will seem familiar to foreigners, although admittedly *The Jetsons* is disconcerting when dubbed in Irish. The image of Irish as a living language, however, gets a major boost from TG4's popular *Ros na Rún*. First broadcast in 1996, this soap opera set in a fictional village near Spiddal, a dozen miles outside Galway, airs three times a week. The story line often features topics and incidents that would have been banned a generation ago: love triangles, abortion, divorce, even the first gay kiss on Irish television. As it does so, it plays against long-held stereotypes of the West; its citizens, "as venal as anyone," include a female vet and a lawyer, but no farmers and fishermen.[8] Although the surface of village life is as realistic as soap opera allows, there is no real-world equivalent of *Ros na Rún*, for English has penetrated even the Gaeltacht more thoroughly than the program suggests. Irish-speaking viewers can appreciate the irony that the Irish spoken on the program represents all three dialects and includes the occasional mistakes and mispronunciations of those for whom it is a second language. Nonetheless, partisans believe that even if *Ros na Rún* does not reflect current reality, it "challenges" the Irish to see new possibilities for the future of their language, to imagine a "linguistic community" that, scattered throughout the country, "finds cohesion through . . . television or internet."[9]

ENGLISH-LANGUAGE RADIO AND TELEVISION

Most Irish programs, however, were broadcast in English. Although originally intended as a public service station along the lines of the British

Broadcasting Corporation (BBC), financial necessity drove Radio Eireann to introducing sponsored programs in 1931. Rather than imitating the catchy jingles and mini-dramas of American radio advertising, Radio Eireann offered sponsors a brief announcement at the beginning and ending of a program. An early and enthusiastic sponsor was the Irish Hospitals Sweepstakes. Forbidden from advertising in British newspapers, it welcomed the opportunity to reach some British listeners. Live sports broadcasting began in 1926, and drama serials, music, news, and a political discussion program modeled on the BBC's *Question Time* gained popularity. Although the Catholic Church's stern morality influenced radio programming as it did other areas of Irish culture, censorship became a serious issue only after 1939, when Britain went to war and Ireland remained neutral. As British newspapers and radio broadcasts were freely available, almost anyone who wished to keep up with the war news could easily do so. Nonetheless, de Valera's government, always mindful of how easily either the Germans or British could occupy the Free State, went to great lengths to ensure that its neutrality would be respected.[10] Enforcing absolute editorial neutrality on the press became an obsession: "news broadcasts had to be read over in advance to the head of the Government Information Bureau, Frank Gallagher, and on occasion to Mr. de Valera himself."[11]

Television flourished in both Great Britain and America after the war. From 1953, BBC-TV could be picked up on the east coast of Ireland. Later in the year, the BBC set up a TV transmitter in Belfast, extending its service along the border. By 1955, Britain's first commercial channel, ITV-TV, could be received along the eastern coast; its Northern Ireland affiliate, Ulster TV, began broadcasting in 1959. Even though no local programming was available, there were probably 50,000 television sets in the Republic.[12] Resistance to the general evils of television, which "horrified" Pope Pius XII when he contemplated in 1955 "the thought that... it may be possible for that atmosphere poisoned by materialism, fatuity and hedonism, which is... breathed in many cinemas, to penetrate... the home," flourished among conservatives.[13] But with 40 percent of Irish homes already within the broadcasting range of BBC-TV, the government could not remain idle.[14] A committee appointed by the Minister of Posts and Telegraphs in 1956 complained not only of too much frankness "in sex matters" on the BBC but of "constant emphasis on... the British view of world affairs... British... achievements.... [and] every movement of the royal family."[15]

As the 1950s progressed, an Irish television channel came to seem inevitable, but whether the broadcasting service should follow a BBC public service or an American free-enterprise model was sharply debated. In 1960, a new Broadcasting Act resolved that question, establishing an Authority to manage state-sponsored radio and television. Although there were injunctions to keep in mind "national aims" such as restoring Irish, RTE was to be surprisingly autonomous. As was the case with radio, commercial sponsorship was part of the mix, although the government still limits the amount of advertising on RTE to a daily average of six minutes per hour. The first Irish TV broadcast went out on December 31, 1961. It featured the representative of the old order, Eamon deValera, who warned his audience about the "immense power" of the media and his fear that it might "lead... to decadence and dissolution."[16]

About television's power, at least, the old warrior was right. By 1973, RTE's annual report noted that 77 percent of homes in the Republic had television sets; by 2004, the figure was 99.5 percent, with 50.4 percent of homes including two or more sets.[17] True, in the early years, programming had a heavily Catholic slant. The unspoken assumption was that everyone, from the characters on situation comedies to viewers, was a conservative Catholic. Masses and other religious ceremonies were broadcast; the papal visit of 1979 was given "extravagant coverage."[18] Even in 2005, twice a day, at noon and six, RTE pauses its broadcasting for a minute. As a church bell tolls, the camera pans over a multicultural cross section of the Irish population, each figure briefly stopping the day's activity to meditate. No explicitly Catholic language or images are used; yet the Angelus, a devotional practice recalling the angel's announcement to Mary, is hardly nondenominational. The revolutionary effects of the medium became obvious as early as 1962, when Gay Byrne's *Late, Late Show* aired for the first time.

Byrne hosted this two-hour talk show until 1999. In 2005, it was still going strong with his successor, Pat Kenny. From Mother Teresa to Jerry Springer, the show's guest list has been a who's who list of contemporary celebrity, but Byrne's willingness to talk about controversial topics was what mesmerized and helped to transform Irish society. There was, for example, the business of the Bishop and the nighty. In 1966, a guest on the program, asked about the color of the nightgown she had worn on her wedding night, responded that she could not remember; "perhaps she had not worn one."[19] Bishop Thomas Ryan telegraphed RTE to let them know how disgusted he was, and he preached a sermon on the same theme the next day. Subsequent publicity, however, only heightened the show's popularity. In time every sexual taboo, every religious or social or political controversy, could be sure to air on the *Late, Late Show*. A social historian speaks of the Irish women's movement as being "launched" on the program in 1971.[20] "In Enniscorthy when I was a lad," notes novelist Colm Toibin, "we all sat glued to it.... If any other programme talked about sex, it would have been turned off. Turn that rubbish off. But nobody every turned the *Late, Late Show* off."[21] One reason Byrne was so successful may have been that he himself shared many of his audience's values, and he knew how to pitch topics to their sensibilities. In the late 1970s, the program aired a long interview with an Irish lesbian in which she spoke of the many difficulties she encountered. This program met no resistance, possibly because "the discussion was social in emphasis and avoided explicitly sexual references."[22]

Drama programs also brought changing, sometimes critical, perspectives on Irish society into the home. Because RTE, within its financial limits, aspired to the BBC model of public service television, promoting the best indigenous writers was a major goal. The actor and producer Hilton Edwards who, with his partner Michael MacLiammoir, had founded the Gate Theater in 1928, was the first director of RTE's drama department. In its first three years under his leadership, RTE produced such Irish classics as John Synge's *The Well of the Saints,* Sean O'Casey's *The Moon Shines on Kylenamoe,* Yeats's *Purgatory,* and Oliver Goldsmith's *She Stoops to Conquer.* RTE also commissioned dramatic adaptations of works of fiction such as Frank O'Connor's "In the Train" and "Guests of the Nation" (1963, 1969), Somerville and Ross's *The Real Charlotte* and *The Irish R. M.* (1966, 1982), and Liam O'Flaherty's *Land* (1967). RTE also produced new plays by rising local playwrights such as Eugene McCabe, Brian Friel, Neil Jordan, and Tom Murphy. Severe financial cutbacks led RTE to close its drama department in 1990, but to some extent collaboration between television and Ireland's prominent writers continues. In 1994, RTE commissioned a series of plays called *Two Lives,* each to run for half an hour and to feature two characters in one location. The list of distinguished Irish writers who contributed to the series includes Dermot Bolger, Thomas Kilroy, Pat McCabe, John Banville, Anne Enright, and Roddy Doyle. Plays in the *Two Lives* series explored such topics as highly dysfunctional parent-child relationships and the lives of Irish immigrants abroad. Doyle's *Hell for Leather* (1998) consisted of dialogue between a Catholic single mother and a Protestant career woman who have discovered that they shared the same lover, a recently deceased Catholic priest.

But soap operas and situation comedies provide a further glimpse of how the "social drama" of late twentieth-century Ireland's transformation "played itself out in television drama."[23] Perhaps the most influential early serial was *The Riordans,* which repeatedly topped the audience ratings in 15 years (1965 to 1979) of production. The program was set in a fictional rural village, and its characters ran the full social range from moneyed farm owners to poor farm workers. Initially somewhat didactic, with many messages about modernizing agriculture, the series developed sociological and psychological interests. Its scriptwriter, Wesley Burrows, wanted to represent real life, and if "an issue of wider social significance was suggested by a story, he preferred to plunge into the heart of the issue."[24] Such issues included attitudes to mental illness, travellers, single mothers, mixed marriages, and religious vocations. *The Riordans* often satirized the society lightly, as in an episode in which a character was required to paint clothes on naked figures done for a new mural in the village pub: "It was a laugh, but a laugh that said more about the Irish mind and its cultural consequences than many a tedious commentary."[25] The program even drew praise from the well-known English cultural critic, Raymond Williams, who praised the way the characters were embedded in a recognizable social and economic context, just like characters in Dickens or Thackeray.

Irish society, however, was not ready for the harder-hitting satire of Patrick Gilligan's *The Spike* (1978), set in a vocational school that the author described as a "scrap heap" for the "undeserving poor."[26] The program depicted characters sharply divided, usually along the lines of class: the principal's daughter versus the working-class students, the ill-educated principal versus his well-educated faculty, rich women taking night school classes versus poor women cleaning the toilets. It focused on problems "rooted in class inequality: poverty, prostitution, illiteracy, anti-social behavior in social institutions, domestic violence, child labor . . . lack of career opportunities, political hypocrisy and power struggles for control of the education system."[27] Having already provoked negative reviews, condemnation by individual clergy, and letters-to-the editor denouncing its vulgarity, *The Spike* was cancelled after a firestorm greeted the infamous fifth episode, in which art students were shown drawing a naked female model. The founder of the League of Decency, J. B. Murray, suffered a heart attack while phoning the newspapers to complain about "the filthy play." He attributed the attack to "the stress caused by the sight of the naked female body"; his wife "told the papers that the family had tried to stop him watching . . . but he insisted."[28]

As might be expected, the next two decades produced an Irish television audience less susceptible to shock. Two of the most popular serials on RTE were *Glenroe* (1983–2001) and *Fair City*, which debuted in 1989 and was still running in 2005. With its rural setting, *Glenroe* harked back to *The Riordans*. Its format, with 24 episodes a year, allowed for plenty of interwoven stories. Normally a middle-of-the-road program that depicted a world untouched by the Troubles in the North, *Glenroe* characters included more independent women and the full soap opera range of adulterous wives, babies born out of wedlock, and couples struggling with the Republic's continuing refusal to grant legal divorces. *The Spike*'s Patrick Gilligan wrote several episodes in 1988 featuring a traditional priest trying to come to terms with liberation theology, liturgical dance, and colleagues whose views about teaching were influenced by Paulo Freire's radical *Pedagogy of the Oppressed*. These episodes were praised for their "sensitivity to both sides," although more radical critics continued to deplore *Glenroe's* tendency to view social problems "at a safe distance."[29]

Fair City, on the other hand, returned to Dublin and the working class. This program, while certainly no rigorously accurate documentary, continues to reflect Ireland's changing mores: a storyline about a gay man in a relationship first with a bisexual, married man and then with a man whose partner was dying of AIDS, a story about a couple agonizing over whether to terminate a pregnancy after testing revealed that the child would be born severely disabled. The woman went to England for an abortion her partner could not accept: "the edgy painful relationship between them after it" was depicted in a "sophisticated way, although it did not seem to be popular with the audience."[30] Although *Fair City*, like *Glenroe*, is more wish-fulfilling soap opera than rigorous deconstruction of contemporary Ireland, contrasting its popularity with *The Spike's* quick demise offers one measure of how far public tastes have changed. Indeed, American viewers accustomed to Federal Communications Commission restrictions on obscenity may find themselves surprised at the freedom with which four-letter words are uttered on today's RTE.

Television Journalism

With its broadcasting monopoly in the Republic, Radio Telefis Eireann's influence on local issues was substantial from the beginning. Public affairs and news programming played a central role in the early years of Irish television, accounting for more than half of the "home-produced programming" in 1962.[31] According to regulations establishing the broadcasting Authority in 1960, information about "matters of public controversy" was to be presented "objectively and impartially and without any expression of the Authority's views."[32] This unobjectionable, if undefined, principle was supplemented by Article 31, which said that "the Minister may direct the Authority in writing to refrain from broadcasting any particular matter of any particular class."[33] In the early years, few politicians were actually interviewed on RTE, and, on the whole, the Taoiseach, Sean Lemass, was inclined to protect the station's freedom of speech from complaining viewers.

A crisis occurred, however, when, in 1966, the Minister for Agriculture, Charles Haughey, objected strongly to a broadcast in which one of his pronouncements on a milk price dispute was juxtaposed with a statement by a representative of the National Farmers' Association. Haughey insisted that placing his words on a par with an ordinary citizen's violated the station's obligation to present news impartially and persuaded Pearse Kelly, then Head of News, to order that the segment be cut from the 9 o'clock news. When a debate about the matter erupted in the Dail, Lemass replied that "Radio Telefis Eireann was set up by legislation as an instrument of public policy and as such is responsible to the Government."[34] To Lemass's opponents, it seemed as if he was saying that the government had the right to silence broadcasters, as they were its employees. The immediate crisis was resolved when the Authority's chair challenged the Minister of Posts and Telegraphs to invoke Section 31, and he backed down.

But the question of RTE's relationship to the government remained unresolved in 1969, when the Troubles erupted in Northern Ireland. While the situation was less immediately perilous than in 1939, Irish military vulnerability and reluctance to be pulled into conflict were once more critical. A British government was again pressuring an Irish government for at least tacit support. Then, too, the Irish state emerged out of a guerilla war between the Irish Republican Army (IRA) and Britain; and, on one reading, the same forces were again arrayed against each other in the North. Although the Free State had declared the IRA illegal in 1936 and interned its leadership during World War II, many Protestants in the North saw the government in Dublin and the paramilitary organization in Belfast as blood brothers. Naturally, too, most people in the Republic identified with Catholics in Northern Ireland and reacted with outrage when they saw television coverage of police beating civil rights protesters. It was inevitable that the IRA would find sympathizers in the Republic willing to shelter a bomber on the lam or turn a blind eye to the neighbor who was doing so. And while the vast majority of people in the Republic opposed violence, in 1972 an out-of-control mob responded to Bloody Sunday by burning down the British embassy in Dublin[35]. Just the previous October, Conor Cruise O'Brien, then Minister for Posts and Telegraphs, had invoked Article 31.

O'Brien was already a leading public intellectual. A gifted writer and scholar whose doctoral dissertation on Parnell was published by Oxford University Press, he had served with distinction in the diplomatic corps, a career that culminated with his mission as United Nations (UN) special envoy to the Congo in 1961. O'Brien developed a highly critical view of the UN role in Africa, on which he elaborated in *To Katanga and Back* (1963), a book prefaced with a copy of a letter from UN Secretary-General, U Thant, warning that unauthorized disclosure of UN affairs was against regulations. A member for years of the small, left-leaning Irish Labor party, O'Brien seems an unlikely advocate for press censorship. Yet he went to the Dail to speak in favor of an order "to refrain from broadcasting any matter...calculated to promote the aims and activities of any organization which engages in, promotes, encourages or advocates the attaining of any...objective by violent means."[36] O'Brien told legislators that "the democratic state has the right to enact repressive legislation, provided that it represses the right things in the right way."[37] Words do lead to blows, he argued; language appeals powerfully to the emotions. A government that establishes a broadcasting system and collects fees from its citizens to run it has a duty to protect itself and them from speech that endangers both. The state must not confuse its citizens, must not "accredit the idea that the IRA is a quasi legitimate institution, or that it is appropriate for citizens to be neutral as between the democratic state and the armed conspiracies which seek to usurp its functions."[38] In 1973, O'Brien extended the ban to include other organizations "proscribed by the *British* government in Northern Ireland."[39]

The Dail renewed the broadcasting ban annually until 1994, when it was allowed to expire in anticipation of the cease-fire; Section 31 remained on the books until 2001. Various court challenges and a 1989 appeal to the European Commission of Human Rights were all unsuccessful. One low point in relations between government and TV was reached in 1972, when RTE's Director-General refused to turn over production materials that might help the Irish and British security forces find IRA Chief of Staff Sean MacStiofain. When the broadcasting Authority supported his decision, its members were all dismissed. After 1976's amended Broadcasting Authority Act, the RTE was not only forbidden to broadcast a terrorist's call to arms but was also prevented from allowing members of a political party affiliated with an outlawed organization to speak on any topic: "a Sinn Fein member who kept bees could not be interviewed on his hobby."[40] Fear of accidentally including a quotation from someone associated with a proscribed organization led many reporters to avoid the North, or to shy away from stories about working-class neighborhoods where paramilitaries and their affiliates thrived. In retrospect, some observers argue that the ban provided an excuse for ignorance in a Republic already inclined to distance itself from the North. A strong argument can be made that investigative reporting leads to political solutions, and that its absence reinforced the paramilitary argument "that only violence could change things."[41]

NEWSPAPERS

As elsewhere in the twenty-first century, newspapers in Ireland face stiff competition from television and the Internet. Nonetheless, the nation's Joint National Readership Survey reported that in 2005, newspapers had picked up 100,000 new readers. They claimed that 91.4 percent of Irish adults currently read a newspaper, and that young people "show no sign of losing interest in newspapers either."[42] Although increased prosperity and population growth doubtless play a part in this success story, a spokesman for the National Newspapers of Ireland says that the newspapers have "raised their game" by investing in "new printing facilities, formats, new supplements and new color magazines."[43] Ever since 1996's Freedom of Information Act gave journalists access to government documents previously kept confidential, newspapers have played a vigorous role in exposing the many scandals in church and government that marked public life. Newspaper writers used this new tool "with more enthusiasm and to greater effect than their colleagues... to embarrass both governments and public servants."[44] Investigative reporters became celebrities in their own right. A Dublin woman whose name became the title of a film, *Veronica Guerin* (2003) was also the model for the heroine of *When the Sky Falls* (1999). An investigative reporter for the *Sunday Independent,* Guerin had written stories about organized drug-dealing. In June 1996, as she sat in her car at a traffic light, she was shot dead by a gunman on a motorcycle. Evidently her name remains a watchword in the criminal world. In 2005, a Dublin court heard a case in which the crime editor of another Irish newspaper, *The Sunday World,* claimed to have been told by a potential interviewee that he would soon "be meeting Veronica Guerin" if he published his name.[45]

Today there are six nationally circulated morning newspapers and nine Sunday newspapers in the Republic. Of these the *Irish Independent,* founded in 1905, has the largest circulation at 612,000. Since 1973, the *Independent,* traditionally the newspaper of the Catholic middle classes, has been owned by Tony O'Reilly, the Rupert Murdoch of Irish journalism. O'Reilly's Independent News and Media (INM) is now a global giant that owns newspapers and magazines in Australia and India, as well as Ireland, the United Kingdom, New Zealand, and South Africa; all told, the company publishes 175 titles. The company's Annual Report for 2004 states that it employs more than 11,000 people and puts its assets, which include television, radio, and communication technologies, at more than $2.5 billion in 2004.[46] In 2005, INM owned 67 percent of Irish daily newspapers and almost 87 percent of Irish Sunday newspapers.[47] Since 2000, it has also owned *The Belfast Telegraph,* traditionally a middle-of-the-road, moderate Unionist newspaper. Mindful that it might be accused of exploiting its market dominance, before completing the purchase INM committed itself not to "change employment structures in its Northern titles... not [to] change *The Telegraph's* editorial policy, and not to introduce cross-border deals with the group's titles in the Republic."[48] Concerns about INM's dominance in the Republic are frequently expressed, but as of 2005, the Minister for Enterprise, Trade and Employment was refusing to criticize the conglomerate publicly.

Although with a circulation of 323,000 *The Irish Times* has only about 11 percent of the Republic's readership, it is undoubtedly the nation's elite paper. Founded in 1859, it was the newspaper of the Ascendency, politically identified with moderate Unionism. After independence, Irish Catholic voices were more often heard. To take the most famous early example, from 1940 until his death in 1966, Flann O'Brien wrote a popular humor column, sometimes even in Irish. In O'Brien's day largely centered on Dublin, the paper expanded its size, staff, and geographical reach dramatically after 1986, the year it introduced its first color press. Averaging around 18 pages in 1986, 15 years later the typical issue had more than 50 pages. The paper added special features on science, legal affairs, environment, health, social affairs, media, and food. A staff of 190 in 1986 had expanded to 280 by 1996. In 1986, its most "foreign" bureau was in Brussels: "ten years later it had Moscow, Washington, Beijing, Paris, Rome and Bonn and a lot of new stringers."[49] After it had established bureaus in these distant places, the *Times* also opened up regional offices in its own country, in Galway and Tullamore. Like its counterpart in New York, the *Times* is now a national paper that maintains a good reputation for completeness and objectivity in its reporting, even as its editorial policy is understood to be liberal. And as in New York, artists, writers, actors, directors, dancers, singers, and other performers prize a favorable review from the *Times* above all others.

MAGAZINES

Competition from English and American publications poses a greater problem for Irish magazines than it does for newspapers, which can rely to some extent on interest in Irish law, politics, and local affairs. Creating a niche market for, say, Irish fashions or Irish computer gaming is more difficult. It is perhaps surprising, then, that 24 publishers offer more than 400 titles to the Irish market. Some of these are, as expected, highly specialized journals tailored to a well-defined audience: *Irish Nursing,* the annual *Journal of the Irish Georgian Society,* and the *Irish Farmers Journal* are good examples. There is a monthly *Ireland's Horse Review,* a weekly *Auto Trader,* and, for bicyclists, the monthly *Irish Cycling News.* It is probably a bad sign for a nation's magazine industry when its bestseller is a television guide, and the British *Sky Magazine* has recently been outselling the home-produced *RTE Guide.* With a circulation of 114,000 in 2003, *RTE Guide* easily outsells anything in the general interest category, such as *Ireland's Own* (43,000) and *Magills* (25,000).[50]

One of the more colorful upscale magazines is *The Dubliner,* which started publishing in 2001. The magazine bills itself as "the definitive guide to Irish culture"; among its features are lists of Dublin's best restaurants, Ireland's best hotels, and "ten great Dublin bars."[51] But unlike similar glossies seen around the world, *The Dubliner* has tackled serious issues, such as Irish racism and pedophile priests. Its October 2003 issue featured an interview with Gerry Adams.

Smurfit Communications, long a leading publisher of women's magazines, suffered a major public relations blow in 2002 when it was revealed that the company had been "overstating the circulation figures of… *Woman's Way, U Magazine,* and *IT Magazine* (Irish Tatler) since 1998."[52] Two of these publications, the upscale *IT* and the more down-market *Woman's Way,* have since recorded substantially lower sales than Smurfit had been reporting. But even under close supervision of the Audit Bureau of Circulations, circulation figures for *U Magazine* more than doubled in 2003, making it, at 50,000 copies, the most popular Irish women's magazine. In 2004, Smurfit was bought out by Norah Casey's Harmonia publishers. Perhaps inevitably nicknamed "Hormonia," by its critics, the company gears *U* to women 18 to 27 "at the more politically and sexually liberal end of the… market."[53] Casey, who has a diverse list that includes the Aer Lingus flight magazine, *Cara,* has sought to revitalize *Woman's Way,* which will remind Americans of *Women's Day.* One of her goals is to "free it from its stodgy menu of endless food recipes and arts and crafts." She has also purchased a Web site, iVenus.com, which offers such features as "horoscopes," and "soapdish" in addition to teasers about the women's magazines.

GLOBALIZATION AND IRISH MEDIA

While one Irish newspaper has grown rich from the globalization of media, its effects on Irish journalism more generally remain unclear. English newspapers have always posed a threat to their Irish counterparts. In 1932 , the government imposed a tariff on imported newspapers and periodicals that within a couple of years cut their profit margin by a little more than half.[54] This tariff, of course, was impossible to maintain if the Republic were to enter the Economic Union and was abolished in 1971. In 1999, the total circulation of daily newspapers from the United Kingdom in the Republic was 194,000. Major English newspapers such as the *Times* of London, *The Guardian,* and the *Daily Telegraph* each sell a few thousand copies daily, but most of the English newspapers sold in the Republic are tabloids.[55] In Northern Ireland, locally published newspapers have had a more difficult time. In 2005, a new offering, the *Daily View,* was forced to shut down after publishing for only five weeks. Circulation figures for *The Belfast Telegraph* had fallen 8.3 percent in six months. Only *The Irish News,* which largely sells to the growing Catholic population in the North, has had modest success.[56]

As for television, any discussion must take into account that more than half of the programs available are imports, mostly from Britain and the United States. *Dallas, Friends, Will and Grace,* and *Desperate Housewives* are as much a part of popular culture for the average Irish person as *The Riordans* or *Fair*

City. A phenomenon called "localization" permits the formats of many popular American and British TV to be adapted for Irish TV: the Canadian corporation that owns Ireland's TV 3 repackages ABC's *20/20* with an Irish anchor.[57] Localized versions of *The Weakest Link* and *Who Wants to be a Millionaire* have had a mixed reception. The reality format, first used in the Netherlands for *Big Brother,* has spawned almost as many variants in Ireland as in the United States. Even TG4 got into the act with *SOS,* an Irish-language version of *Survivor.* Economic and technological realities frustrate anyone who wants Irish television to be culturally distinctive. "Transnational commercial media," notes the current Chairman of RTE, Farrel Corcoran, "have an ideological interest in framing globalization in the language of privatization and social divestment and in pursuing their own self-preservation by perpetuating the political and social systems that permit them to exist."[58] As the United States exports its television programs to countries where public broadcasting still remains influential, it tends to export its private enterprise model for the media. Corcoran worries about the "caribbeanisation of Irish broadcasting," a state in which "scores of television channels from North America are available but almost no TV of any significance is produced locally."[59] Others are more hopeful that globalization will produce new markets for Irish programs, noting as a promising sign the modest success of BBC-Northern Ireland's *Ballykissangel* on both BBC-America and PBS. And, of course, the same technologies that drive globalization offer opportunities for small communities and minority voices. The 32-county Community Media Network, a nonprofit organization established in 1993, advocates innovative uses of the Internet, video, and desktop publishing by persons who wish to offer an alternative to the corporate giants.

THE IRISH IN BRITISH AND AMERICAN FILM

If Irish television is inevitably a hybrid, with local programming competing with British and American programs, Irish film is even more strongly marked by British and American actors, directors, audiences, and capital. Film was already a popular medium when the Free State was born. By 1916, about 150 Irish theaters were showing movies, and there was even a film magazine, *Irish Limelight.*[60] But the financial difficulties that pushed Radio Eireann into courting commercial sponsors were close to prohibitive when it came to making indigenous movies. Thus the earliest Irish movie most people will think of, Robert Flaherty's *Man of Aran* (1934), although long accepted as a truthful documentary, was in fact a romantic myth produced by a Michigan-born director who made his name with *Nanook of the North* (1922). The film depicts the lives of fishermen on the Aran Islands, a locale made famous by

John Synge, whom Flaherty had read with enthusiasm. Its respectful vision of the islanders' bravery, self-sufficiency, and strong ties to family, church, and tradition accorded perfectly with de Valera's idealized Gaelic Ireland. After the Taoiseach attended the film's Dublin premiere, it became a regular on the parish hall circuit. In fact, it is still shown daily throughout the summer to tourists visiting the islands' Aran Centre in Kilronan.

Although Flaherty spent two years on the main island, producing 37 hours of film using actual Irish people as actors, he took many liberties with real life. Take for example the stunning white thatched cottage featured in the film: although constructed authentically, it was built to order "on the more exposed, dramatic side of the island," which natives avoided.[61] The film's most spectacular sequence is a shark hunt on a stormy Atlantic, undertaken because the islanders need its oil. In fact, kerosene had been routinely imported from Galway for 100 years, and the islanders had to be taught how to hunt in the traditional way. What was authentic was the danger. The storm that Flaherty filmed so stunningly put local men at a risk they would not otherwise have taken. And although the islanders' ancestors had indeed created the soil of their picturesque fields with seaweed, the famous soil-making scenes were equally anachronistic. Film techniques contributed to mythologizing the islanders. Low camera angles often put the viewer in the position of looking up at a heroically sized figure framed against a bleak sky or rock face. In one such shot, as the camera returns from the sea to the hero's face, "he turns his head slightly to offer a perfect profile of his chiseled good looks, framed against the skyline by the 'tam-o-shanter' headgear which Flaherty insisted that the characters wear."[62] Flaherty's Irish were like his Inuits: virtuous primitives pitted against harsh and unrelenting nature. Extraordinary visual beauty and an awe of the natives' resolution make *Man of Aran* a welcome departure from demeaning images of the stage Irish, but the film evades the harsh economic and social realities of Irish life during the Depression.

Although U.S. and British films about Ireland seldom measure up to *Man of Aran*'s artistry, they often imitate it: even if set in the putative present, they portray Ireland as a rural backwater untouched by modernization. Millions of people around the world, to take one example, saw American director John Ford's *Quiet Man* (1952), in which John Wayne plays an American boxer who, after accidentally killing an opponent, retires to Ireland and finds love in a rural idyll with Maureen O'Hara. The camera pans over scenic landscape as hero and heroine go for long rides in a horse-drawn jaunting cart. A horse race along the beach provides vistas of the Atlantic as seen against a full-Technicolor sky and a white beach. Bicycle rides offer more glimpses of green fields intersected by stony walls. As in travelogue, minor characters—women in shawls, a man in a top hat fit for a leprechaun—are as picturesque as the white horses

and sheep, and as undifferentiated. Millions more marveled at the scenery sur-
rounding the apparently authentic Irish village built from scratch for the production of British director David Lean's *Ryan's Daughter* (1970), which netted
Oscars for Sarah Miles and John Mills. Almost 30 years later, British director
Kirk Jones's *Waking Ned Devine* (1998) offered yet more gorgeous scenery and
colorful characters, "two old boys who grew old but never grew up" attempting
to claim a huge lottery prize in the name of a dead man.[63] This time, in spite of
the story's Irish setting, the filming was actually done on the Isle of Man.

ARDMORE STUDIOS AND THE QUEST FOR AN IRISH FILM INDUSTRY

It remains difficult to distinguish clearly between British or American
films about Ireland in which some native actors appear, and the more elusive category of the authentic Irish film, the one, as actor Stephen Rea puts
it, that is "Irish in the way that a French movie is French and an Italian
movie is Italian."[64] In 1958, the Irish government partially underwrote the
new Ardmore Studios with a view to developing an indigenous film industry.
Headquartered a few miles south of Dublin, in Bray, the studio originally
filmed plays and actors from Dublin's famous Abbey Theatre. One of its most
distinguished productions was *This Other Eden* (1959), in which Irish writer
Walter Macken played the lead in a script based on his own work. The plot,
conventionally enough, revolves around a romance between an Irishwoman
and an Englishman freshly arrived in the country. Yet unlike *The Quiet Man,*
the film debunks some of the pieties of Irish nationalism and "is notewor-
thy for constructing an image of Irishness that emanated from within the
national culture, rather than being imposed from without."[65]

However, the project of producing a wholly Irish film industry faltered
amid financial difficulties and disputes about Ardmore's mission. Between
the 1960s and the mid-1980s, Ardmore's facilities were primarily rented out
to foreign companies. Some films produced there, such as John Ford's *Young
Cassiday* (1964) and John Strick's *Ulysses* (1967), had Irish themes; but many,
such as *The Spy Who Came in from the Cold* (1966) and *Lion in Winter* (1968),
did not. Such productions did not necessarily provide Irish jobs; "foreign film
companies," as the Irish film maker Louis Marcus complained, "aren't there
to prove that Irish men and women can make films: they . . . want to use their
own people."[66] In 1973, with Ardmore Studios in deep financial trouble, the
government purchased it outright. It has changed hands several times since
1982 and continues to rely on foreign film productions.

In 1981, in another move to create an indigenous film industry, the government established the Irish Film Board (IFB), which underwrote 10 films

before being suspended for economic reasons in 1987. The IFB offered partial subsidies; the remainder of the funding came from such partners as the
British Film Institute and Channel 4. The films produced from 1981 to 1987
were not international blockbusters, but they were fresh and original, praised
for examining Irish society both honestly and critically. Bob Quinn's *Poitín*
(1978), for example, an Irish-language film, portrayed the rural west unsen-
timentally as, in the words of one angry character, "a dead place for dead
people."[67] *Maeve* (1981), based on Pat Murphy's screenplay, offers a feminist perspective on the Troubles. As its heroine returns home from London
to Belfast, she encounters sexual harassment from British soldiers but also
confronts the male violence embodied in her own nationalist community's
traditions. Technically innovative, the film "used unmarked flashbacks, direct
address to camera, and sequences of non-naturalist dialogue to disrupt a stable point of view." Rather than identifying with either Maeve or the Irish
nationalists, the viewer was encouraged to question them.[68] Perhaps most
memorably, *Angel* (1982; released as *Danny Boy* in the United States), also
set in the North, was the first film for director Neil Jordan and actor Stephen
Rea. The story of a saxophonist who kills members of a Protestant parami-
tary gang one by one after he witnesses them murdering a mute girl, the film
tried to "deconstruct the political mythologies which underpin the Troubles
by showing their psychic roots."[69] In another departure from formula, the
leader of the Loyalist gang turned out to be a police detective, a point apparently lost on most of the film's English reviewers, who assumed that all Irish
terrorists belong to the IRA.

Although the IFB failed to produce them, Irish blockbusters were just
around the corner. Jim Sheridan's *My Left Foot* (1989) and Neil Jordan's *The
Crying Game* (1992; starring Stephen Rea) both scored critical and box office
success in the United States. So, with Anglo-American funding, did *The Commitments* (1991), a film version of Roddy Doyle's novel about a successful
rock band from working-class Dublin, and Sheridan's *The Field* (1990). The
latter, starring Limerick-born Richard Harris in a memorable, if grandiose,
performance as an Irish King Lear, is set in the 1930s. Harris's character, Bull
McCabe, is the classic land-hungry farmer. For years he and his sons have carried wagon loads of seaweed up what looms almost as the side of a mountain
to create soil for a once-barren field they rent from an Anglo-Irish widow.
He is single-mindedly determined to own the field and pass it on to his sons.
The first son, however, commits suicide after being unable to bear his father's
browbeating. Then the widow sells the land to an American, who plans to
pave it and build a hydroelectric station, and McCabe's second son runs off
with a traveller woman. McCabe murders the American and provokes a cattle
stampede in which his son accidentally dies. In a scene straight out of Yeats's

poem about the hero Cuchulain, who also unwittingly killed his son, the old man walks raving into the sea.

When the Irish Film Center and National Film Archive opened in Dublin's Temple Bar in 1992, it was a banner year. For the first time, there was a central depository for Irish film and a site for its study. The center featured two cinemas showing art films from around the world; the center operated as a private club, which moviegoers could join for a modest fee, that enabled them to view films were banned in public cinemas. The center also housed Film Base, a resource center for low-budget productions, and now the publisher of the journal *Film Ireland.* In 1992, the government also published a report on *The Film Industry in Ireland,* which noted its potential for economic growth. In 1993, the government reestablished the IFB, again providing loans and partial subsidies to Irish filmmakers and further restructuring the tax system to encourage private investment in film as well. The number of films produced annually rose immediately. By 2000, the government reported that the industry raised roughly $100 million dollars for the Irish economy on a tax investment of about $40 million.[70]

For purists, the revived IFB adopted an "explicitly commercial policy to create jobs and provide support for a global audiovisual product," thus making it harder for filmmakers to produce the "culturally incisive" films of the 1980s.[71] Others would argue that Irish film policy simply acknowledged the realities of the global electronic market, which pressures filmmakers to take British and American audiences into account. If an Irish director such as Neil Jordan or Jim Sheridan relies on Hollywood backing, then his film must play well in the United States. To ensure this result, an American superstar is often cast in a role for which a talented local actor might easily be found. Jordan's *Michael Collins* (1996) featured Irish actor Liam Neeson in the title role, but his (mostly fictional) love interest was Julia Roberts. Meryl Streep was imported to star in Pat O'Connor's film version of Irish playwright Brian Friel's *Dancing at Lughnasa* (1998). Perhaps so few British soldiers and officials are seen in popular films about the Troubles, such as Terry George and Jim Sheridan's *Some Mother's Son* (1996) and *The Boxer* (1998), because producers know that a British audience might resent seeing its own people in an unfavorable light. Some even argue that George and Sheridan's *In the Name of the Father* (1993), a film about the Guildford Four, who spent 15 years in an English prison after being wrongfully convicted of a pub bombing, soft pedals political criticism by focusing on the melodramatic theme of father-son reconciliation. And even when the influence of foreign money and sensibilities are kept to a minimum, the simple fact that most English-speaking people live outside the Republic guarantees that local references, jokes, and even accents will need to be cut, modified, or explained.

The difficulties of an Irish film for outsiders are apparent in Margo Harkin's *Hush-a-bye-Baby* (1989). Even though filmed in a part of Ireland under British rule and relying on some British funding, it comes about as close as possible to being wholly indigenous. Harkin belonged to the Derry Film and Video Collective (DFVC), a group that originally received funding from British Channel Four to do documentaries. A suggestion of DFVC's relative independence is that its *Mother Ireland* (1988), an analysis of the role of female imagery in Irish nationalism, was "promptly banned in Britain."[72] Harkin's group spent two years interviewing women in Catholic, working-class Derry, with a view to telling a fictional story that would be faithful to their understanding of themselves. The story line involves a 15-year-old girl named Goretti who becomes pregnant after a brief relationship with teenage Ciaran, who is subsequently jailed by the British for suspected ties to terrorism. The actors are Irish, and the settings—the working-class Creggan area of Derry and a farmhouse in the Donegal Gaeltacht—are scrupulously realistic. Most of the hot-button issues of the times, from abortion to the internment of terrorist suspects without trial, play a part in the story, but the director avoids polemic by eliminating obvious targets.

There is a great contrast between the girls giggling in the schoolroom as a good-looking priest talks to them about marriage and the streetwise way they smoke, swear, and talk about sex in the neighborhood. But teachers are not seen disciplining the girls brutally or threatening them with hell. Goretti's father is unemployed, but a school friend notes enviously that her mother has a job; the family's house is overcrowded, but clean and modern. Her parents are loving, but distracted with a large family and the stresses in their own relationship. A few glimpses of holy pictures and disapproving references to abandoned babies establish the shame that leads Goretti to conceal her pregnancy from them, but there is no suggestion that she fears parental violence. The Troubles are simply taken for granted. Leaving the neighborhood means being searched at a checkpoint; coming home means seeing the sign announcing "You are now entering Free Derry." No one talks about politics, but no one is especially shocked or outraged when a 16-year-old is "lifted" and jailed on suspicion of terrorist activities. The film's ending is ambiguous. Goretti wakes up screaming after a nightmare in which, dressed as the Virgin Mary, she breaks out of a glass case. Her parents run in, obviously alarmed. The continuing screams suggest that she might be going into early labor, but the film ends abruptly, without explanation.

The film was especially successful when shown on RTE, where it attracted 650,000 viewers. Aside from the attractions of excellent acting and a recognizable vision of contemporary urban life, the film raised topical issues that had a special resonance in Ireland. One was abortion, which the Republic banned after a constitutional referendum in 1984. Subsequently it faced the trauma of Anne Lovett, the 15-year-old who died in childbirth at a grotto of the Virgin Mary, and of Joanne Hayes, falsely accused of being the mother of a dead baby who washed up on the beach in Kerry and determined in the course of the investigation to be the mother of another dead baby. Emer McCourt's luminous Goretti was, to people who had lived with such headlines, only too recognizable. Many of them had shared Goretti's experience of going to the Gaeltacht to study Irish and sneaking away to speak English with a friend. They might not have known anyone by the name, but they were sure to recognize the allusion to Maria Goretti, a 12-year-old rape-murder victim whom Pius XII canonized in 1950 as a model of chastity and forgiveness. When Dinky, Goretti's loyal friend, shakes a finger at a roadside shrine of the Virgin Mary and says, "Now don't ya f–kin' move, I'm warnin' ya," the Irish audience could recognize the miraculous moving statues of the summer of 1985. They did not need a voice-over to explain what "Free Derry" was, and they could understand all of the dialogue, even slangy off-color jokes exchanged in a working-class Ulster accent that outsiders can find impenetrable. Yet the very reasons for the film's popularity in Ireland are, of course, the reasons it did not find an American distributor.

Irish filmmakers who wish to do more than underwrite a couple of hundred years of stage Irish stereotyping face the challenge, then, of designing a film that a foreign audience can understand, which nonetheless offers the Irish a recognizable reality. One step in this direction has been the evolution of an urban film, usually set in Belfast or Dublin, that depicts Ireland as a contemporary country with its share of ugly housing projects and factories. Two good examples are Stephen Frears's *The Snapper* (1993) and *The Van* (1996), both based on novels by Roddy Doyle, who also wrote the screenplays. The director is British, but the actors, including Colm Meaney, who stars in both, are Irish. *The Van* centers on a couple of unemployed Irishmen who rehabilitate a motorless old "chipper," a vehicle in which fish and chips can be prepared and from which they are sold. Although the story is told with great humor and verve, showing the men's temporary success at selling their wares to excited crowds of soccer fans, it faces the problems of working-class men who lack the skills to succeed in the new economy. At the end, having been cited for failure to meet government standards for selling food, the men abandon the van at low tide in Dublin Bay, surely an ironic comment on the idealized rural scenery of films such as *The Quiet Man*. *The Snapper* deals with unwed pregnancy, acquaintance rape, and the changing roles of women in a working-class neighborhood. Sharon, age 19, spends her evenings at a local pub, where she and her friends often drink heavily. After one such evening, George, a middle-age neighbor with a daughter Sharon's age, accosts her and they have sex in the pub's parking lot.

Unlike *Hush-a-bye Baby,* where Goretti listens to a discussion of abortion on the radio, *The Snapper* ignores the possibility. In this it is probably faithful to a residual Catholicism in the family. Sharon makes no serious effort to conceal her pregnancy, and her parents set her brothers and sisters down to explain it. Yet in spite of the family's generous acceptance, shame becomes an issue: Sharon is ashamed to name the child's father, but then George humiliates both her and her father by boasting of his conquest. Neighborhood children mock Sharon's younger brothers and sisters. Like *The Van,* the film remains largely comic, although the realities it confronts, including a couple of episodes in which heavily pregnant Sharon becomes drunk, are grim. In the shadow of the Kerry Babies Tribunal and public discussions of infanticide, a line where Sharon and her father are talking around the baby's paternity comes close to gallows humor. What will they do, asks Sharon, if the baby is a girl and looks like George? "Oh, feck," says Dessie. "Then we'll have to smother it and leave it on his [door] step."[73] The ending, with the baby safely born and the family celebrating, might even be considered a happy one. Like most of Doyle's work, *The Snapper* evinces "a faith in the essential strength and goodness of the working-class Irish, a goodness... not rooted in religious faith necessarily, nor in airy notions of Celtic myth, but in the simple sense of fair play practiced by the decent, hardworking people who have long inhabited the poorer housing estates of Dublin."[74]

A different kind of contemporary urban realism can be found in films that explore Dublin's underworld, where crime and drug addiction burgeoned throughout the 1990s. Two films focus on Martin Cahill, nicknamed "The General," a career criminal who was gunned down in a Dublin suburb, probably by the IRA, in 1994. British-born director John Boorman filmed *The General* (1998) with Irish actor Brendan Gleason in the title role. Shot in color, the film was released in black and white, a medium Boorman values for its ability to suggest "a parallel world that's somehow different."[75] He intended to disturb viewers by making Cahill human, even as he engages in such brutal activities as nailing a suspected informer to a table. But quite a few reviewers saw the film's Cahill as a Robin Hood, "a lovable brigand," as one explained, "who will win your heart with his funny, brash, brawny Irish ways."[76] Similarly, Irish Director Thaddeus O'Sullivan's *Ordinary Decent Criminals* (2000), which features Kevin Spacey as Cahill, was both praised and derided for turning him into a folk hero for the Irish inner city. Spacey's accent, which "reduced local audiences to unsolicited laughter," further undermined the film's claims to portray Ireland's underclass realistically.[77]

The story of Veronica Guerin, the determined investigative report for the *Irish Independent,* seems in some ways a more promising vehicle for a realistic view of the new criminal underworld. After all, a story focusing on

Cahill always risked asking the viewer to share his perspective, to celebrate such accomplishments as stripping a mansion, Russborough House, of its Vermeers in the biggest art theft in the Republic's history. Identification with Guerin, on the other hand, invited viewers to share the perspective of a spirited upper-middle-class woman as she draws closer to Dublin's drug underworld. The 1999 version, *When the Sky Falls,* starred American actor Joan Allen as Sinead Hamilton, a character closely based on Guerin. Before Guerin's murder, she was consulting with Irish writer Michael Sheridan about making a film based on her life. *When the Sky Falls* was based in part on Sheridan's original script and respected Guerin's wish that some elements of the story be fictionalized. Yet the result was a lackluster production that one reviewer calls "well-meaning but poorly organized". Although available in the United States as a video, the movie was never released in American theaters.[78] Four years later, American director Joel Schumacher's *Veronica Guerin* offers a substantially more satisfying version of the heroine's personality and motives and a far clearer picture of the impact of drugs on inner-city Dublin.

Some of the film's most dramatic scenes simply show Guerin walking through the city's poor neighborhoods, knocking on doors in public housing estates, trying to talk to a comatose teenage addict, observing children playing with abandoned hypodermic needles. That the children are so obviously the native Irish, not Third World immigrants, underscores how thoroughly heroin has become an Irish problem. In contrast, an early scene in *When the Sky Falls* establishes the heroin problem by having the Martin Cahill character gesture at the lights of the city below, remarking that there is a needle for every point of light. The 2003 film also adds to Guerin's complexity. She was, by most standards, extraordinarily reckless, cultivating contacts with criminals, spending hours in disreputable pubs, going alone to interview dangerous men in isolated places. Admirable as her persistence and courage were, more conventional viewers are bound to wonder about her young son's safety, or whether she found close connections with violent men somewhat too emotionally satisfying. In *When the Sky Falls,* this conflict is played out as a domestic one, with an exhausted Veronica arriving home after dark, after an evening of marching in an antidrug demonstration, her son asleep on her shoulder. Her husband's lecture on thinking about their family comes off as petulant jealousy. In *Veronica Guerin,* the much warmer relationship between the couple suggests an unusual degree of both love and acceptance. Little Cathal enjoys a nurturing relationship with his father and grandmother. Viewers still do not understand the full sources of Guerin's zeal and ambition, but they cannot put them off to a need to get out of the house.

All of the films about Dublin's underworld are violent, but *Veronica Guerin* may do the best job of portraying its sheer unglamorous brutality. Irish actor

Gerard McSorley plays the film's chief villain, John Gilligan, with extraordinary menace. The scene in which Guerin, totally unprotected, confronts Gilligan on his doorstep, is deeply disturbing for the cold-blooded efficiency with which he swings a fist in her face and then keeps on beating her after she is down. When she presses charges against him, he telephones her with an equally chilling threat to rape and kill her son. Australian actress Cate Blanchett's performance is also remarkable. An *Irish Times* review noted that the actress not only manages "to look uncannily like Guerin herself...and crucially pulls this off in the intense close-up shots, but she also achieves a convincing accent that strongly resembles Guerin's familiar voice."[79] Backed up by a mostly Irish cast and crew, and benefiting from its director's conscientious effort to avoid the clichés of the gangster movie, *Veronica Guerin* provides a convincing vision of a city where drug addiction has devastated poor neighborhoods, and even suburbs are targets for crime and violence. A lengthy voice-over at the end irritated Irish reviewers but addressed the foreign audience's interest in the political impact of Guerin's reports and murder.

For a country so long accustomed to seeing itself imagined as a timeless Eden, cinematic representations of the present have a special importance. To the extent that the lives of well-off urban professionals arguably resemble those of their counterparts in Manhattan or London, it should not be surprising that some popular films pay little attention to the questions of national identity that have traditionally engaged Irish filmmakers. Irish director Gerard Stembridge's *About Adam* (2000), the story of a handsome rogue who seduces three sisters in an upper-middle-class family, might as easily have been set in Los Angeles or Edinburgh. Although its screenplay was written by Roddy Doyle, Kieron Walsh's *When Brendan Met Trudy* (2001), the improbable story of a schoolteacher film buff (played by Peter MacDonald) who falls in love with a thief (Flora Montgomery) seems almost equally placeless. Indeed, it makes more references to the French and American movies in which MacDonald's character is steeped than it does to Irish reality.

But an increasing number of films have also looked critically at the past. Sydney McCartney's *A Love Divided* (1999) is based on events that took place in Wexford in 1957 when a Protestant woman married to a Catholic man was ordered by a local priest to send their children to a Catholic school. She takes the children north, where they are sheltered by kindly Protestants. Back home, Catholics boycott the Protestant neighbors with whom they have lived in peace for generations. Eventually, as in real life, the couple reconcile and home school their children. The film's depictions of Protestants as part of the texture of rural life in the Republic and its acknowledgment that they suffered discrimination at the hands of the Catholic majority revises the familiar vision of Gaelic Ireland. Two films with British directors, Alan

Parker's *Angela's Ashes* (1999) and Peter Mullan's, *The Magdalene Sisters* (2002), although admired for excellent acting, received mixed reviews for their scathing treatment of the past.

The unrelenting bleakness of *Angela's Ashes,* based on American Frank McCourt's memoir of growing up in Limerick in the 1930s and 1940s, offended people who preferred their accounts of Irish poverty to focus on pre-Independence Ireland. Lacking the wit of the original novel, the film, with its depressing vistas of endless rain and harsh Catholic institutions, suggested to some a "reactionary and regressive" resignation; others deplored its idealization of American immigration.[80] By the time *The Magdalene Sisters* was released, Irish audiences had had a decade of clerical scandals and accounts of child abuse in Catholic orphanages and industrial schools to prepare them to see sadistic nuns screaming at young women left in their care. Perhaps it was all precisely true, or perhaps, as some Catholic writers hoped, in real life such a place would have contained a few gentle and courageous sisters. But whatever the case, the cinematic stereotype of Ireland as a tranquil refuge, where a wounded John Wayne could expect healing, was gone forever.

NOTES

1. Iarfhlaith Watson, *Broadcast in Irish: Minority Language, Radio, Television and Identity* (Dublin: Four Courts, 2003).

2. Watson, 52.

3. John McQuillan, quoted in Watson, 54.

4. Watson, 33.

5. Watson, 67.

6. Market Research Bureau of Ireland, quoted in Watson, 68.

7. "Succeeding Beyond the Pale," *The Irish Times,* 28 November 2001.

8. Ruth Lysaght, "Pobal Sobail: *Ros na Rún,* TG4 and Reality," in *Keeping It Real: Irish Film and Television,* ed. Ruth Barton and Harvey O'Brien (London: Wallflower Press, 2004), 147–158.

9. Lysaght, 152. Lysaght argues that the image of a language in the minds of those who do not speak it influences its fate. If the Irish public sees Irish as a living language, it is more likely to remain one.

10. After Irish independence, Britain remained in control of several key ports in the Free State, relinquishing them only in 1938. Churchill fiercely opposed this move and spoke openly of taking them back after the outbreak of war. Provoked by deValera's condolences to the German government on the death of Adolf Hitler, Churchill gave a victory speech on 13 May 1945 that suggested few qualms about an English invasion of Ireland: [in 1940] "the approaches which the southern Irish ports and airfields could so easily have guarded were closed by the hostile aircraft and U-boats. This indeed was a deadly moment in our life, and if it had not been for the loyalty and friendship of Northern Ireland, we should have been forced to come to

close quarters with Mr. de Valera, or perish from the earth. However, with a restraint and poise to which, I venture to say, history will find few parallels, His Majesty's Government never laid a violent hand upon them." http://worldatwar.net/timeline/ireland/18–48.html.

11. John Horgan, *Irish Media: A Critical History Since 1922* (London: Routledge, 2001), 48

12. Horgan, 83.

13. Quoted in Horgan, 80.

14. Helena Sheehan, *The Continuing Story of Irish Television Drama: Tracking the Tiger* (Dublin: Four Courts, 2004), 80.

15. Quoted in Horgan, 79.

16. Quoted in Horgan, 84.

17. Quoted in Horgan, 119; statistics for 2004 come from Joint National Listenership Survey 2004. http://www.medialive.ie/General/durables.html.

18. Helena Sheehan, *Irish Television Drama,* 2nd ed. (Dublin: Four Courts, 2004), CD-ROM.

19. Tom Inglis, *Lessons in Irish Sexuality* (Dublin: UCD Press, 1998), 39.

20. Pat O'Connor, "Ireland: A Country for Women?" *Jouvert: A Journal of Postcolonial Studies* 4.1 (Fall 1999). http://social.chass.ncsu.edu/jouvert/v4i1/oconn.htm.

21. Colm Toibin, *The Trial of the Generals: Selected Journalism 1980–1990* (Dublin: Raven Arts, 1990), 87. Quoted in Horgan, 89.

22. Maurice Earls, "*The Late Late Show*: Controversy and Context," In *Television and Irish Society: 21 Years of Irish Television,* ed. Martin McLoone and John MacMahon (Dublin: RTE-Irish Film Institute, 1984), 120.

23. Helena Sheehan, *The Continuing Story of Irish Television Drama,* 1. I am indebted to Sheehan for the examples in this paragraph and the next.

24. Helena Sheehan, *Irish Television Drama. A Society and Its Stories* (Dublin: RTE, 1987), 129.

25. Sheehan, *Irish Television Drama,* 133.

26. Gilligan, *RTE Guide,* 20 January 1978. Quoted in Sheehan, *Irish Television Drama,* 164.

27. Sheenhan, *Irish Television Drama,* 164.

28. Sheehan, *Irish Television Drama,* 169.

29. Sheehan, *The Continuing Story of Irish Television Drama,* 33, 36.

30. Sheehan, *The Continuing Story of Irish Television Drama,* 55.

31. John Horgan, *Broadcasting and Public Life: RTE News and Current Affairs: 1926–1997* (Dublin: Four Courts, 2004), 26.

32. Horgan, *Broadcasting and Public Life,* 23.

33. Quoted in Alex White, "Section 31: Ministerial Orders and Court Challenges," in *Democratic Censorship and the Democratic State,* ed. Mary Corcoran and Mark O'Brien (Dublin: Four Courts, 2005), 34. The Minister in question was the Minister of Posts and Telegraphs, then in charge of broadcasting. The title has since been changed, but is still being laughed at: a racing greyhound on *Glenroe* was named after the Minister for Arts, Culture, and the Gaeltacht.

34. Quoted in Horgan, *Broadcasting and Public Life*, 41.

35. A survey in 1978 showed most citizens in the Republic opposed to partition (72%), but only 21 percent supported the IRA's activities. However, 42 percent claimed to support the IRA's "motives," as opposed to 33 percent who opposed them and 25 percent who remained neutral. E. Davis and R. Sinnot, *Attitudes in the Republic of Ireland Relevant to the Northern Ireland Problem* (Dublin: Economic and Social Research Institute, 1979). Quoted in Mark O'Brien, "Disavowing Democracy: The Silencing Project in the South," in Horgan, *Broadcasting and Public Life,* 49.

36. Quoted in White, 37.

37. Conor Cruise O'Brien, "Broadcasting and Violence: The Case for Media Restriction," in Horgan, *Broadcasting and Public Life,* 25.

38. O'Brien, 37–38.

39. Luke Gibbons, *Transformations in Irish Culture: Critical Conditions. Field Day Essays* (Notre Dame, Ind.: University of Notre Dame Press, 1996), 79.

40. Desmond Fisher, "Getting Tough with RTE," in Corcoran and O'Brien, 71.

41. Ed Moloney, "Censorship and 'The Troubles,'" in Corcoran and O'Brien, 109.

42. "Media Release," 8 March 2005, Joint National Readership Survey, http://www.jnrs.ie/whats.htm.

43. "More and More Irish Adults Reading Newspapers," National Newspapers of Ireland, 8 March 2005, http://www.nni.ie/presrel28.htm.

44. Horgan, *Irish Media,* 166.

45. "Journalist Threatened Twice, Jury is Told," *The Irish Times,* 5 May 2005.

46. Independent News and Media PLC. Annual Report 2004. http://www.implc.com/annualreport04/IndoA04.pdf.

47. "Media Group 'Abused' Its Position," *The Irish Times,* 25 February 2005.

48. Horgan, *Irish Media,* 172.

49. Horgan, *Irish Media,* 144. The statistics in the preceding three sentences also come from this source and page.

50. Information on circulation figures comes from "Ireland." Media Update: Magazines, *The Media Map Yearbook 2004* (Carlsbad, Calif.: PriMetrica Limited, 2004), 161–162.

51. *The Dubliner,* Home page, http://www.thedubliner.ie/.

52. *The Media Map Yearbook 2004,* 161.

53. Hugh Oram, "In Tune with Publishing," *Marketing: Ireland's Marketing Monthly,* 5 March 2005, http://www.marketing.ie/mar05/article1.htm.

54. Horgan, *Irish Media*, 35. "The value of imported newspapers fell from 216,000 pounds in 1932 to 99,000 pounds in 1934."

55. Horgan, *Irish Media,* 191. Of the 194,000 circulation figure, *The Sun* accounts for 102,000 and the *Daily Mirror* for 62,000. Both have local editions featuring substantial Irish content.

56. "North Proves a Tough Market for New Titles," *The Irish Times,* 12 May 2005.

57. Farrel Corcoran, *RTE and the Globalisation of Irish Television* (Bristol: Intellect, 2004), 202.

58. Corcoran, 199.

59. Corcoran, 204–205.

60. Brian McIlroy, *Irish Film: An Illustrated History* (Dublin: Anna Livia, 1988), 19.

61. Lance Pettit, *Screening Ireland: Film and Television Representation* (Manchester: Manchester University Press, 2000), 78.

62. Martin McLoone, *Irish Film: The Emergence of a Contemporary Cinema* (London: British Film Institute, 2000), 40.

63. Charles Ealy, "Writer-Director Kirk Jones Based *Waking Ned Devine* on His Grandfather," Interview with Kirk Jones, 10 December 1998. *The Dallas Morning News*. Newspaper Source. The phrase is actually a quote from one of the film's leading actors, David Kelly.

64. Stephen Rea, Interview with Ted Sheehy, Barton and O'Brien, 199.

65. Ruth Barton, *Irish National Cinema* (London: Routledge, 2004), 81.

66. Quoted in Pettit, 97.

67. Quoted in Pettit, 104.

68. Pettit, 105.

69. Pettit, 106.

70. The actual figures are 58,659,880 Irish pounds and 21,576,037 Irish pounds. Office of the Revenue Commissioners. Quoted in Barton, 107.

71. Kevin Rockett, "Bord Scannan na hEireann," in *The Encyclopedia of Ireland*, Brian Lalor, ed. (New Haven, Conn.: Yale University Press, 2003), 108.

72. Pettit, 121.

73. Quoted Pettit, 124.

74. Terry Byrne, *Power in the Eye: An Introduction to Contemporary Irish Film* (Lanham, Md.: Scarecrow Press, 1997), 40.

75. Paula Hunt, "Voluntary Outsider John Boorman," Interview, *MovieMaker Magazine,* 32 (February 1999). http://www.moviemaker.com/issues/32/32_boorman.html.

76. Frank Avruch, Review of *The General*. Boston's Man about Town. http://www.bostonman.com/frankarchive.html.

77. Barton, 185.

78. Harvey O'Brien, Harvey's Movie Reviews, "Veronica Guerin (2003)." http://homepage.eircom.net/~obrienh/veronica.htm. O'Brien is a professor of film studies at University College Dublin.

79. Michael Dwyer, "Story That Retains Power to Shock," Review of *Veronica Guerin. The Irish Times,* 12 June 2003. http://www.irishtimes.com. Harvey O'Brien agrees about Blanchett's accent, which he characterizes as "very good, but even better is the uncanny way she has captured the gestures and vocal rhythms of the real Guerin." "Veronica Guerin (2003).

80. McLoone, 182.

7

Performing Arts

THE OFTEN-VOICED IRISH dislike of the "stage Irishman" goes back to nineteenth-century British music hall routines featuring a drunken mud-stained Paddy whose improbably thick brogue barely allowed the audience to understand his protestations of innocence when accused of petty theft. To say that the Irish are a nation of performers is perhaps too close for comfort to the hated stereotype, but the nation has a rich heritage of dance, music, drama, and storytelling that asserts a distinctive cultural identity. From actors and vocalists such as Stephen Rea and Sinead O'Connor to groups as diverse as the Irish Tenors, Riverdance, and Boyzone, Irish performers have achieved global reputations. In Ireland the performing arts often involve a performance of national identity, whether perpetuating threatened traditions, such as oral storytelling in the native language, or asserting the distance between the nation's identity and the travesties of it that foreigners confuse with reality. With interest in Irish traditional culture growing at home and abroad, the 1990s saw renewed interest in historically accurate recreations of the older forms of storytelling, dancing, and music-making. But they also brought artists such as Enya and Riverdance's Irish-American Michael Flatley, who sought to fuse elements of the tradition with contemporary styles and technologies. In rock music especially, since the 1970s, performers such as Van Morrison and the U2 band have refused the old markers of Irish identity in favor of a contemporary style with roots in the United States and Britain.

REVIVING THE TRADITION

Along with reviving the Irish language and Irish sports such as Gaelic football and hurling, the Irish nationalists of the late nineteenth century sought to document and preserve elements of Irish culture that 50 years of radical depopulation had nearly destroyed. To promote performance of the Irish arts, nationalists organized the first *feis* or step-dancing competition in 1897. In 1929, the Free State created an Irish Dancing Commission to certify teachers and set rules for competitions now held around the world. Today's competitions are tightly controlled, requiring performers at the advanced "hard-shoe" level to master traditional "set" dances, in which every step is prescribed. Although the *feis* rhetoric suggests that the rules derive from an ancient past, set dances are a product of modern times, and it would be impossible to tease out the native and foreign elements in the older Irish dance forms.

Accounts dated before the famine suggest that dancing was a satisfying, highly social event. Rural people often danced outside, at a conveniently spacious crossroad. Apparently the dancers were exuberant; when men and women danced together, "there was also sexual theater—expressed through the heavier 'hit' of the male dancer (culminating in the 'batter,' heavy rhythmic drumming with the full foot), counterpoised against the quicker, buoyant step of the female performer."[1] Soloists, however, were valued for their ability to "dance on a six-pence," to dance in a small space without moving their upper body. One sometimes finds the folk explanation that people adopted this style so that an Englishman glancing in the window would not know that the apparently impassive person with arms held rigidly against the body was actually dancing, but it is more likely that the skill evolved because rural families were crowded into small cottages, the only available indoor space.

From the mid-eighteenth century, itinerant dance masters went from community to community, introducing elaborate dance patterns such as the French quadrille, a square dance performed by four couples. The dance masters respected the tradition, incorporating older styles rather than declaring them obsolete. "Lancers," the dance pattern performed by guests at the famous party in James Joyce's story "The Dead," is just one such descendent of the quadrille. After the famine, the Catholic Church "turned against the robust tradition of dance," making efforts to "domesticate its wilder energies and to control the time and places of performance."[2] Unwittingly, the Gaelic revival contributed to this toning down and standardizing of Irish dance. Fionan MacColuim, a Gaelic League member who in the early twentieth century wanted social events to promote the language revival, found the monotony of Irish dance forms discouraging and wished for "large-scale, rapidly moving dances, covering the entire floor space of a hall that could involve everybody as participants."[3] Armed with ideological purpose, he went to Kerry with one of the few surviving dance masters, Patrick Reidy, and came away with a wider repertoire of local dances.

MacColuim's work established a "new canon" of Irish dance that ignored the traditional dances of Connemara and Donegal and eliminated the innovation and openness to foreign influence that had characterized pre-famine dance.[4] After Independence, the Free State relentlessly promoted Irish dance along the lines officially adopted in 1929, with frequent assurances that it was not only more patriotic to step dance than to waltz, but more chaste. The Dance Hall Act of 1935, passed after substantial lobbying by Catholic clergy, outlawed dances in private homes, moving dance to public spaces subject to meddling and regulation. As a result, the official if historically dubious version of Irish dance was preserved, but largely in the form of stage performances in which most competitors were schoolchildren.

Dance shoes and costumes became part of the "tradition"; pre-famine dancers were mostly barefoot, but soft shoes for female dancers called "gillies, which resemble black ballet slippers with intricate lacing," were introduced in the 1920s. Men wear hard-soled shoes for so-called soft-shoe dances such as the light jig; for "hard-shoe dances" such as the set dances, both men and women "use hard shoes with a sort of tap on the toe and heel."[5] An early recommendation that performers wear Gaelic dress has evolved into giving male dancers a choice between trousers and a kilt, worn with a jacket and white or black shirt; female dancers wear school dresses. Each dance school has its own distinctive full-skirted dress, often featuring lace or an embroidered pattern copied from one of the designs in the medieval Book of Kells. Such costumes can cost hundreds of dollars. A highly successful female dancer earns a right to a "solo" costume with a unique design, and an even higher cost. For women, the practice of wearing ringlets has become traditional, with wigs sometimes adopted to achieve the look.

While the waltz and fox-trot quickly displaced traditional Irish dance as the casual entertainment of ordinary people, step dance competitions remained popular in the Free State. In 1951, a group of musicians founded Fload Cheoil na h'Eireann, an annual festival celebrating tradition Irish dance and music. The organizers of Donegal's 2005 Fload expected 250,000 visitors for what is now an eight-day event.[6] Regional versions of the Fload are held all over Ireland and in the United States, Australia, and Britain. A new era in Irish dance, however, began in 1994, when a dance group led by Michael Flatley, the first American-born winner of the World Irish Dance Championship, performed during an intermission in the Eurovision Song Contest, a televised musical competition for residents of Economic Union (EU) countries conducted along the lines of Fox TV's *American Idol.* Although not actually an entrant, Riverdance was catapulted into instant fame. A videotape of the group's 1995 performance at the Point Theatre in Dublin still communicates the audience's excitement at the great technical skill of the performers and the daring innovation of their program. The performance features a series of tableaux that include artists from several other nations, including a Spanish flamenco dancer, a Russian ballerina, and an African American group singing a freedom song. Strobe lights, dramatic backdrops, and glittering costumes mark a radical departure from the *feis* tradition. Even when Flatley and Jean Butler dance to recognizably Irish music and incorporate traditional steps, they make dramatic hand gestures or switch into tap or ballet movements.

To a purist, Riverdance is an entirely unacceptable adulteration of the tradition by foreign elements. Indeed, its commercial success demonstrates its betrayal. But its defenders argue that Riverdance takes the tradition into a newly global culture. Flatley, born in the United States of Irish parents, represents Irish emigration and its assimilation into the world. Then, too, as when dancing masters introduced the quadrille, Irish culture had historical ties to continental (and Catholic) Europe; the insularity of de Valera's Ireland was the exception. Besides, Riverdance's popularity has stimulated interest in Irish dance more generally. Still, particularly in Flatley's 1996 production, *Lord of the Dance,* an allegorical struggle between the powers of good and evil for the soul of the protagonist, the risks of welding incompatible styles become apparent. A postmodern audience may well decry the apparent lack of irony about costuming the blonde Good Woman in a white shawl, and when the Power of Darkness emerges masked, an audience reminded of Darth Vadar may have trouble suppressing a giggle.

IRISH MUSIC

The fourteenth-century "Brian Boru" harp, its triangular frame made of willow and strung with brass wire, now exhibited at Trinity College Dublin has long been an emblem of Irish nationalism. Stone carvings featuring stringed instruments, most likely lyres, were made in the ninth and tenth centuries; a late eleventh-century shrine offers the first depiction of the harp. Varying in size from small instruments held on the knee to free-standing ones five feet tall, harps were sometimes works of art, intricately carved and set with jewels. Harpers were trained in special schools, and travelers' accounts of their music emphasize "the sweet and bell-like tone, the skill, speed and liveliness of the playing, and the 'sporting of the grace-notes' above the heavier sound."[7] The bardic, even Homeric, harper was, like the poet, an important figure in aristocratic households as long as the old Gaelic society survived. Some even found employment in the houses of wealthy Anglo-Irishmen.

Carolan (1670–1738), a blind harper and composer, wrote songs with both Irish and English lyrics. The early musicologist Edward Bunting transcribed them into European musical notation. Such songs remain the best source of information about a tradition in which players learned by ear and lyrics were transmitted orally.

With the decline of Irish fortunes, the aristocratic harp gave way to smaller instruments, including the fiddle, which is identical to the classic violin but played with distinctive techniques that vary from one region to another. Other traditional instruments include various forms of the flute, the tin whistle, and the bodhran, a one-sided drum made by stretching a goatskin over a wooden drum. The uilleann pipes are a variation of the more familiar Scottish bagpipe in which air is pumped into the bag by a bellows worn under one arm, and squeezed by the player's elbow (*uillinn* in Irish). It is played while the musician is seated, with the bag under the opposite arm and the remainder of the instrument with its keys and pipes resting on the player's lap. A quieter instrument than the Scottish bagpipes, the uilleann pipes are said by their admirers to offer more "sensitive tonal quality and...complexity."[8] A relatively late development, its design fixed in the late eighteenth century, uilleann pipes nearly died out after the famine. Their revival began in 1944, when an association to promote them was established, and prospered after 1968, when the current players' association, Na Piobairi Uilleann, was formed. In their absence, two quite different instruments, the nineteenth-century melodeon and the twentieth-century accordion, replaced the uilleann pipes in local performances.

Traditional Irish singers sang in the old-style (*sean-nos*) manner, typically as unaccompanied soloists. Their songs, like other traditional music, were learned by ear and transmitted orally. The old Irish modal tunes, lacking "overt dynamics" and having "a certain nasal intonation," often struck foreigners as unpleasant, even discordant.[9] Today, *sean-nos* singing is supported by Oireachtas, an annual festival of traditional music started by the Gaelic League in 1897. In modern times, the greatest of these was Seosamh O hEanai (1919–1984), who worked as a laborer on construction sites in England and Scotland for much of his adult life. A gold medalist at Oireachtas in 1955, he was featured in a 1965 Clancy Brothers show at Newport. O hEanai immigrated to the United States in 1966, teaching folklore part-time at Wesleyan University and then the University of Washington, and achieving a modest celebrity for his appearances on the *Merv Griffin Show*.

What most of the world thinks of as traditional Irish music is not, of course, *sean-nos* singing or the playing of uilleann pipes, but the sweetly romantic tunes of Thomas Moore, perhaps as sung by John McCormick, and the rousing patriotic ballads and drinking songs of the Clancy Brothers and the Dubliners. Had the famine never occurred, an increasingly educated Irish-speaking population probably would eventually have written down its own music, perhaps creating a notation that would have preserved subtleties now lost. Indeed the first event consciously organized around preservation-ist principles was the Belfast Harp Festival of 1792. Many of its organizers were associated with the United Irishmen, the revolutionary movement that briefly brought Protestant and Catholic together. Performers were limited to Gaelic music, and the romantic nationalism of the time and place set the terms in which traditional Irish music has often been studied since: "a fear of extinction... drive towards active transmission and performance, and... concern for purity and authenticity."[10] The political and economic condi-tions that followed the defeat of the 1798 rebellion, however, ensured that English tastes would be consulted when Irishmen with English educations wrote down the notes of Irish music.

THE NEW TRADITION

The first successful transmitter of Gaelic music to a wider audience was Thomas Moore, the Trinity-educated son of a Catholic grocer in Dublin. His 10 volumes of *Ancient Irish Melodies* (1808–1834) were set to Sir John Stevenson's accompaniments, which were based on musicologist Edward Bunting's transcriptions. Quite a bit was lost in translation. The harmonic aesthetic of Stevenson's arrangements, so well suited to Moore's nostalgic, even sentimental lyrics, offended Bunting. Moore retorted that he was adapting the traditional forms to communicate and preserve them, lest "they remain sleep-ing in 'their authentic dross.'"[11] Cynics might suggest that Moore's laments for a defeated nation appealed to English audiences because that was how they liked to thinking of the Irish, but his songs also appealed to the Irish Catholic middle classes. Doing so, they helped to create something new and potentially "incendiary": "Through his prudent foregrounding of melodic attractiveness and muting of aspects unpalatable to the colonial status quo, Irish audiences could hear claims to a national identity distinctly, if softly, voiced."[12] It must have taken an unusually complacent Victorian to overlook the revolutionary overtones of "The Minstrel Boy," which celebrates a harper who destroyed his instrument because its "songs were made for the pure and free." To generations of immigrants, songs such as "She Is Far from the Land" spoke to homesickness and displacement. It would take an unusually stern purist to deny that "The Harp That Once through Tara's Halls" and "The Meeting of the Waters" are authentic Irish music.[13]

John McCormick (1884–1945) was the most celebrated lyric tenor of his time, performing opera and lieder, as well as the Irish songs of Moore and other adaptors. Continuing this tradition, the Irish Tenors, a trio composed of Ronan Tynan, Anthony Kearns, and John McDermott (soon replaced by Finbar Wright) recorded their debut album in 1998 and instantly became successful both in the British Isles and the United States. Their repertoire includes Moore's songs and other Irish and Irish American favorites—"The Rose of Tralee," "Galway Bay," "When Irish Eyes Are Smiling"—as well as a few Protestant hymns, such as "Amazing Grace" and "Nearer, My God to Thee," which acquired an Irish connection when it was played by the orchestra on the sinking *Titanic*. In 2005, Tynan decided to strike out on his own with a solo album, *Ronan,* which largely eschews Irish music in favor of new songs by composers Richard Marx and Desmond Childs and show tunes such as the theme from *The Man of La Mancha.* Tynan's performance of this last piece provoked a reviewer to remark that it made one understand why Don Quixote had been cast as a baritone, but he remains the best-known Irish tenor in the United States.[14] His appearance at Ground Zero, singing "Danny Boy" to rescue workers as their efforts were ending in April 2002, the culmination of a series of appearances at funerals and benefits, became part of unforgettable iconography of the September 2001 attacks for many Americans.

The Clancy Brothers—Tom, Pat, and Liam—and Tommy Makem formed a ballad and instrumental group in the late 1950s. Liam played the guitar, Pat the harmonica, and Makem the tin whistle and banjo. The group largely sang in unison, appearing live to enthusiastic audiences in the United States and Ireland. Part of the Clancy Brothers' appeal was their relative lack of sentimentality. U.S. audiences, who were developing an interest in folk music in the early 1960s, embraced them along with Joan Baez and The Weavers. Liam Clancy had accompanied an American musicologist studying traditional music when she traveled around Ireland in 1955 and was well acquainted with the *sean-nos* tradition and practitioners such as O hEani. The group popularized some elements of the *sean-nos* style and such old traditions at the singing of the "Wren Boys" on St. Stephen's Day, December 26. Legend said that St. Stephen, the church's first martyr, was betrayed by a wren, and on his day mummers would go from house to house carrying a dead wren in a bush, collecting money for its funeral that they promptly spent on drink and celebration. The Clancy Brothers' raucous and irreverent version of this song introduced something of the old tonality to foreign audiences.

At the same time, the Clancy Brothers tried to get away from the mournful tones often associated with Irish music. Liam Clancy recalled that one source of inspiration was a couch in Greenwich Village: "'Brennan on the Moore' was a famous old ballad but it was sung mournfully.... I was sitting on this couch that had springs in it. And I said 'Let's try and get the sound of

it.... bouncing up and down on the springs, beating out the sound of a gal-
loping horse and singing to its rhythm. We knew we had established something new—a new way of singing old songs."[15] A similar, perhaps somewhat
edgier ballad group, The Dubliners, formed in 1962. In 1967, when their
"Seven Drunken Nights," a song about an alcoholic recounting his discovery
of his wife's adultery, was one of the top five songs in England, it was banned
from being played on Radio Eireann. The same song, sung in Irish by O
hEani, faced no such obstacles.

In 1963, uillean-piper Paddy Moloney formed The Chieftains. The group
is still active more than 40 years later, but its membership varies, typically
including four to six traditional musicians on instruments including the flute,
the fiddle, the harp, the bodhran, and the tin whistle. The popularity of the
Clancy Brothers and the Dubliners probably helped the Chieftains gain an
American audience for their new arrangements of traditional instrumental
music, although they appeared for the first time on U.S. television only in
1979. In the 1980s, the Chieftains started appearing with step dancers, most
notably giving early opportunities to Jean Butler and Michael Flatley. The
1980s also saw the gradual rise of a younger group called Altan, which has
proved equally successful at finding a wider audience for spirited performances
of traditional music. Founded by Belfast flute player Frankie Kennedy and
soprano and fiddler Mairead Ni Mhaonaigh, 2005's Altan has six members
playing instruments ranging from the fiddle and tin whistle to the bouzouki
and guitar. Like the Chieftains, Altan plays many instrumental pieces, but Ni
Mhaonaigh's lovely soprano performances of Irish lyrics are always among the
highlights of their performances.

ROCK, PUNK, AND THE NEW AGE CELTIC

Although famed for their commitment to the tradition, the Chieftains
recorded 1988's *Irish Heartbeat* in collaboration with the Belfast-born rock
star Van Morrison. Reviewers praised the album for assimilating rock style
and sensibility to songs such as the old John McCormick favorite, "The Star
of County Down," and Seasamh MacCathmhaoil's "My Lagan Love." Such
fusions of the traditional and contemporary have become popular since. Perhaps the most celebrated band is the Pogues, formed in the early 1980s by
Shane MacGowan. Having begun with a punk group whose name is usually
shorted to "the Nips" for the sake of decency, MacGowan saw the creative
possibilities of assimilating the raucous and unmelodic expressiveness of punk
with a similar aesthetic in the tradition. The Pogues' albums include some
traditional favorites, such as Brendan Behan's "The Old Triangle" and the
"Irish Rover," but they typically speak to the contemporary Irish experience

in London, where they were especially popular with expatriates. The music is played on drums, guitar, banjo, bass, accordion, and tin whistle. For many listeners, MacGowan's lyrics, sung in a raspy voice and working-class accent, are a major attraction. Songs such as "Dark Streets of London" and "Streams of Whiskey," are praised for "disciplined lyrics" that combine "rawness" with a "poetic sensibility."[16] The title of their 1985 album, *Rum, Sodomy and the Lash,* already suggests the distance traveled from Moore and McCormick.

"The Sickbed of Cuchulain," from this album, provides a marvelous example of what happens to Irish music when it is inflected not only with the punk sensibility, but with twentieth-century European history and the expatriate experience. Cuchulain, of course, is the legendary hero beloved of poet W. B. Yeats. The song imagines inglorious Irishmen gathering around the dying hero, to whom they bring their own stories. One is a drinker who, when refused service in a London pub, kicked out its windows. Another caught syphilis in Cologne, where he heard death trains whistling by. A third, a client in a Spanish brothel, knocked down a Blackshirt he heard "cursing out the yids." Belligerent and drunken Paddy, the hated stereotype, fuses with others whom the twentieth century dehumanized, including London's Pakistani and Afro-Caribbean immigrants. They will all assemble to pray at the bedside of the dying Cuchulain, but not before ordering another round of drinks.

For more soothing music, sometimes explicitly marketed as suitable for meditation and deep relaxation, one can turn to Celtic New Age performers. Although the term is imprecise, "Celtic" as used here evokes the literary "Celtic Twilight" of the late nineteenth century. Like Yeats's early poems, the music invites adjectives such as "ethereal," "haunting," and "otherworldly." Unlike Yeats, today's Celtic New Age performers often use the Irish language for original compositions that may or may not refer to figures from Celtic mythology. Although the style has many imitators in the United States, Canada, and Scotland, its roots are in Clannad, a family group that formed in Donegal in 1970. The Irish-speaking Brennans and Duggans combined an interest in traditional songs and instruments with knowledge and appreciation of jazz and rock. Moya Brennan reminisces that her father played Nat King Cole, the Everly Brothers and Elvis Presley, while the children played Joni Mitchell or the Mamas and the Papas.[17] Early Clannad music often featured lyrics in Irish with family members playing bass, guitar, harp, tin whistle, and even mandolin. Later albums feature more jazz instrumentation, including the keyboard and the not-at-all Irish saxophone.

An original composition with Irish lyrics that Clannad produced for a British television production, "The Theme from Harry's Game," sold more than a million copies in 1982 and was used again in the background of the film *Patriot Games* in 1992. The lush melody proved that Irish could be a successful medium for pop music, a point that was proved again several times in the decade that followed. Daughter Enya, who joined Clannad in 1980, left two years later to pursue a solo career that has produced such albums as *Watermark* (1988), *Shepherd Moons* (1991), and *A Day without Rain* (2000). Her beautiful voice achieves some of its characteristic "haunting" quality with the help of contemporary technology. On CDs her voice is electronically "overdubbed" with previous recordings, so that echoes from a chorus of virtual Enyas seem to float above her strong soprano. She has perfected this technique both for songs of her own composition and for music from other cultures, from "Caribbean Blue" to the American Shaker "How Can I Keep from Singing?" Like Tynan, she became further enmeshed with American culture when her song "Only Time" became what one reviewer called a national "lullaby" as it was played and replayed on U.S. radio in the weeks after the September 2001 attacks.[18] Enya's sister, Moya Brennan, won a similarly warm reception for her own solo albums, *Perfect Time* (1998) and *Whisper to the Wild Water* (2002), which contain a number of religious songs such as "Follow the Word" and "Mary of the Gaels."

In spite of its worldwide popularity, Celtic New Age music, with its mist and moonshine, has many detractors at home, and most of them would argue that the authentic voice of today's Ireland is urban rock. U2, inducted into the Rock and Roll Hall of Fame in 2005, formed in Dublin in 1976 but achieved widespread fame only in 1983, when their third studio album, *War,* and *U2 Live: Under a Blood-Red Sky* went to the top of the charts in the United States. Perhaps best-remembered from *War,* an album that addressed Ireland's Troubles directly, was *Sunday, Bloody Sunday.* Its title refers to the British Army's 1972 killing of 13 unarmed civil rights protesters in Derry, but the song goes on more generally to indict a larger world that confuses headline news with entertainment: "We eat and drink and tomorrow they die." U2's capacity for reinventing itself is legendary. For many, 1991's *Achtung Baby,* with its "distorted keyboards" and even, in Bono's "The Fly," "spooky Gothic-electro-glam-goth-rave-up," was the highpoint, a time when the band's blend of "organic with electronic" was at its most exciting.[19] Fans who liked U2 at its edgiest and most ironic were inclined to regard the group's 2004 release, *How to Dismantle an Atomic Bomb,* as a bit of an "artistic retreat." On the other hand, new songs such as "Yahweh" and "Sometimes You Can't Make It on Your Own" reflect U2's ability to combine "rock passion and spiritual fervor" as well as any of their earlier work.[20] U2 has gained the respect of many people outside rock for its social activism. The band was a key player in 1985's Live Aid concert and performed in July 2005 for the Live 8 global telecast that promoted debt relief for Africa.

Another major talent who defies stereotypical expectations for Irish musicians is Van Morrison. Growing up in Belfast, Morrison immersed himself in rhythm and blues and jazz. By the time he turned 13, he was playing the guitar, saxophone, and harmonica. Even when he performs a song with an Irish theme, such as 1986's "Tir na Nog," which has lines such as "We stopped in the Church of Ireland and prayed to our father," the rhythms, intonations, and voicing of African American music are unmistakable. In the less brilliant work of other bands, in songs like the Corrs' 1995 "Runaway" and "Someday" or "Burn Baby Burn" from Ash's 2002 album, *Free All Angels,* American influence seems fatal to Irish performers. Such charmless music seems indistinguishable from the blur of Top Forty hits one might hear in the background of any long drive on a U.S. interstate, and one may wonder why anyone who started out with an Irish accent would practice so long to sound like a Midwesterner. But an artist like Morrison uses an American aesthetic to express urban Irish experience.

A rather different but powerful example of an Irish artist working with American models can be found in Sinead O'Connor's 2000 *Faith and Courage.* Her "Daddy I'm Fine" casts an Irish story in American accents, as a girl born in Dublin explains to her father why she had to leave home: "And I told my poor worried father/Said ain't gonna go to school no more/Cuz see I wanna look cool and look good." Similarly, "The Lamb's Book of Life," returns repeatedly to Yeats's lines, "Out of Ireland have I come/ Great hatred, little room/Maimed us at the start," running through the variations "Out of Ireland I have run" and "Out of history we have come." In O'Connor's version of the emigrant's story, the singer comes to the United States, not for political or economic freedom, but to follow a tenuous hope for salvation, perhaps from "your preachermen," perhaps from "the Rasta man." Such music invites the audience to feel the emotional connection between Ireland and the United States, rather than to see their edges blurred in some mid-Atlantic sea of popular culture.

IRISH STORYTELLING AND DRAMA

For reasons lost in the mists of antiquity, traditional Irish culture had no drama but placed a high premium on storytelling. By the nineteenth century, oral storytelling was an important part of rural life. Perhaps it had been so for centuries, but it is also possible that it was a relatively late development, replacing the minstrel with his harp. One house would be designated the *teach airneain,* "the house frequented by night visitors," and from November to May men would gather there after work was done. After catching up on the news, they would spend the evening singing songs and telling long folk tales.[21] "Booleying," the practice of sending girls and women to watch over livestock at a remote summer pasture, was another occasion for exchanging traditional stories. This continuation of traditional storytelling at a time when it had disappeared in many parts of Europe made the West of Ireland a paradise for nineteenth- and early twentieth-century folklorists, who preserved many of the stories. Today the storyteller, or *seanchai,* still performs at Irish arts festivals, telling stories both in English and Irish. Many would say that the premium placed on lively conversation, especially in pubs, proves that this tradition survives.

Without an ancient dramatic tradition of their own, the Irish long associated theater with the English. The first Irish theater was built by the Lord Lieutenant, close by the seat of his power in Dublin Castle, in 1635. From Richard Brinsley Sheridan to Oscar Wilde and George Bernard Shaw, the Anglo-Irish became celebrated playwrights, but their careers centered on the London stage and their works avoided Irish topics. One exception was Shaw's *John Bull's Other Island* (1904), written at Yeats's request for the Irish Literary Theatre. In other cultural areas Irish nationalists wanted to restore a heritage on the verge of extinction, but theater offered the opportunity to invent something new. Debates about what would constitute an authentic Irish theater flourished, with some nationalists willing to tolerate bad writing and poor acting if only the performers could speak the national language with a credible accent. Others sought to banish the hated stage Irishman and in the process transform the theater into a place where "an idealized image of the Irish nation" might be acted out.[22]

The Queen's Royal Theatre, Dublin, in spite of its name, became "the most proletarian of the licensed theaters, and its drama came to reflect the aesthetics desires and political beliefs of its mainly lowbrow, working-class and middle class audience."[23] Here were played satisfyingly patriotic works by Desmond O'Grady and J. W. Whitbread on the lives of heroes such as Wolfe Tone and themes such as the famine, emigration, and land reform. Audiences loved this fare, and although more genteel theaters were teaching audiences the rules of polite spectatorship, actors at the Queen's expected to be booed, hissed, and pelted with missiles when they portrayed the villainous English. Audiences, in short, also performed, and played their part in making theater a "public sphere" in which people might "register...nationalist sentiments."[24]

When Yeats, Lady Gregory, George Moore, and Edward Martyn founded the Irish Literary Theatre in 1899, they certainly shared the nationalists' political and cultural ambitions for an identifiably Irish drama. But their idea of a literary, rather than a popular, theater meant freedom to experiment, to adapt new dramatic forms developed by, for example, the Scandinavians Henrik Ibsen and August Strindberg, and to express Irish themes. Although the Irish Literary Theatre project ended within three years, its founders continued to work with other nationalists in the National Theatre Society, better known after 1904 by the name of its home, the Abbey Theatre. Early productions included Yeats's *Cathleen ni Houlihan* (1894) and *The Countess Cathleen* (1902), both romantic and historical, the first set in 1798 and the second during the famine. The most memorable production of *Cathleen ni Houlihan* was the first, in 1902, with the heroine's part played by the great love of Yeats's life, Maud Gonne. This six-foot tall, beautiful redhead was already famed for advocating Irish nationalism, so when she took the part of a character whose name personified the nation, its message was unmistakable. The plot centers on Michael, a young man shortly to be married, who falls into conversation with a mysterious old woman and leaves bride and parents to die for Ireland. In the play's famous last line, Michael's parents ask his brother if he had seen the old woman on the road, and he responds: "I did not, but I saw a young girl, and she had the walk of a queen."[25]

Not all Abbey plays made such appeals to revolutionary sentiment, and the most famous of them all, John Synge's *Playboy of the Western World* (1907),

Synge's *Playboy of the Western World,* which once caused a riot, is now a staple of Irish theater. This photo shows a 2002 production. © *Irish Times.*

produced a riot. Synge was the son of a Church of Ireland minister who studied Irish at Trinity and followed Yeats's advice that he leave Paris to go to the
Aran Islands to "express a life that has never found expression" in literature.[26]
At the time, the Aran Islands were entirely Irish speaking, and although boats
from Galway and Clare kept their inhabitants in touch with the Irish West,
modernization was slow to change them. Synge loved the people, finding their
"imagination...and the language they use...rich and living."[27] Although
Synge's claim, that the turns of phrase in his Aran plays were those actually
used by servant girls in the kitchen, evokes skepticism, he saw his writing as a
"collaboration" with the "folk imagination."[28] If Synge's English was flavored
with Irish syntax, his explorations of role-playing and the element of performance in daily life were colored by his knowledge of the French symbolists
and Irish expatriate Oscar Wilde. *Playboy* centers on the mythic theme of a
stranger, Christy Mahon, coming into a rural community with a tale of having murdered his father that induces women to fall madly in love with him.
Christy has just won a series of athletic competitions when his father turns
up in the community with a bandaged head and reveals that the "Playboy" is
neither a murderer nor a hero. The town turns on Mahon and his new fiancée
participates in an attack in which he is burned.

Synge's admiration for his characters' wit, imagination, and language seems
obvious to most contemporary audiences. How could one not see poetry in a
man who tells his fiancée that when he kisses her he feels a "kind of pity for
the Lord God who is all ages sitting lonesome in his golden chair?"[29] Yet in
1907, the Abbey's audience, many of whom expected an Irish play to present the Irish as a wholly admirable people long overdue for self-government,
found Synge's characterizations demeaning. Like the music hall's stage Irishmen, the men in the play were drunken, belligerent, and untrustworthy. The
women's sexual frankness, bordering on aggression, belied the chastity of
Gaelic maidenhood. When Pegeen used the word "shift" (chemise, an under-
garment) in Act II, the audience could bear no more and rose to its feet,
with many howls that no Irish woman ever used such a word. Thus did an
audience trained for the Queen's Theatre exasperate Yeats and Lady Gregory.
Nor did the Irish realist Sean O'Casey always succeed at the Abbey. Although
full of compassion for the urban poor, O'Casey had no patience for the sentimental nationalism that in his view too often led to "people...dyin for the
gunman."[30] Even after Independence, *The Plough and the Stars* (1926), with
its blunt depictions of tenement life and its ironic, even satiric treatment of
the Easter Rising of 1916, produced another riot. Although O'Casey's fame
was at its heights, Yeats and Lady Gregory rejected his next, and more experimental play, *The Silver Tassie* (1928). So like another famous playwright from
Dublin, Shaw, O'Casey became permanently alienated from the Abbey.

In 1925, just two years after the pro-Treaty forces emerged victorious in the civil war, the Free State began subsidizing the Abbey. A national theater offered the new state prestige, and many of the plays it was to produce in the next three decades evoked "an impression of consensus and national unity" and reinforced a distinction between the state's legitimate "political agency...and what was seen as the threatening illegitimacy of socialist or republican militancy."[31] The Abbey, like the Free State, grew conservative. At mid-century, Ireland's most brilliant playwright was living abroad and writing in French. Samuel Beckett's *Waiting for Godot* (1952) is the classic existential, or absurdist drama: life as the banter of Estragon and Vladimir, two tramps by the side of the road waiting for the figure who never arrives, aware from the first line of Act I that "there is nothing to be done."

In 1955, when the play was first performed in Dublin—at the smaller Pike Theatre, not the Abbey—Irish audiences claimed to recognize "subtle nuances which would be lost" on foreigners; an Irish translation, *Ag Fanacht Le Godot,* was soon forthcoming.[32] The most Irish of Beckett's plays is the one-act *Krapp's Last Tape* (1958), which was originally written in English as a monologue for the Irish actor Patrick Magee, whom Beckett admired. Throughout the course of the play, Krapp, the protagonist, listens to recordings of his own voice, an audio diary kept for more than 30 years. He mostly jeers at the tapes, expressing disbelief that he could ever have been the young whelp they disclose. One tape records a moment of profound revelation, "never to be forgotten," but Krapp switches it off irritably to listen again to his youthful description of a sexual encounter, "my hand on her breast."[33] While Beckett would have been the last writer in the world to produce local color, the Irish references in the play, as to a Miss McGlome, from "Connaught, I fancy," whose singing Krapp is accustomed to hear in the evenings, add romantic cultural nationalism to the dustbin of discarded beliefs that the protagonist catalogues. Against Synge's peasant plays and the urban realism of O'Casey's most famous plays, Beckett established a "counter-tradition" that would encourage the next generation of Irish dramatists.[34]

CONTEMPORARY THEATER

By the 1960s, Irish theater was enjoying a revival, partly as a result of the multiplication of venues in which new work could be presented. Especially key was the inauguration of the Dublin Theatre Festival in 1957, with a commitment to producing international as well as Irish plays. New dramas first presented at the Festival include Brian Friel's *Philadelphia, Here I Come!* (1964), Eugene McCabe's *King of the Castle* (1964), Thomas Kilroy's *The Death and Resurrection of Mr Roche* (1968), and John Boyd's *The Assassin*

(1969). Such playwrights introduce new topics, such as life in working-class Belfast (Boyd's *The Flats*, 1970) or push the old ones further, as in Tom Murphy's *The Sanctuary Lamp* (1975), which centers on three derelicts gathered in a city church exchanging stories that "incorporate a scathing account of divine power."[35] Some, such as Friel's *Philadelphia* and Kilroy's *Double Cross* (1986), require innovative staging. The protagonist of *Philadelphia* is presented on stage as two people, a public self and a and a private self whom the other characters cannot see. *Double Cross* moves back and forth between the intersecting and contrasting stories of two Irishmen who probably never met.

One is Brendan Bracken, Minister of Information in Churchill's wartime cabinet and later British M.P. Born in Tipperary, he was so thoroughly anglicized that he was rumored to be Churchill's illegitimate son. The other is Brooklyn-born William Joyce, whose family moved back to Ireland when he was three. After serving as an informer for the Royal Irish Constabulary in 1920, Joyce went to England, where he eventually joined the British Union of Fascists. During World War II he broadcast propaganda from Berlin to England, where he was nicknamed Lord Haw-Haw. The British hanged him in 1946. In the first part, the "Bracken play," Bracken is on stage in London. After he turns off Joyce's radio broadcast, a ghostly Joyce appears on a video screen, mocking and correcting Churchill's minister. In the second part, set in Berlin, Bracken appears on the video screen. To further emphasize the fragility of identity, cardboard cutouts used to play Churchill, King George V, and fascist sympathizer Oswald Mosley in the first part are reversed to become Goebbels, Hitler, and Mosley in the second. The ease with which these Irishmen reinvent themselves as Englishmen, one to serve the Crown and the other to betray it, recalls the role-playing of Synge's *Playboy*. Writing during the Troubles, Kilroy says that he wanted to demonstrate the "dangerous absurdity" of "basing one's identity, exclusively, upon a mystical sense of place rather than in personal character."[36] This concern identifies Kilroy's play with the company for which it was written, Northern Ireland's Field Day.

Founded by Protestant actor Stephen Rea and Catholic playwright Brian Friel in Derry in 1980, Field Day explicitly asked the Irish to reimagine their country, to get past the fixed narratives of Unionism and nationalism. Its frequently evoked metaphor of creating an imagined "fifth province" on stage to promote peace in the four historical provinces of Ireland suggests a faith in the power of art that flies in the face of Beckett's pessimism.[37] Joined in 1981 by Protestants Tom Paulin and David Hammond and by Catholics Seamus Heaney and Seamus Deane, and supported by the Arts Councils of both the Republic and Northern Ireland, Field Day eventually produced a series of books and pamphlets on Irish culture, as well as what by 2001 had become a five-volume anthology of Irish literature. But its chief activity, between 1981 and 1991, was producing one new Irish play a year, and then touring each through towns on both sides of the border that normally had no access to professional theater. Only one of the Field Day plays, Stewart Parker's *Pentecost,* set in Belfast during a Unionist workers' strike in 1974, dealt directly with the Troubles. Several—Friel's version of Chekhov's *Three Sisters* (1981), Derek Mahon's translation of Moliere's *The School for Husbands* as *High Times* (1984), Paulin's translation of Sophocles' *Antigone* as *The Riot Act* (1984), Heaney's translation of Sophocles' *Philoctetes* as *The Cure at Troy* (1990)—were European classics put into the English language as actually spoken in contemporary Ireland.

Field Day's activism, in short, stopped well short of propaganda. Many of its plays deal with the politics of language, explore issues of Irish identity, or offer a wider context for viewing Northern Ireland's problems; "above all there were plays exploring the idea of history as an imposition on the past of one narrative or another."[38] Friel's *Translations* (1980), the first Field Day production, is the classic example. Set in rural Derry in 1833, the action is triggered by the arrival of a contingent of British soldiers and engineers charged with mapping Ireland. Accompanying them as a translator is Owen, son of Hugh, who conducts a local hedge school with the help of his other son, Manus. Irish-language hedge schools, set up in such places as abandoned barns, date from the days when the English forbade Catholic schools. From 1831 on, they were gradually replaced by British National Schools, in which English was the medium of instruction. Mapping itself is a form of translation, turning a landscape into a paper chart and, in this case, requires translating or at least anglicizing place names so that the British can pronounce them, for example, "Burnfoot" for "Bun na hAbbann," which really means "mouth of the river." The contingent of mappers arrives just as Hugh is offered a position as schoolmaster in the new National School, so the play captures a moment when the old Irish culture is threatened, not by Cromwellian massacre, but by English as an instrument of modernization. A modern empire requires a bureaucracy with maps and school systems, and the persons who establish them may be personally courteous, even enlightened. Issues of language and translation define other key actions: Manus's success in teaching the mute Sarah to speak aloud; Yolland, an officer, falling in love with a local woman, Maire, although they can only communicate in sign language.

Even this brief summary suggests why one critic argues that Field Day simply produced more "unreconstructed nationalism."[39] The play rehearses familiar nationalist grievances; the potato blight even comes up in Act III. When Sarah uses her newfound speech to report seeing Yolland kissing Maire, catastrophe ensues: Yolland disappears, probably killed by local men. Manus runs off, knowing his love for Maire makes him a likely suspect. The

British threaten to evict the whole community if Yolland is not produced in 48 hours, and someone sets the British camp on fire. One can easily draw some grim message to the effect that even enlightened colonialism always resorts to violence when threatened, or that a community's historical griev-ances always destroy persons who wish to set them aside. But Friel's defend-ers would say that Field Day was never about forgetting history, but about reimagining it and discovering that it need not dictate intractable violence. Although Hugh has faithfully kept his hedge school and taught the local people to speak and read classical languages, and although he has articulated strong reasons for keeping Irish alive, he nonetheless resolves at the end to teach Maire English, which will allow her to emigrate. He realizes that the rural Irish can no longer ignore modernization; he even concedes that words are only signals: "it can happen . . . that a civilization can be imprisoned in a linguistic contour which no longer matches the landscape of . . . fact."[40] Survival requires adaptation, negotiation, and the empathic imagination that allows us to "interpret between privacies," to understand a dimension of the self that is more than its tribal affiliations.[41]

The work of a younger playwright, Frank McGuinness, has many affini-ties with Friel's. Indeed, McGuinness wrote the screenplay for Pat O'Connor's 1996 film adaptation of Friel's *Dancing at Lughnasa,* first produced at the Abbey in 1990. The Field Day project of encouraging Irish people to reimag-ine their history is central to McGuinness's best-known play, *Observe the Sons of Ulster Marching Towards the Somme* (1985). The British Army lost almost 20,000 men on July 1, 1916, the first day of the battle of the Somme. Approxi-mately 2,000 of that number were Protestant Ulstermen. For most people, the Somme looms up as the defining military catastrophe of World War I, a mis-calculation that cost the combined armies 1.3 million casualties and produced no real strategic advantage for either side. But for Protestant Ulster, it is a story of loyalty betrayed by incompetent generals but also by an English parliament that had already conceded Home Rule and would grant independence to the Free State in 1922. On the other hand, for nationalists the Easter Rebellion was the sacred event of 1916, and the tens of thousands of Irish Catholics who died fighting with Britain between 1914 and 1918 truly became a lost and forgotten generation.[42] Coming from a Catholic and nationalist back-ground, McGuinness set himself the difficult task of recovering the humanity of Ulster's soldiers. He took the additional risk of imagining the perspective of a young gay man in a regiment of Christian fundamentalists.

Observe the Sons of Ulster begins and ends with an old man named Pyper, at first glance a caricature of intransigent, "no surrender" loyalism. But he is an old man haunted by ghosts, including that of his younger self, a very different man. The four parts of the play, Remembrance, Initiation, Pairing, and Bonding, allow Pyper's ghosts to materialize on the stage, as he takes us back to his first days with the regiment. The young Pyper was a destabilizing element, a gay man alternately shocking other recruits with camp announcements about his "remarkably fine skin" or a coy invitation to "kiss" his bleeding thumb "better."[43] But although several initially express revulsion at this "milksop," his wit and his greater experience of the world, perhaps abetted by their naivety, lead them to accept him. As time goes on, even McIlwaine, who earlier seemed more mad dog than human being when he tackled a fellow soldier suspected of being Catholic, concedes that Pyper's cynicism about military rhetoric is well founded: "We're all going to die for nothing."[44] But in the final scene, just before the men rush out to attack the Germans, it is Pyper who seems to lose touch with reality, imagining that the Somme has been transformed into the Boyne, that to fight this war is to fight for Ulster.

The heaviest irony is that the other men go out to die and only Pyper survives. But his closest friend, and perhaps lover, Craig, has accurately predicted that no one really survives such a massacre: "Whoever comes back alive, if any of us do, will have died as well."[45] Just before the battle begins, the men recognize Pyper as one of their own, giving him a loyalist orange sash to wear into battle. McGuinness's play makes no effort to explain the stages in Pyper's transformation into a fundamentalist preacher. It simply ends with the young Pyper and the older one juxtaposed. As young Pyper tries to explain the horrors he saw that day, the older one has no response to him but the single word "Ulster." After he has made this response eight times, the young Pyper tells him to dance in the Lord's "deserted temple," and the older Pyper responds laconically "Dance." Nothing in the play excuses historical intransigence or makes a man frozen in the political certainties of his youth anything but pathetic. But seen in the local context, of its first production at the Peacock Theatre, Dublin, for example, the play offers an extraordinarily moving representation of a generation of young men whose humanity is concealed by both loyalist and nationalist rhetoric.

WOMEN IN THEATER

Women became more visible in Irish theater in the 1980s. In 1983, in Belfast, a group of unemployed actors—Marie Jones, Carol Scanlan, Eleanor Methven, Brenda Winter, and Maureen Macauley—decided to put on their own production. After a successful premiere, they formally set up the Charabanc Theatre Company, named after an open wagon with benches once used for excursions. They articulated the goal of "presenting plays which reflect Northern Irish society." In the early 1990s, they added the phrase "putting women's experiences to the fore."[46] Charabanc's early work was collaborative; the group did library research and extensive interviews with working-class women, so that some of their dialogue was based on oral histories. But collaboration had further implications for Charabanc: they did not produce written texts, and hence most of their work remains unpublished. And they usually dramatized groups of women creating meaningful responses to difficult circumstances, just as the actors themselves were doing. What emerges is the identity of a group, for example, of linen mill workers who went on strike in 1911, or of residents of Belfast's notorious Divis Flats, rather than a clearly defined protagonist or even a plot. Like Field Day, Charabanc toured extensively, often in places that would otherwise not have access to professional theater. A Charabanc production was reportedly marked by great vitality, with songs and jokes and a rapid succession of incidents that made it seem "more like a revue than a play...Theatre of the Absurd in which the absurdity is all too real."[47] Finding the company's demands on their energy exhausting, and troubled financially, Scanlan and Methven disbanded it in 1995. Marie Jones, who left in 1990, subsequently wrote *Stones in His Pockets* (2000), a play about an Irish town overrun by the cast and crew of a Hollywood movie, which enjoyed long runs both on Broadway and in London, where it won an Olivier Award for the Best New Comedy of 2001.

The best-known contemporary feminist playwright in the Republic is Marina Carr, author of, among others, *Low in the Dark* (1989), *The Mai* (1994), *Portia Coughlan* (1995), and *Ariel* (2002). One sign of her reputation at home is that in 2003, Carr won the American Ireland Fund Annual Literary Award, which carries a $25,000 stipend and substantial prestige, as previous winners include such contemporary luminaries as Seamus Heaney, John McGahern, Brian Friel, and Edna O'Brien. Carr's best-known play is *By the Bog of Cats* (1998), which opened at the Abbey and in the winter of 2004–2005 played in London's West End, where it was nominated for an Olivier for the Best New Play. Most of Carr's plays are set in the Irish midlands, in an imaginary version of County Offaly, where the playwright lived as a child. This setting is quasi-mythical, gaining part of its significance from its having been neglected in the Irish theater, which has more often focused on Dublin or the West. A similar point might be made about women, who seldom appear as protagonists of Irish plays, and even then are mostly found in the stereotyped roles of innocent beauty or beleaguered mother. With less romantic and political baggage than other places in Ireland, the midlands are home to the bogs that have preserved, as well as buried so much of the nation's ancient past. Noting in an interview that "landscape is another character," providing the author does not belabor it and turn it into something "overly symbolic and self-conscious," Carr adds that the "archaeological treasures" found in the bog have "a Greek quality…as well as being very Celtic."[48] Certainly, the psychological landscape of *By the Bog of Cats* is as Greek as it is Celtic—full of classical allusions and dire prophecies of grim fate worked out inexorably in the lives of the proud, the blind, and the obsessed.

Set in the eponymous bog during a cold spell that leaves it white and frozen, the play begins with omens. First Hester, the protagonist, appears on stage "trail[ing] the corpse of a dead black swan"; then a "ghost fancier" suggests to her that she will die by sunset; then the bog's resident madwoman, or rather cat woman, reminds her that Josie Swane, Hester's absent mother, had prophesied that her child would remain alive only so long as the swan did.[49] A brief exposition of Hester's circumstances makes these warnings even more compelling. She is dangerously unhinged, for Carthage, the lover who deserted her, will be marrying a woman half her age later that day. She is under pressure to leave her house, which she repents having signed over to Carthage; and her loving relationship with her seven-year old daughter Josie is threatened by her own erratic behavior, which includes wandering through the bog all night while the child sleeps alone. As if that were not enough, Mrs. Kilbride, Carthage's mother, seems determined to take control or, as she puts it to Josie, "I'll break your spirit yet and then glue ya back the way I want ya."[50] By the end of Act I, in short, the audience is prepared for a reenactment of Euripides's *Medea*—bride poisoning, child-killing, maybe even the magical survival of the witchlike protagonist.

Reviewers who find the play pretentious point to the heavy-handedness of these allusions, which can hardly be denied. For others, however, the allusions define the tone of the play, which is alternately blackly humorous and poignant. Carr, they would argue, is trying to create a new myth, not inflate a domestic drama with classical trappings. Medea's rage, after all, centered on losing Jason, for whom she killed her brother and betrayed her father's trust. But while Josie protests that she loves Carthage and wants nothing more than to reestablish their home and family, the mild-mannered rationalizing man who reminds her that she signed them away seems an unlikely object of such desperate passion. What really drives her is hunger for the mother who abandoned her when she was seven. Her terror of leaving the Bog of Cats stems from the desperate hope that her mother will return, and the certainty that she will never find her anywhere else. Hester, it turns out, has killed her brother and used his money to start the cattle business that supported her and Carthage, but her motive for doing so was the intolerable realization that her mother abandoned her to start another family. And Medea-like, she kills her child, but only because she realizes that if she commits suicide and leaves Josie alive, the girl will wait and watch for her all of her life, just as she waited for her mother.

Without idealizing women, Carr's play makes relationships among women central to understanding them. *By the Bog of Cats* represents the strength of the mother-drive, and the hunger for mothering, in dangerous, even grotesque forms, as when Mrs. Kilbride appears at her son's wedding in a bridal gown. But it prevents the sentimentalizing of motherhood that many Irish women associate with their culture's traditional emphasis on the Virgin Mary, Cathleen ni Houlihan, and self-sacrificing and repressed womanhood. Not only does it place a woman's struggles and decisions at the core of the action, but it also touches on another social theme. The Kilbrides reject Hester in part because her mother was a Traveller or, as Mrs. Kilbride puts it to Josie, "That's what yees are, tinkers."[51] As Carr notes, "I chose to make her a traveller because travellers are our national outsiders."[52] Hester's penultimate act of vengeance, just before killing her daughter and herself, is to burn down the house and cattle the Kilbrides insist that they have bought from her. As the Irish audience knows, burning down a house before moving on is an old traveller custom, one anathema to a contemporary Ireland of soaring property values. In depicting a newly respectable, property-owning Ireland beset by its outsiders, by ghosts, superstitions, and irrational desires, Carr offers what a credible version of what one reviewer sees as her overriding goal, "to find public myths for a society that no longer knows what anything means."[53]

THE LEENANE TRILOGY

Remnants, not only of Greek mythology but also of *Hamlet*, Hollywood, and Irish drama from Synge to Beckett, color Martin McDonagh's representations of the rural West, so long concealed in the mythologies of romantic nationalism. McDonagh, like the Pogues' Shane MacGowan, is London Irish, a man whose Irish-born parents took him on annual summer holidays to Sligo and Connemara. McDonagh's *Leenane Trilogy—The Beauty Queen of Leenane* (1996), *A Skull in Connemara* (1997), and *The Lonesome West* (1997)—has been highly successful in London and on Broadway. *The Beauty Queen,* for example, won four Tony Awards. Reception at home, where the plays premiered at Galway's Druid Theatre, has been more mixed, with accusations that McDonagh earns his popularity by reintroducing the stage Irishman and inviting audiences to congratulate themselves on their superiority to him. Or as one critic puts it, the "repellant" characters on stage are Irish versions of "white trash," whose "actions conform to barbaric norms established at the plays' outset and left intact at the end."[54] Certainly the actions of McDonagh's characters are far from edifying. They murder their mothers and fathers, steal from their brothers, and commit suicide at an alarming rate. And unlike similar figures in classical tragedy, they are beset by senility, alcoholism, and a range of unattractive personal habits and afflictions.

Had Samuel Beckett rewritten Synge's *Playboy*, the result might well have resembled *The Beauty Queen of Leenane*. Leenane, a tiny town on Ireland's only fjord, is in the heart of Connemara, a few miles from the sacred mountain, Croagh Patrick. It is an astonishingly beautiful setting, and one that witnessed some of the worst suffering of the famine, yet none of this loveliness or pathos is evident in the play. The opening dialogue pits daughter against mother. One senses that the same resentments, in the same language, feature in all of their conversations. What once might have scandalized has become, thanks to the television set that flickers in the background, as free of novelty as their daily lives. When one character reports that a priest "has had a babby with a yank," another replies that it would be hard to find one who had not, and adds that it would only be news "if he'd punched that babby in the head."[55] The mother, Mag, and her daughter, Maureen, plot against each other in large and small ways. Mag conceals a party invitation from Maureen apparently because she fears Maureen's attraction to Pato Dooley, a laborer home from England to visit his family. Maureen, in turn, inflicts petty torments on her mother that range from purposely making her Complan (a milk drink similar to Ovaltine) lumpy to buying a brand of biscuits her mother loathes.

What hope can there be for Maureen, except that Pato Dooley might fall in love with her, and her monstrous mother might die? These possibilities come within her reach in Scene 3, when Pato stays overnight and calls her a "beauty queen," although the next morning, disquietingly, he can think of no better way of reassuring her than to reiterate, "You don't sicken me."[56] But with Maureen boasting of Pato's sexual prowess, Mag's gloves come off, and she reveals that Maureen's career as a cleaning woman in England had been cut short by a spell in a mental hospital, and that the scars on her own hand are a result of Maureen's deliberately scalding her. Perhaps Mag lacks credibility, but amazingly Pato writes from England to propose marriage and an escape to America. This time, however, Mag does manage to destroy the letter, but then lets that fact slip. Maureen tortures her mother to get at the truth, holding her hand over the stove and horribly splashing her face with boiling oil. While she is screaming, Maureen muses romantically on Pato's love, and then rushes out to say goodbye to him just before his train takes him away. When she returns, she is reminiscing fondly about their reunion, and how she will join him in Boston, but she is also wielding a poker. As Mag's body slides to the floor, she cheerfully concocts her cover story about how her mother tripped over a stile.

It was all for nought, of course. The final scene reveals that Maureen's story of meeting Pato at the train station was pure fantasy, and the man himself has become engaged to an American woman. Maureen's crime has been suspected, for there is talk of a funeral delayed a month, and an inquest, but in the end she is not charged. As in *Playboy,* the illusion is shattered and the lovers parted; but where in *Playboy* the resurrected father and his son go off together, in *The Beauty Queen* Maureen, alone, is turning into a replica of her mother. Meanwhile the banal illusions of family and nation persist as though nothing had happened. The last voice heard comes over the radio, as a Chieftain's song is followed by Delia Murphy's "The Spinning Wheel."[57] The announcer's words have as little connection to reality as any of Maureen's fantasies: the song is a birthday wish for Mag from Maureen's sister: "Well, we hope you had a happy one, Maggie, and we hope there'll be a good many more of them."[58] The image of an Ireland whose delusions are more powerful than its moments of truthful insight, an Ireland for whom modernity offers no meaningful contact with the world, but only an endless feedback loop of Free State propaganda, is hardly one to gratify a contemporary Dubliner. But given the long half-life of the sentimental vision of Ireland, as witnessed in global phenomena such as the synthetic Irish pub and Internet marketing of shamrock-strewn pottery, McDonagh's insistence that the audience examine the relationship between Irish identity and its images may be well worth pondering.

NOTES

1. Kevin Whelan, "The Cultural Effects of the Famine," in *The Cambridge Companion to Modern Irish Culture,* ed. Joe Cleary and Claire Connolly (Cambridge: Cambridge University Press, 2005), 143.

2. Whelan, 143.

3. Whelan, 144.

4. Whelan, 145.

5. Pat Friend, "Irish Step-Dancing: A Living Tradition," AllAboutIrish.com. http://www.allaboutirish.com/library/dance/dancehist.shtm. Friend's article is also the source for the definition of "gillies" given in the previous sentence.

6. Actual attendance varied from 40,000 to 60,000 people per day during the weekend. There were 4,000 musicians and 131 competitions.

7. Brian Lalor, "Harp," in *The Encyclopedia of Ireland* (New Haven, Conn.: Yale University Press, 2003), 473.

8. Lalor, "Uilleann Pipes," 1088.

9. Lalor, "Sean-nos Singing," 976.

10. Lillis O Laoire, "Irish Music," in *The Cambridge Companion to Modern Irish Culture,* 270.

11. O Laoire, 271.

12. O Laoire, 271.

13. "The Meeting of the Waters" evokes a beauty spot in Wicklow where the rivers Avon and Avoca meet. Its evocation of a lost rural paradise brought tears to the eyes of immigrants exiled to city slums. A. D. Godley, *The Poetical Works of Thomas Moore* (London: Oxford University Press, 1929), 184–185.

14. Christina Roden, Review of *Ronan*. Amazon.com.

15. Ronan Nolan, "The Clancy Brothers and Tommy Makem" (RamblingHouse, 2000). http://www.iol.ie-ronolan.

16. "The Pogues," Lalor, 881.

17. "'Ethereal' Irish Music," *The Washington Times,* 26 February 2004. http://web22.epnet.com.

18. Marc Weidenbaum, "Into the Mystic," February 2002. Disquiet: Ambient/Electronic. http://www.disquiet.com.

19. Troy Carpenter, "Review of *Achtung Baby* by U2," Nude as the Nineties: The Most Compelling Albums of the Decade. http://www.nudeasthenews.com/90s/reviews/final25/19achtung.htm.

20. George Varga, "25 Years in the Game, U2 is Still Flying High Creatively," Review of *How to Dismantle an Atomic Bomb*. 24 March 2005. *San Diego Union-Tribune*. http://www.u2ground.com.

21. "Storytelling," Lalor,1022.

22. Mary Trotter, *Ireland's National Theaters: Political Performance and the Origins of the Irish Dramatic Movement* (Syracuse, N.Y.: Syracuse University Press, 2001), 6.

23. Trotter, 59.

24. Trotter, 65.

25. Quoted in Trotter, 93.

26. Quoted in Colm Toibin, "Love of the Land," in *The Observer,* 9 July 2005. http://www.guardian.co.uk.

27. J. M. Synge, *The Playboy of the Western World,* Preface. 1911. http://www.bartleby.com/1010/100.html.

28. Synge, Preface.

29. Synge, *Playboy,* Act III.

30. Sean O'Casey, *The Shadow of a Gunman*. 1923. *Literature: The Human Experience,* 4th ed., Richard Abcarian and Marvin Klotz, eds. (New York: St. Martin's, 1986), 310.

31. Lionel Pilkington, "The Abbey Theatre and the Irish State," in *The Cambridge Companion to Twentieth-Century Irish Drama,* ed. Shaun Richards (Cambridge: Cambridge University Press, 2004), 239.

32. John P. Harrington, "Samuel Beckett and the Countertradition," in Richards, 171.

33. Samuel Beckett, *Krapp's Last Tape. Modern Irish Drama,* ed. John P. Harrington (New York: Norton, 1991), 316.

34. John P. Harrington, "Samuel Beckett and the Countertradition."

35. D.E.S. Maxwell, "Contemporary Drama: 1953–1986," in *The Field Day Anthology of Irish Writing,* vol. 3, ed. Seamus Deane (Derry: Field Day Publications, 1991).

36. Thomas Kilroy, Headnote to *Double Cross. The Field Day Anthology,* vol. 3: 1274.

37. Eric Binne, "Friel and Field Day," in John P. Harrington, *Modern Irish Drama* (New York: Norton, 1991), 565.

38. Marilynn Richtarik, "The Field Day Theatre Company," in *The Cambridge Companion to Twentieth-Century Irish Drama,* 202.

39. Richtarik, 201.

40. Brian Friel, *Translations* (London: Faber and Faber, 1981), 67.

41. *Translations,* 67.

42. Approximately 200,000 Irish men served in the British Army during World War I, and about 35,000 died. In recent years, the Republic has made an effort to memorialize these casualties. A precise breakdown on casualties by region or religion is unavailable, but *The Encyclopedia of Ireland* notes that the British raised three New Army Divisions in Ireland during World War I. Of these the 36th was entirely Protestant and Unionist; the 10th and 16th were "predominantly Catholic and nationalist," 391.

43. Frank McGuinness, *Observe the Sons of Ulster Marching Towards the Somme. Frank McGuinness: Plays One* (London: Faber and Faber, 1996), 103, 134.

44. McGuinness, 154.

45. McGuinness, 188.

46. Helen Lojek, "Playing Politics with Belfast's Charabanc Theatre Company," in *Politics and Performance in Contemporary Northern Ireland,* ed. John P. Harrington and Elizabeth J. Mitchell (Amherst: University of Massachusetts Press, 1999), 83.

47. Fintan O'Toole, *Critical Moments: Fintan O'Toole on Modern Irish Theatre,* ed. Julia Furay and Redmond O'Hanlon (Dublin: Carysfort, 2003), 62.

48. "Marina of the Midlands," Part Two, *Irish Times,* 4 May 2000.

49. Marina Carr, *By the Bog of Cats* (Loughcrew, Ireland: The Gallery Press, 1998), 13.

50. Carr, 25.

51. Carr, 25.

52. "Marina of the Midlands."

53. O'Toole, 190.

54. Vic Merriman, "Staging Contemporary Ireland: Heartsickness and Hopes Deferred," *Cambridge Companion to Twentieth-Century Irish Drama,* 254.

55. Martin McDonagh, "The Beauty Queen of Leenane," in *Plays I* (London: Methuen, 1999), 10.

56. McDonagh, 33.

57. Delia Murphy was a famous singer of the 1930s and 1940s; "The Spinning Wheel" is a romantic ballad about a young man luring a young woman away from her work.

58. McDonagh, 60.

8

Art and Architecture/Housing

ALTHOUGH IRISH WRITING AND MUSIC are better known abroad than the visual arts, Irish painting, sculpture, and architecture are all flourishing. The Irish Museum of Modern Art in Dublin allows one to experience all three simultaneously: some of the best of Irish and international art housed in an award-winning restoration of a retirement home for British soldiers built in 1684. Indeed, the building and its exhibitions make a natural metaphor for a culture that has become increasingly adept at using its past. One notes a striking continuity from the austere parallel lines of the museum's Georgian architecture to the strong horizontal and vertical lines that make up a new painting by Sean Scully. Across town, the National Gallery of Ireland, the Douglas Hyde Museum, and the Hugh Lane Municipal Gallery offer an opportunity to trace the span of twentieth-century Irish art. The city's streets, parks, and squares offer an introduction to sculpture and design. Here, too, one notes visual continuities with the past; "Sean's Spiral" a metal "triangular spiral" by Richard Serra installed in the cobbled pavement of Dublin's Crane Street in 1984 picks up a motif carved into the wall of a tomb at Newgrange 5,000 years ago. Yet not all Irish artists have wished to insert themselves into a national tradition. As for twentieth-century Irish art, it is helpful to begin by distinguishing artists in the Republic who supported the general goals of the Irish Renaissance and those who, turning their backs on the Free State, looked to Europe for inspiration.

IRISH LANDSCAPES: THE TRADITION

In painting during the Irish Renaissance, a movement to "de-Anglicize" Ireland, to restore the native language and culture, there was a fascination with the landscape of the Gaelic West and a determination to produce images of the Irish as strong, sympathetic figures, freed of colonial stereotypes. Even painters outside the movement, such as Dermod O'Brien, elected President of the Royal Hibernian Academy in 1910, produced such works as his "A Winding River, West of Ireland."[1] A peaceful, almost pristine, landscape without human figures, the painting is dominated by a luminous ivory and lavender sky whose tones, repeated in the river, contrast with the dark greens and browns of the shoreline and an adjoining pasture. Trained at London's Slade School of Fine Art, O'Brien is doubtless interested in suggesting the scene's beauty, which he evokes in a formally balanced composition, not in making nationalist propaganda.

Yet imagine a suitably Celtic figure in this green and silver landscape, and one sees immediately the potential for a political statement: perhaps about the unspoiled naturalness of the Irish peasant, so preferable to the degraded English factory worker, or about the ironic contrast between humanity's coarse black rags and the soft, silky textures of sky and water. Jack B. Yeats (1871–1957), for example, often painted the Western landscape, but people usually loom large in it. The brother of W. B. Yeats shared his enthusiasm for the West of Ireland, traveling with their friend playwright-poet John Synge through Mayo and south Connemara in 1905. Jack Yeats illustrated the articles about the trip Synge wrote for the *Manchester Guardian* and his *Aran Islands* (1907). Yeats published his own *Sketches of Life in the West of Ireland* in 1912. Like Synge, Yeats recognized the poverty of his fishermen and farmers, but what interested him more was their individual courage and the strength of a culture that has taught them to endure in such a cold and stony place. The subject of *The Man from Aranmore,* a 1905 watercolor, dominated his dockside setting, looming up through a trick of perspective over the misty hillside behind him, larger than the inlet of the Atlantic to his left. The dominant colors of the painting are muted blues, reds, and purples. The Atlantic glows in a red-tinged gold, as if seen against a brilliant sunset. The man's clothing, even the colors of his hands and face, are the colors of the landscape and the stone flags on which he stands. He belongs in this landscape against which he is posed, his right foot thrust forward, the fingers of his right hands curled under in a loose fist "not devoid of menace."[2]

Similarly, "Kelp-Making," an ink drawing from *The Aran Islands,* presented the worker as a tall, almost noble figure, leaning back from a fire whose smokes billows in the opposite direction, as he turns the kelp with a shovel.

Far from being an object of pity for his labor, the man seems confident that he is doing valuable work skillfully. He perfectly embodies the tone of the accompanying text, in which an islander says to Synge, "Isn't it a great wonder that you've seen France and Germany, and the Holy Father; and never seen a man making kelp till you come to Inishmaan?"[3]

Two of Yeats's contemporaries, Paul Henry and Sean Keating, both first-rate craftsmen, were equally celebrated for their rural landscapes. Henry, son of a Baptist minister in Belfast, seems a strange figure for the Free State to adopt, but his paintings of the West might have been designed as illustrations of de Valera's ideal of "frugal comfort," of a self-sufficient Gaelic peasantry carrying on the traditions of their fathers. "The Potato Diggers" shows a white-haired man and a woman hunched over their spades. Again, perspective makes them dominate over the pale Atlantic and the cliffs behind them.[4] The man's clothing is in shades of the brown used for the soil and the potatoes, its thick rough wool bunched in spots, so that its texture too matches the field. The woman's blouse is a darker shade of the gray used for the mountain and sky. The only bright color is provided by the red in the woman's skirt and the scarf that entirely obscures her face; but these, too, are "weathered to a variety of tones" that the painter himself described as "'barbaric.'" In the 1920s, several of Henry's landscapes, reproduced in train posters, were widely distributed, becoming "the standard view of the west of Ireland in tourist literature and in government publications."[5] In a sense Henry "became the victim of his own imagery," supplying the demand for more of the same rather than developing further, and this identification of his paintings with the repressions of de Valera's Ireland made him an establishment figure a younger generation of artists would reject.

The rural poor in the three paintings examined offer a contrast to English depictions of the ragged Irish as figures of comedy or pathos. Sean Keating transformed them into saints, or rather, the inspiring figures of a social realism that strikes more than one critic as downright Stalinist. As a young man, Keating also visited the Aran Islands, "a revelation," as he put it, "a wonderful background of barren landscape with very agile handsome men."[6] Versions of them figure prominently in Keating's more political paintings, such as *Men of the West* (1917). In this painting, which features three mustachioed men armed with rifles and wearing hats perhaps, too, suggestive of the Stetson, the setting seems "more reminiscent of being west of the Rio Grande than west of the Shannon."[7] Keating was commissioned by the Electricity Supply Board to record the building of the hydroelectric dam on the Shannon from 1926 to 1929. His 26 paintings and drawings wonderfully evoke the Shannon Scheme's importance to the young state, and not incidentally reveal how its commitment to ancient Gaelic values could be made to jibe with a heroic vision of engineering feats propelling Ireland into the future. But the solemn mixture of near-photographic realism, the giant dam rising in its concrete blocks, with allegorical figures—the priest, hopeful youth, earnest labor, even a skeleton for the famine dead—make a painting like *Night's Candles Are Burned Out* seem slightly absurd to a modern viewer. The next generation would reject all such official images of Ireland along with the narrow patriotism with which they had become associated.

REVISING THE TRADITION: LANDSCAPE

One pair of photographs by Willie Doherty, "Longing/Lamenting," (1991) provides the clearest illustration of what his generation dislikes in conventional nature paintings. The first is a photograph of a sky, the upper three-quarters bright blue, a few white clouds scattered through the lowest quarter. The word "longing" in white capitals is centered just above the clouds, or about two-thirds of the way down the page. In the second photograph, a field is covered with rough grass; some of it a faded green, some bleached to lighter shades, yellow and white. The grass is partly covered with dried brown leaves. The lighting suggests that the picture was taken in bright sunlight. Across this autumnal scene the word "lamenting" appears, again centered in white capitals, but this time about one-third of the way down the page. For Declan McGonagle, the photographs make "an unambiguous statement that landscape is ideological, that we constantly project meaning on to nature and that this has been a particularly visible and damaging feature of the Irish situation."[8]

Kathy Prendergast, an artist from the Republic, raised an even stronger challenge to the landscape tradition with her 1983 *Body Map Series*. The series plays with the conventional representation of Ireland as a woman: where Americans have Uncle Sam, Irish nationalism has always had the dark Rosaleen, Cathleen ni Houlihan, the "old woman," the shan von vocht, Mother Ireland. One measure of how firmly this image was stamped into the public consciousness is that John Lavery's painting of his American wife, Hazel, costumed as Cathleen ni Houlihan appeared on Irish currency from 1927 until 1975. But feminists saw the irony of depicting the nation as a woman even though its laws limited the rights of actual women. One explanation of this paradox emphasizes that the Free State was a fledgling postcolonial nation. Men newly freed from the humiliations of submitting to a colonizer are prone to assert authority over women. Thus "women were to serve, not only as the passive emblems of the nation, but also as the territory over which patriarchal power was exercised."[9]

In Prendergast's water color and ink drawings, a faceless woman's body is literally mapped, in sections, as a geographical entity. In *Enclosed World in*

Open Spaces, there are lines marking longitude and latitude and labels assigning geographical names to body parts: the abdomen is a desert, the breast volcanic mountains, the naval a crater, the vulva a harbor. Several provide cross sections of the map, with suggestions about how to "alter" or "control" it. Thus *To Control a Landscape: Oasis* depicts a shaft driven into the abdomen (desert). A windmill pumps water through the shaft and irrigates the desert's surface. This process is delineated in a text attached to the drawing, ending with the explanation: "Thus instead of emitting fire and smoke, the mountains will now exude water and irrigate the soil."[10] These are witty drawings, capable of sustaining multiple interpretations. One can easily imagine an ecological reading that stresses the folly of exploiting one natural resource, such as subterranean water, without taking into account the damage caused to others. But in its immediate context, Ireland two years before the rejected abortion referendum, the idea of a faceless system that forces fertility on the female body without considering the woman's wishes or the costs of extinguishing her sexual energy, her fiery spirit, is a focus.

As graphic artists mixing images and text, Prendergast and Doherty represent the most obvious subversions of the romantic Irish landscape. But other professional artists have revised that landscape in images. Two of the most successful of these are Gwen O'Dowd and Maria Simonds-Gooding. In O'Dowd's paintings, of which her 1992 "Over by Clogher Head" gives us a good example, images hover "between representation and abstraction."[11] Against a black background, giant white waves rise out of a blue and green sea. The painting, in the style of abstract expressionism, offers no photographic detail. In the center of this turmoil a handful of small brown shadows are visible, but there is no way of knowing whether they suggest boats, rocks, or some other objects tossed up by wind and sea. If O'Dowd has "little Celtic mist in her work," Maria Simonds-Gooding has even less. Her landscapes are not only abstract but "ethereal: the physicality of the landscape is very much implicit and the impression has indeed been likened to an x-ray." Her 1990 etching, "Enclosure on a Mountain" is dominated by the mountain itself, a dark mass against which is a four-sided white and gray object from which a white strip, suggestive of a road, leads into a wider vertical strip that links to a horizontal strip leading from one edge of the mountain to the other. Parallel, but unconnected, another horizontal strip crosses near the bottom of the dark mass. Again, there are no human figures; at the center of the white and gray object there is etched another four-sided object from which two parallel lines extend: the enclosure, presumably, within the larger enclosure. The etching has been seen as a portrait of the "vestigial remains" of a primitive civilization: "man has marked the land with his enclosures, and nature has worn away the walls that 'humanize' the landscape." Or, as the artist herself puts it, "I portray the effect that *people* have had on the landscape as opposed to the natural phenomena."[12]

AGAINST REPRESENTATION: THE TRADITION OF EXPERIMENT

The elements of abstract expressionism that have been noted in O'Dowd and Simonds-Gooding landscapes of the early 1990s could be found as well in the later paintings of Jack B. Yeats, for although the Yeats, Keating, and Henry landscapes discussed are the most overtly "Irish" paintings of their time, many painters of their generation resisted nationalist pressure. Such artists studied abroad and produced paintings that reflect the dominant European schools: postimpressionism, cubism, and abstract expressionism. Mainie Jellett (1897–1944), arguably "the greatest woman painter the country has ever produced," was the embodiment of this modernist tradition.[13] Jellett, born of Protestant Unionist parents in Dublin, studied in London during World War I and went to Paris in 1921. There she studied with André Lhote, a great admirer of Cézanne and himself an early Cubist painter. Lhote believed that students should analyze the Old Masters to "see how the background and figures were combined and developed on mainly geometrical lines and basic forces in the composition," and encouraged them to produce "Cubist developments" of these paintings.[14] This influence is obvious in her early portraits and figure drawings, which remain representational while showing the cubist interest in geometrical form. Jellett, however, expressed an interest in a more "extreme Cubism," with its emphasis on balance, harmony, and "the essential flatness of the picture plane–painting was to be true to its nature as an essentially two-dimensional art."[15] She turned to the studio of Albert Gleizes, author of an influential book on "Cubism and the Means to Understand It."

In the 10 years she spent with Gleizes, Jellett was persuaded to abandon not only perspective, but "the cinematic vision," the effort to represent movement by drawing the same object from multiple perspectives that we see in Picasso's *Demoiselle d'Avignon*. Instead, Gleizes taught, the painter must accept "the two-dimensional and essentially static nature of the picture plane" and create "a different movement, the movement of the eye from one thing to the other, established by the most elementary means available to the painter, the inter-action of plane surfaces, line and color."[16] This influence is obvious in her paintings of 1922–1925, several of which are titled simply *Abstract Composition* and feature geometrical shapes in solid color. When she exhibited some of these paintings with the Society of Dublin painters in 1923, the *Irish Times* reviewer identified one in particular, a five-sided worked called "Decoration," as a "freak painting." George Russell, poet and painter of the Irish Renaissance, referred to "the sub-human art of Miss Jellett."[17] The controversy that followed, which included robust defenses from other artists, ranged over the whole question of whether the visual arts should imitate music in making a harmony of forms, rather than representation or narrative, its central impulse. Thus within Dublin's art world, Jellett became identified with the Parisian and the modern, with the artist's claim to reject the local and parochial along with the conventional and realistic. Combining her study with Gleizes with periods of teaching, exhibiting, and giving public talks in Dublin, she became a major influence on the next generation of Irish artists. She argued forcefully that "painting is … not an imitation of objects" but an effort to reveal the spirit which lies beneath their surface; for the best painters, "the reality of the exterior world serves as a departure."[18]

THE TRADITION OF EXPERIMENT: LIVING ART

The modernism for which Jellett was such a strong proponent began to flower in Dublin only after the outbreak of World War II brought an influx of artists trained abroad. The pacifist White Stag Group, whose members included the Hungarian Basil Rakoczi, left London for the neutral Irish capital. The war also caused a number of Irish artists to return from their adopted homes in Paris, Berlin, and Florence. Prominent among them was Louis le Brocquy, whose paintings *The Spanish Shawl* and *Image of Chaos* were rejected in 1941 by the Royal Hibernian Academy (RHA), the guardian of the Keating and Henry school that its detractors had come to call "National Realism." Le Brocquy's mother, Sybil, a well-established writer, resolved to establish a new vehicle for promoting and exhibiting modernist art, organized a group that came to be known as "Living Art." Having elected Mainie Jellett as president, Living Art put on its first exhibition in 1943. For the next 40 years the Irish Exhibition of Living Art (IELA) was an annual event, providing encouragement to Irish artists to experiment with not only modernism, but all of its avant-garde successors, op, pop, and minimalism. It also gave encouragement to artists who wished to find new ways of interpreting the Celtic heritage.

After Mainie Jellett's early death in 1944, her place as president of Living Art was taken by Norah McGuinness, a younger artist who had also studied with Lhote. Mc Guinness's work, like that of Jellett's partner, Evie Hone, and the Drogheda artist Nano Reid, provides striking examples of a fresh and experimental art that takes its direction from European rather than local models. One particularly interesting example that illustrates these qualities is Nano Reid's "The Backyard" (1959). An oil painting dominated by oranges, yellows, and browns, it has the flatness, or refusal to simulate "depth" or perspective, that Lhote admired. On the painting's left, the viewer sees a bright orange cat on a stone wall, four blue-gray cylinders (barrels? ashcans? glasses?) in a blue enclosure, and a rectangular table with a basket (bowl?) containing bottles. In the middle a human figure, its back, drawn as a nearly straight vertical, turned away from the objects on the left. The hands are raised, holding up a length of white material. In the lower right hand, another rectangular object (a basket? a box?), lined with white, holds several yellow objects and what appears to be a gray bottle. In the lower left-hand corner, another orange cat, this one striped, appears to leap forward. Everything is painted with bold lines and broad brush strokes, but the vertical lines dominate. It is an absorbing and accomplished picture. One understands why critics compare her style with Matisse's, but also why one expresses some frustration that "in her mature work she does not describe; she hints and suggests, leaving the viewer to break her code."[19] There is just enough representation to bring out the viewer's impulse to construct a narrative or an ideology, to make, for example, the brown and gray figure hanging up laundry a symbol of oppressed womanhood. But any such effort is baffled by the painter's refusal to be more specific: the figure is as genderless as it is faceless.

Perhaps the most famous contemporary Irish artist is Louis le Brocquy, the young artist whose rejection by the RHA led his mother to start the IELA. The only living artist ever to be included in the permanent collection of the National Gallery of Ireland, he has had a long career not only spanning, but embodying, several of the key movements in Irish art since World War II. In the early 1950s, during a "grey period," le Brocquy painted a series of bleak cubist interiors, each representing several naked figures staring off in different directions.[20] In several senses, these paintings give fresh meaning to the phrase "nuclear family": the emotional isolation, charged with obscure tension, of a family whose members coexist but offer no comfort to each other. In "Man Writing" the family dog offers a quite human smile to the writer, who stares past him into the middle distance. In "A Family," a cat huddles next to a reclining woman, its stripes fading into her prominent ribs, its eyes fixed outward. Faded, nearly colorless rooms suggest an institution, part prison, part hospital; in "A Family," a woman inclines on a bed, a stark white plane on a dark rectangular with only one visible leg. One thinks immediately of "operating tables or mortuary slabs."[21] In "A Sickness" (also known as "Family Illness") a seated female nude holds a hand that dangles down the side of a white-draped female invalid who appears to float from the ceiling. In the foreground, the head and shoulders of a third, draped in gray, her eyes downcast, suggests the shawled rural women of another generation. Again the figures make no eye contact; indeed the averted eyes of the woman in the foreground are the only hint that she is aware of the other two. Although family estrangement is an obvious theme, le Brocquy comments on the relevance of the political context: "in these post-war, Cold War days, we all of us walked in fear of potential nuclear disaster obliterating civilized life."[22]

In the mid-1950s, le Brocquy began a series of White Paintings; he himself attributed the change to a visit to southern Spain, where "all dull color ... is lost, irradiated into brilliance by a white sun."[23] Indeed the white background, against which is a shadowy figure sometimes accented with thick strokes of white paint (*impasto*) remains characteristic of le Brocquy's paintings as late as 1996. In discussing his white paintings, le Brocquy emphasizes the importance of shadow, how it can be a "stronger presence" than the "object itself"; and the paintings do bear out his suggestion that we are looking at "figures bleached away into evanescence, giving substance only to shadow."[24] It has been argued that the "shadow," as in Jung, acts "as a contrast to the persona, or visible, 'public' self," and that for le Brocquy incorporating "this awareness into his work became central." One of his most accessible "White" paintings is "Young Woman (Anne)," a 1957 image of Anne Madden, whom he married a year later. Shortly after the couple met, Anne was severely injured in a car accident and spent almost a year having a series of spinal operations, after each of which she was encased for months in a fullbody cast. The shadowy figure who faces the reader is headless; its body ends at its knees. As in an X-ray, short dark horizontal lines locate six vertebrae on a shadowy spine. A short, bright red line suggests a surgical wound. In the otherwise white and gray painting, there are only two other touches of red, one on the subject's left shoulder and the other near the pelvis. Horizontal gray lines, resembling markings or smears on an X-ray, divide the pelvis from the abdomen and upper from lower thighs. A slash runs from one horizontal line to another, as if marking an X over the figure's erogenous zone. Here impasto imitates the rough plaster of a cast; the impression given is not just that the painting reproduces "the visual circumstances of the artist's life" but its psychological consequences, "apprehensions of mortality ... separations ... enforced celibacy."[25]

Le Brocquy also occasionally painted Irish subjects. In the mid-1940s, for example, while still very much under the sway of the cubists, he undertook a series of paintings of Irish travellers whom he had seen at Tullamore.

But it is the portraits of Irish writers—James Joyce, William Butler Yeats, and Samuel Beckett—that reflect his most mature interest in "the Irish imagination."[26] Paradoxically perhaps, le Brocquy's interest in painting the isolated human head was first triggered by seeing an exhibition of Polynesian skulls in Paris. In 1965, when he visited the south of France, he saw his first examples of a Celtic "head cult." For le Brocquy it "acted as a confirmatory revelation ... of the image of the head as a kind of magic box that holds the spirit prisoner."[27] Ideally, a le Brocquy portrait frees that spirit, or rather "reconstructs" it, much as an anthropologist recreates a human face from the skull outward. Since this living spirit has many depths, le Brocquy came to believe that the artist must produce a series of reconstructions, each offering the possibility of new interpretations. And as he continues to use many of the techniques of the White Paintings, the head often seems to emerge from the shadows, requiring the viewer to examine it carefully, from several angles. Although the Yeats and Joyce paintings show the head floating in the center of a white canvas, his 1994 charcoal "Image of Samuel Beckett" goes back to the X-ray motif seen in his 1957 painting of his wife. Here the viewer can see the "skull beneath the skin," the lines of the skull beneath the dramatist's thatch of white hair, the head tenuously attached to a shadowy spinal column.

THE TRADITION OF EXPERIMENT: ROSC AND AFTER

Although IELA exhibitions continued to be held into the late 1980s, many people in Dublin's artistic community became frustrated that the city provided so few opportunities for people to see the best contemporary international art. In 1967, the architect Michael Scott and the former Guggenheim Museum director, James Johnson Sweeney, opened the first Rosc exhibition with a view to filling this gap. Rosc (Irish variously for "the poetry of vision" or "battle-cry") exhibitions, to be held once every four years, were to include three to five works by each of 50 living artists to be selected by a jury of experts on international art. The purpose was to bring in artists from abroad, so Irish artists were excluded from the first two exhibits and not "definitively" included until 1980, when performance and installation art were added. Although in 1977, the Office of Public Works, citing safety hazards, had refused French artists Christo and Jeanne-Claude permission to wrap St. Stephen's Green in gold-colored woven nylon, in 1980 Marta Minujin found a more welcoming atmosphere. This installation artist reconstructed a life-size model of the Martello Tower, which Joyce uses in the opening scenes of *Ulysses,* using only loaves of Downe's bread, a brand mentioned in the novel. Afterward, she distributed the loaves to the public so that "later in the day, the bright orange 'Butterkrust' wrappers could be seen all over the city."[28]

With perhaps more lasting consequences for Irish art, 1980 also saw the installation of James Coleman's *Strongbow.* Now perhaps Ireland's best-known installation artist, Coleman displayed an effigy of man who came to Ireland in the twelfth century at the invitation of the King of Leinster, bringing a host of Welsh-Norman knights whom England's Henry II followed into Ireland. Traditionally Strongbow, who married the king's daughter Aoife, is a hero, but his role in Ireland's colonization makes him an ambiguous one. The effigy lies in a darkened room, its face and hands lighted. Near this medieval scene is a color television monitor, presenting the image of a pair of hands, one orange and one green. The hands begin to clap, first slowly and then "rising to a crescendo sufficient to wake the dead. But Strongbow slumbers on ... impotent to intercede in this conflict between the present sons of Ulster."[29]

Rosc's last exhibition was in 1988. There was general agreement that the era of large-scale international exhibits was waning, and after opening in 1991, the Irish Museum of Modern Art filled the need for a venue that would bring contemporary art from around the world to Ireland.[30] Although the judgments of one's contemporaries are notoriously fallible, the Dublin-born painter Sean Scully is widely regarded as the most important Irish artist of the 1980s and 1990s. An admirer of abstract expressionism educated in London and at Harvard University, he belongs to the tradition of experiment, to the line of Irish artists-in-exile rejecting nationalism in favor of a timeless and universal art. "I'm more interested in what unites us than what divides us," he told an interviewer in 1997. "My feeling is that people who do work that is overtly topical or political are very interested in what divides us."[31] Having turned away from representation in the early 1970s, Scully began painting in horizontal and vertical stripes. Scully sees his horizontal and vertical lines as a "motif as capable of functioning as a metaphorical expression of social reality."[32] The artist frequently speaks of the grids of the contemporary city, its streets, its suspension bridges, its skyscrapers. But he also sees a fascination with "large structures, trying to get to the heart of them" as a theme of classical painters such as Giotto.[33] In his early paintings, a pattern runs over the whole canvas, often in the form of multiple grids superimposed one above the other. The lines are precise, geometric, and often created through taping.

Since a 1982 painting called *Heart of Darkness* that Scully and his critics regard as a significant breakthrough, he has continued to use stripes; but they are imperfect, created with uneven or blurring brush strokes. Typically, as in *Landline Blue,* a 1999 painting at the Irish Museum of Modern Art, a layer of thick under-painting remains visible beneath the broad, short brush strokes of the stripes. *Landline* is divided horizontally into two halves, the lower dark blue and the upper a beige that coats the blue so lightly that the effect from a distance is a shimmering gray-blue. Each half has a centered rectangle of six white and indigo stripes. The upper rectangle, however, is less than half the width of the lower. Given the title's suggestion of a landscape, and the possibility of seeing the blurred beige and blue of the two halves as forming a horizon, one viewer noted that the broad but short horizontal brush marks that are especially visible in the upper half of the painting suggest distant buildings.

In interviews, Scully explains that, by 1980, he had lost faith in modernism, by which he apparently means trying to suggest the inner spirit of a subject by abstracting it into perfect geometrical structures. He continued to use the stripe, which he associates with modernism, even calling it a "signifier for modernism," but as "something that had failed, 'had the beauty of failure,'" which he could transform. "Since formalism was dead in relation to abstraction ... I understood that the form had to be knocked down, taken apart. And not simply put together: *but put back together for a different reason.* The issue was now content, and.... an art of relationships."[34] Deliberate imperfections, such as allowing the under-painted color to bleed through to the surface or blurring the dark blue horizon with the beige one, are a means to a goal, to "endow geometry with a human aspect."[35] Thus, although none of his work represents the world directly, Scully himself insists on its metaphorical, expressive intent. A painting such as *Landline Blue* invites viewers to feel, to meditate, to sense if not spell out a connection between the painting and their own lives. As one notes the relationship between the larger striped rectangle in the lower half of the painting and the smaller one above it, which seems to glow out of its dark blue background, one can be reminded, for example, of Scully's claim that his paintings are about power relationships: "It's interesting that something small can stand up and be in a composition, dynamically, and have to deal with something much bigger. There's a sort of equal relationship there."[36] This statement offers a way of talking about the painting's apparent life and energy, but certainly does not provide a definitive key for interpretation.

PAINTING THE TROUBLES: VERNACULAR ART

A distinction between Irish artists who have responded directly to the nation, its landscapes, its political circumstances, or its distinctive cultural traditions and those who come out of a tradition of experiment that follows European models and prefers universal forms and colors to representation is always, as has been seen, in some danger of breaking down. Louis le Broquy turned to portraits of Joyce, Yeats, and Beckett after a lifetime of formalism. He also produced illustrations for a 1986 Dolmen Press edition of Joyce's *Dubliners,* and even Sean Scully, without abandoning his horizontal and vertical stripes, produced a series of illustrations for Joyce's *Pomes Penyeach* in 1994. Political commentary and experiment were readily blended, as in the James Coleman installation that juxtaposed a medieval-looking image of Strongbow with a video evocation of the mutual antagonism of Republicans and Unionists. Indeed Northern Ireland's Troubles pressed a compelling theme on the visual arts. That is not to say that the whole province was one continuous combat zone. High levels of violence in South Armagh, or in working-class Derry or Belfast, coexisted with life as usual, or nearly as usual, in upper-middle-class suburbs. Between 1969 and 1989, fatalities in the urban north and west of

"Irish Out," proclaims a wall painting in Protestant Ulster. © CAIN, http://cain.ulst. ac.uk/photographs, 2000.

Belfast totaled 1,099. In the same period, "the number of residents of the province's gold coast' [North Down] who lost their lives to political violence was the remarkably small total of eight."[37]

But as long as the Troubles remained the central and intractable reality of the North's politics, even to avoid them was a political decision. As the artist Brian O'Doherty put it, "You discover that response to any oppression generates its own clichés. The darkness is your midst ... evicts a whole family of emotions and strategies that more peaceful times engage."[38] Thus even artists with a preference for abstraction, or inclined to find the countryside a more congenial subject than a bombed-out pub, acknowledged the violence. For most professional artists, finding a way to represent the suffering without playing into the hands of the terrorists was a high priority. In a society where victims' images are associated with calls for revenge, a painting of a wounded child might incite further casualties.

As these Irish artists well knew, the first paintings of the Trouble were vernacular murals. Working-class people in the North's cities traditionally lived in two-story gabled row houses, with windows front and back. The houses on either end offered a windowless wall that could be decorated for patriotic holidays. Protestants painted the Union Jack, orange lilies, King William on a white horse, and silhouetted men in World War I uniforms, a reminder of

Ulster's losses at the Battle of the Somme. Because Catholics who attempted to decorate their neighborhoods with the orange, white, and green tricolor of the Republic or white lilies recalling the Easter Rising usually found themselves in trouble with the law, the mural tradition came to their neighborhoods only after the outbreak of the Troubles, when paintings were no longer a police priority.[39] After 1969, the usual iconography of the two communities was supplemented with new images of hooded paramilitaries and of the H-Blocks/Maze/Long Kesh (all names for the prison outside Belfast where suspected and convicted terrorists were held). The Red Hand of Ulster, often against an outline map of Northern Ireland, became a favorite icon for Protestants. Depictions of Bloody Sunday and the Irish Republican Army (IRA) hunger strikers became part of the repertoire in Republican neighborhoods.

Today this tradition thrives. Reproduced in books and on the Internet, the paintings have attracted a wide audience. In Belfast, busloads of tourists are driven to see the hundred or so murals extant at any one time.[40] Today's wall painters are generally skillful, erecting scaffolding and spending days on each image. Seeking murals to promote peace and pride rather than serve as "territorial markers," community organizations have sponsored competitions and solicited suggestions from neighborhood children.[41] One such mural foregrounds children sliding down a brightly colored rainbow, with the only political reference a group of civil rights marchers in the background, painted in shades of black and white. Yet many others, especially in Loyalist neighborhoods, retain the fierce images of sectarian war. One, completed in 2001, depicts a figure in black against a bright red background, his face hooded, his gun aimed directly at the viewer. A bloody dawn breaks in the center of a wall painted black in 1999. The Union Jack and Ulster flag provide the only other color. A text reproduced in shadowy letters takes up most of the space: "Soldiers 36th Ulster Division UVF Belfast Brigade. They arose in the dark days to defend our native land. For God and Ulster. And when the Lord thy God shall deliver them before thee, thou shall smite them and utterly destroy them, thou shalt make no covenant with them nor show mercy unto them. Deuteronomy 2: 7."

The militant wall paintings not only offer the simple propaganda that most professional artists eschew, but suggest a mythic view of the conflict. One keeps on painting King William because one sees nothing strange about preserving the hatreds of 1690. A new subject, say the hunger striker Bobby Sands, appears in the pose and attitude of an old icon, the martyred Christ, and the message that Republicans are fated to die for their people gets reiterated. Yet the paintings that have fascinated so many outsiders exert a similar pull on Ireland's professional artists. One sees artists reshaping their icons, using their harsh primary colors in a new context, or experimenting with the juxtaposition of text and image that links the wall painting to the poster or billboard. Michael Dunn's 1999 *Showers* provides an example of "this ironic adaptation."[42]

PORTRAYING THE TROUBLES: PROFESSIONALS ARTISTS, SCULPTORS, AND PHOTOGRAPHERS

An acrylic weather map of Northern Ireland in light green is set against a blue Atlantic and the edges of a Republic colored in a darker green. Black text in a yellow rectangle in the upper left-hand corner reads "Outlook." Sprinkled over the map are the BBC weather service's symbols for clouds, with their trefoil shape, and small circles with numbers indicating temperatures in Celsius. The five yellow circles all contain low numbers, 1–4, and the three black circles indicate higher temperatures, 15 or 20. The elements of the wall painting—crude outline map, the text, nationalist colors, even the blue of the Atlantic, which matches the blue river Boyne in so many images of King William—are juxtaposed with a graphic familiar to television viewers. By scrambling Nationalist and Loyalist motifs, and suggesting that a changeable "weather" has replaced the certainties of history and religion, the artist opens up diverse possibilities and interpretations. Whether one wants to see "showers" as simple realism about Irish weather or a metaphor, there is relief in escaping the harsh dark pieties of the wall painting.

The very different photographic and video work of Willie Doherty, a contemporary Belfast painter, reflects the desire to rearrange familiar images of the Troubles seen in "Showers." Much of Doherty's work is exhibited in pairs, its "double images" compelling the viewer to acknowledge multiple angles, perspectives, and interpretations.[43] "Incident" (1993) and "Border Incident" provide a clear example. The first shows a burned-out car on the verge of a low hill beside a narrow, winding road. The picture appears to have been taken at twilight. The car's original paint color, still visible in spots, is somewhat brighter than the grayed blue of the road, sky, and distant hills. In the foreground the car looms up, its scorched yellows and brown the center of attention. On the right, in the distance, the viewer can identify a picture postcard landscape with green fields divided by stone walls. In "Border Incident" the road and sky are a deeper and brighter blue, which this time matches the paint remaining on another burned out car. This time, there are no yellows and browns. As before, the road is narrow, with no lane markings, but this time it is absolutely straight, bisecting the image. An overgrown hedgerow on the right, where a gabled building can just be glimpsed, sets it off from the pasture on the left.

In other places, a burned-out, abandoned car would probably suggest the aftermath of a lethal wreck, and of course this association is significant.

But a Belfast artist in 1993 knew that a burned-out vehicle, if attached to a plausibly Irish landscape, would suggest a shootout in which British soldiers prevented IRA guerillas from crossing the border to the relative safety of the Republic. In fact, however, the car in the first picture had been burned "as part of the process of dumping it—for 'domestic reasons,' as it were—but the other car had indeed been burnt out after having been used in a paramilitary action close to the border."[44] The images create a disturbing context for each other. They force the viewer to pause over formal similarities, shapes and colors and lines of sight, preventing the more familiar and comfortable response of glancing from image to explanatory narrative. The violent end of terrorists? The progress of British justice? Another martyr for the cause? The pictures provide no answer, except to suggest that the questions are inadequate.

In a dual video projection entitled *The Only Good One Is a Dead One,* Doherty shows two views seen at night, through a car's windshield. There is a strong visual reminiscence of the scene in a sci-fi movie just before alien abductors land. As the video images move, the accompanying soundtrack makes it clear that the driver is approaching a British security checkpoint in Northern Ireland. In one observer's words, "We hear the driver thinking about the attitude among troops and loyalists, regarding nationalists, that the 'only good one is a dead one' his ambivalent monologue works through his apprehensions of being a victim and his fantasy of being the killer."[45] No figures are visible, no landmarks; highway and roadside are obscured in blue and green shadows. In one video the white reflection of the center line marker looms up; in the other, a painted arrow marking a left turn is almost washed out by the glare from the car's headlights. Here the double image seems to force us to follow two views simultaneously, not only mirroring the speaker's ambivalence but acting out the confusion outsiders often experience trying to sort out the differences between the competing visions of Unionists and Republicans. And again, there is no suggestion that this alienated perspective represents truth, only the reminder that any social reality is constituted of multiple points of view.

SCULPTURE

Sculptors, even more than painters, must have felt pressured to present heroic images of the new Free State. One of the legacies of English rule was prominently placed statues of the royal family and British military leaders. O'Connell Street, Dublin's principal thoroughfare, was dominated for more than 150 years by Nelson's Pillar, a statue of the hero of Trafalgar in full Naval dress, standing atop a fluted Doric column mounted on a granite pedestal. Inside the column, 168 steps led to a viewing platform from which visitors could survey the city. Although some people advocated removing all such vestiges of Empire after independence, most Dubliners seemed to accept the landmark as the city center, and expressed regret when perpetrators, never apprehended, blew it up in 1966. Its 2002 replacement, the "Monument of Light," has met a mixed reception. At 250 meters high, the conical stainless steel and glass spire was intended to reflect the city's light and weather; its minimalist design is a deliberate contrast to the political rhetoric of other monuments on the street. Those who immediately nicknamed it the "Spike" are more likely to talk about alien landings and deplore the fact that it would be equally at home in Helsinki or Los Angeles.

Certainly other statuary on O'Connell Street is militantly Irish. The American Augustus Saint-Gaudens's 1911 statue of Parnell seems to have served as the model for heroic statuary all over Ireland. The hero, draped in a heavy coat that suggests a flowing toga, reaches out toward an invisible crowd with outstretched arm. The giant plinth behind him bears a quotation from his speech declaring that "no man has the right … to fix the *ne plus ultra* of Ireland's nationhood." A line of Irish text and an engraved harp complete the inscription; the base of the monument is decorated in "ox-skulls and swags" copied from a nearby rotunda. Circled in garlands are the names of the four Irish provinces.[46] This tradition dies hard, as Eamonn O'Doherty's 1996 rendition of the labor leader and martyr of the Easter Rising, James Connolly, for the Irish Trade Union Congress, demonstrates. Connolly himself has a more contemporary look; he is dressed in a simple suit and depicted as if about to address an ordinary meeting. But the stylized plow and stars behind him (emblems of his Irish Citizen's Army) give this balding, mustachioed man with his piercing bronze gaze a decidedly Stalinist cast. It is a statue that would look at home in the public square of any former Soviet state.

This heroic tradition, and popular Catholic statuary, with its bleeding hearts and upcast eyes, suggests one reason so many contemporary Irish sculptors seem drawn to its opposite: to simple lines, a suggestion of lightness, almost weightlessness, and to unconventional materials, such as the painted canvas that covers a steel frame in Eilis O'Connell's 1989 abstract piece, "Oxala" or the textile scraps of Kathy Prendergast's equally abstract "Stack." The stick-figure skeletons clinging to the ghostly three-masted bronze of John Behan's "Coffin Ship" (1997), the National Famine Memorial near Croagh Patrick in County Mayo, evoke hunger and death. But this unmonumental monument suggests a certain reticence in the face of so much past suffering, a reluctance to turn it to the service of contemporary nationalism. Rowan Gillespie's famine sculpture, a straggling group of five thin, ill-dressed figures carrying their "few possession towards an unseen coffin ship," shares the same impulse to avoid romanticizing or exploiting suffering.[47] Nonetheless, its setting in front of Dublin's contemporary steel and glass International Financial Services Center, seems to invite an ironic interpretation.

Conor Fallon, a contemporary sculptor who admires cubism, says that "avoidance of mass is fundamental to my work."[48] His subjects have often been birds and animals whose energy and movement he wants to convey in sculptures "opening up space." His birds are often hollow, their wings an aerodynamic steel sheet, their legs slender curves. A 1986 horse is all steel curves and open spaces. One flank is entirely exposed. Its shanks open up into two slender branches before converging above its hoofs, short smooth wedges of steel. Fallon brought the same aesthetic to the human head, which he began working on in 1979. Like Louis le Brocquy, he shares the ancient Celtic fascination with the head as the magical source of a person's power. From his perspective, viewers do not see a human head as a mass; they see "the glance of the eye, the animation of the face, the attitude." Thus, strikingly, "My Father's Head" has hollow eyes; made of separate sheets of steel, the head suggests the plates of the skull beneath. His concave "Head of Joyce" has a large curved opening, too large to be an ordinary mouth, beneath a thin sheet of steel that links the familiar monocle to the outlined nose. The skull appears to have been cleaved open between the eyes. Thin, separate bands of steel, also offering glimpses of the hollow space beneath, cover each side. Like the shadows in le Brocquy's portraits, the empty spaces in Fallon's sculptures are often eloquent, suggesting a vitality that flows through his subjects and links them to an unseen world.

But Fallon can also use emptiness as absence. His "Famine" sculpture (1995) incorporates three cast-iron cauldrons, the kind poor farmers used for boiling potatoes, from the famine era. Each is mounted on its side. One, which is whole, faces directly out. The other two, each with a gaping hole cut from its bottom, are turned slightly to face toward the center. A stylized bronze crow is mounted on top of each cauldron; in comparison with Fallon's other birds, they are heavy, static figures. The central one looks down while the crows on the side turn toward each other. Their long, open, predatory beaks are empty. It is hard to imagine a stronger evocation of absolute want, the loss of family, fire, and food, but also of spiritual desolation.

If Fallon reshapes the tradition by resisting physical mass, Danny Osborne seems on the other hand to reshape it by introducing wit. Just across from Oscar Wilde's former home at One Merrion Square, in the formal green park, a life-size marble and granite figure of the playwright lounges on a pile of boulders, a knee and elbow bent, an eye glancing toward two objects mounted on plinths opposite him. The marble face might almost be that of a classical statue, except for its bemused expression. But the green marble smoking jacket with its quilted maroon collar evokes an altogether different era, as do the shapely feet in their elegant, impeccably polished black granite shoes: here there is an unmistakable echo of op art, of an ironic sensibility responding to advertising glamour. One of the plinths holds up a marble torso that might have come from any upper-class Victorian library. On the other, facing away from the playwright, is an equally neoclassic figure who would not have been kept in that library: a full figure naked woman, with a swollen belly. All over the granite plinths, graffiti-style, are hand-written quotations from the author's works counseling the need to assume a pose, wear a mask, and understand hypocrisy as the tribute vice pays to virtue. It is a marvelous subversion of the public commemorative statue, in which marble, granite, and inscriptions play into our sense of Wilde the outsider or Wilde the Anglo-Irishman, which may be much the same thing.

One of the goals of the Irish Renaissance was to restore the integrity of Celtic culture before British rule. The first generation of patriots, however, was not inclined to dwell on one such relic, the Sheela-na-gig. A stone carving found on many medieval Irish churches, bridges, and doorways, a Sheela-na-gig depicts a woman with her legs spread wide open, her hands gesturing toward her remarkably large genitalia. Victorian archaeologists found such images "repulsive, hideous ... and obscene" and suggested that she was either a survival of an old pagan cult or the product of the "wantonness of some loose mind"; everyone puzzled over her association with holy buildings.[49] Modern scholarship suggests she was a Christian artifact first used in the twelfth century, probably meant to warn good Christians of the dangers of lust or female sexuality. Whatever the truth of this view, her presence near doors and windows in secular houses suggests that she was seen as a talisman, having magic powers to protect the owners. By the time of the Reformation, she had become a source of embarrassment for clergy, who issued orders for destroying the images.

Given the repressive official Free State views of female sexuality, Sheela-na-gig became an important figure to many late twentieth-century Irish feminists. Hag or witch or displaced goddess, she was the perfect image with which to counter all of those blue and white plaster statues that taught Irish children to associate the feminine with chaste motherhood. The influence of Sheela-na-gig reveals itself in some of Kathy Prendergast's body maps, and in an installation by Pauline Cummons and Louise Walsh called *Sounding the Depths,* in which a woman's body is reconstructed as three spaces. In one frequently reproduced image, we see a woman's torso, arms akimbo, topped with a giant open mouth from which protrudes a fleshy tongue in a pose of defiant display that recalls Sheela's. Eilis O'Connell has produced a number of sculptures that evoke female sexuality, such as "Cathoid," (1996) a curved object cast in blue lead crystal with a central, almond-shaped opening. "Enmeshed," (1994) an ellipsis woven of brass wire, uses the same motif. In a sculpture done in 1990, O'Connell created two long tapered columns of painted steel, titled "Hot with Inward Heat." From within the figure, a generator emits a cloud of steam. The sculpture was made for a site in England's Bath, where pre-Roman Celts viewed hot springs "as magical" and worshipped goddesses.[50]

ARCHITECTURE: PRESERVATION AND RESTORATION

For visitors, the Irish landscape seems like an architectural museum in which one moves from a seventh-century monastery to a Norman castle and then to a Big House, as the great Anglo-Irish estates are known locally. A temperate climate, failure to develop an industrial economy, and neutrality

Beautiful Georgian door in what was once an urban slum. © Guidescapes.com.

during World War II all contributed to the preservation of buildings that else-where were lost to bombs and aggressive development. Yet independence and modernization threatened parts of this legacy. Burning the Big House was an IRA strategy in 1919–1921. After independence, many Anglo-Irish left the country many others gave up their homes when taxes and upkeep became prohibitively expensive. Approximately 4,000 Georgian houses disappeared in the twentieth century, an irretrievable loss, but in some ways understand-able. It was all very well for Iris Murdoch, the Dublin-born novelist, to call Dublin's Georgian houses "the most beautiful buildings ever constructed to house the human spirit." But in their heyday, ordinary Irish people mainly saw their kitchens, stables, and servants' staircases. By the end of the nine-teenth century, Georgian houses had become, for many of the urban poor, damp, cold overcrowded tenements where everyone shared a few filthy priv-ies out back. Even in 1974, a Georgian enthusiast who bought such a house found 36 families living under its roof.[51] Such people might well be slow to claim Georgian squares as cherished reminders of their past, a point that may explain the demolition of houses on Fitzwilliam Street, the world's longest "Georgian mile," to clear office space in the mid-1950s.

With the new prosperity of the last 25 years has come a housing boom that brought thousands of garish new buildings to the suburbs and countryside. These not only exacerbated the nation's traffic problems, but threaten to destroy some of its most beautiful landscapes. The strenuous efforts of Desmond and Mariga Guinness and the Irish Georgian Society, which they founded, had been highlighting the need to preserve the legacy since the 1950s. The Irish gov-ernment's *Action on Architecture 2002–2005* plan, which promises state over-sight of the "built environment," along with a commitment to "conserve and maintain ... the architectural heritage" testifies to the Guinness's influence. At least as significantly, Irish architects have responded creatively to the need for imaginative renovation and the construction of new houses that enhance their immediate environment, whether it is a street of historical houses or a moun-tain valley. Although a glance through any recent issue of *New Irish Architecture* will reveal many glass, steel, and timber buildings that might be found in any modern city, what is most distinctive in contemporary design are adaptations that incorporate elements of classic Georgian or vernacular architecture with elements designed to meet contemporary safety codes, provide access for the disabled, and allow technology to operate. Whether it is renovating a man-sion, converting early nineteenth-century worker's houses into modern, livable spaces, or building a new house that incorporates the lines and colors of a tradi-tional cottage, Irish architects have demonstrated ingenuity and skill.

Named after the four English kings who reigned from 1714 to 1830, Georgian architecture was inspired by the classical villas, many designed by the Renaissance architect Andrea Palladio, that English noblemen found in Italy when they made their Grand Tours. Externally, it is an architecture that values restraint, symmetry, and harmony. The eighteenth century "rule of taste" dictated that "there must be sufficient spaces left plain so that the ornament in proper places may be more conspicuous and may have their desired effect."[52] Federal, or "colonial" architecture in the United States is one version of Georgian; Irish Georgian, according to one connoisseur, is "less pompous and more ascetic than its English counterpart ... perhaps purer translation of the classical heritage on which the Georgian 'rule of taste' was based."[53] A feature for which many Irish houses are celebrated is their elaborate plaster work, stucco designs, and figures that appear on ceilings and walls or, as at Russborough House in County Kildare, inside a large recessed cupola known as a "lantern." This plasterwork was the "ornament" that, with the vivid colors in which rooms were often painted, set off their plain lines. The excesses of Russborough, however, dismayed one Englishman brought in to decorate it, who observed that the stucco in the stairwell "represents the ravings of a lunatic, and an Irishman at that!"[54] In Dublin's Georgian squares, the "ornament" most visible from the outside was a fanlight above a brightly painted door, its curved "Palladian" lines as much a contrast with the rectangular brick walls as the door's bright color with the dark gray of the bricks.

The Irish Georgian Society raised money to help people purchase and restore historic houses. Much work went into tracing the origins of silk wall coverings and finding artisans who could replace curved glass windows or stabilize "flying" (cantilevered) staircases. Because of the expense and difficulty of restoration, many of the larger houses are still works in progress. A visitor to Castletown House in County Kildare will tour a dozen nearly perfectly recreated studies, portrait galleries, boudoirs, and dining rooms but catch glimpses of other rooms, once equally grand, now bare and bleak, with stained wallpaper and tattered curtains. The state now supports Castletown and many other Anglo-Irish houses. There is also growing pride in the skills Irish artisans contributed to the building of these houses. A visitor to Russborough will now be told that a local man, Henry Kelly, carved its great wooden staircase.

While the Irish Georgian Society homes represent faithful reconstruction and retention of period features—the Guinness home, Leixlip Castle, lacks central heating—a more free-wheeling combination of restoration and adaptation characterizes Temple Bar, a colorful district that begins just south of the River Liffey in central Dublin. In the late 1970s, when the area was in sharp decline, the Irish state transportation company, CIE (Córas Iompair Éireann), started buying up property to build a national bus station. In the meantime, it rented out the dilapidated property, quickly filling the area with artists, writers, musicians, and start-up businesses selling organic food and hip clothing. Without intending to do so, CIE had created a vital alternative-culture quarter for the city, and a growing lobby resisted plans to replace it with a bus terminal. Yielding to pressure, in 1991 the Irish government created a company called Temple Bar Properties to oversee its development and ensure that its distinctive atmosphere remained intact. Group 91, a consortium of eight architectural firms, won the bid to proceed with a major urban renewal project aimed at balancing modernization and preservation, commercial, and residential space. With the help of funds from the European Union, and after five years in which Temple Bar seemed "one giant construction site," the first phase of this ambitious and imaginative urban renewal project was complete.[55]

To its admirers, Temple Bar is a model of successful development. An area that outsiders shunned has become a tourist attraction. Small music shops, theaters, galleries, and design firms prosper. Temple Bar retains its emphasis on locally owned small businesses. Restaurants and coffee houses abound, but Starbuck's and TGI Friday's remain conspicuously absent. A Presbyterian Meeting House built in 1725 is now the Ark, a "children's cultural center"; the former headquarters of the Society of Friends now houses the Irish Film Centre and the National Photographic Archive. Another eighteenth-century building, originally a china warehouse, now houses Designyard, a center for the applied arts. Approximately 2,000 people now live in such stylish buildings as the white and black Printworks, which features "ten apartment laid out around a ... courtyard over shops and showrooms at the street level."[56] The wholly new timber-covered Wooden Building, which contains 191 apartments, has contemporary features such as a central tower with large windows, but its restrained lines allow it to seem perfectly at home in a neighborhood that includes Georgian brick. Soon after the completion of its first phase in 1995, Temple Bar "came to be featured in architectural and lifestyle magazines across the world," both because of the high quality of its architecture and because it epitomized the new Ireland: forward-looking, prosperous, and cosmopolitan.

Meeting House Square transformed a dreary parking lot into "an outdoor room" where, weather permitting, music and theater can be performed. It is even possible to project films from the Photographic Archive building onto the "screen facade" of the Gallery of Photography."[57] The adjacent Irish Film Centre provides a striking example of how Group 91 mixed preservation and innovation. Cinema 1, a 250-seat film theater, set in the former Quaker Meeting Room, retains its almost starkly simple lines. Its lovely Palladian windows, although blocked on the outside by sound-proofing panels, still catch the eye. Rather than disfigure the room with contemporary technological equipment, the builders designed a maple cabinet to contain it. On the other hand, the Film Centre's foyer, which incorporates three walls from the old buildings and the wall of a new building containing offices and a restaurant, deliberately contrasts the contemporary with the traditional. A visitor enters and immediately glances up at a very contemporary steel and glass roof that zigzags across the space between the three old brick walls and the new plaster wall. The limestone floor is decorated with a series of concentric steel circles, and a sign proclaiming "Tickets" in blue neon rather redundantly explains the function of the semicircular office with the wide open window that projects outward from the new wall.

After all of the publicity attendant on Temple Bar's revitalization, criticism was inevitable. One critic deplores the partnership between commerce and culture that made its development possible, believing that Temple Bar demonstrates how "the production, distribution and consumption of arts and culture operate as a cover for capitalist expansion."[58] The critic points out that the Irish Film Centre's construction involved the demolition of all but the front wall of the old Presbyterian Meeting House. When excavations found artifacts from the Viking era, rather than protecting the site, the Dublin Tourist Board created a "multimedia presentation for a new Viking Adventure Center," and displayed the old artifacts selectively. The result is seen as a "mini-theme park" in which the Irish heritage is repackaged for tourist consumption.[59] And even if one argues that the Viking artifacts might well have spent another 1,000 years under the urban wasteland if Temple Bar remained undeveloped, it is clear that renovation meant gentrification. By March 2000, when a "duplex penthouse" in the Wooden Building sold for the equivalent of more than $8 million, it was obvious that today's starving artists were priced out of the neighborhood. As tourists flocked in, the number of restaurants, hotels, and bars increased dramatically, the latter causing residents to complain that streets were clogged with "English stag-party types" on a "seemingly endless pub crawl."[60] Since 1997, the city has responded by refusing to approve further applications for liquor licenses in Temple Bar and went to court when the owner of a hotel opened a huge new bar on his premises.

Living Spaces: Vernacular Architecture and Bungalow Bliss

While landlords lived in their Georgian houses, most Irish people lived in one- or two-room cottages made out of stones from the nearest field, the chinks filled in with mud and clay. The English imposed a window tax, so windows were kept to a minimum. The traditional roof was thatched; in windier areas, stone weights kept it from blowing out to sea. Seen from the

The Irish rural cottage at its most charming: The birthplace in County Tyrone of the nineteenth-century novelist William Carleton. Courtesy of Linda Sichenze.

outside, a white-washed cottage with a thatched roof is an idyllic sight, set off by the gray Atlantic or a vividly green field. Living in such a crowded space, often with the family pig and a smoking fire, was of course another matter. As farm families became more prosperous, they added rooms, floors, and windows. They plastered and painted walls, and acquired a cast-iron stove and some simple furniture. More prosperous farmers built two-story, square houses. Cement block construction, with a coat of plaster and paint or stucco ("pebble and dash"), and slate roofs kept the spare outlines that the great Georgian houses shared with the thatched cottage. House colors were typically sober: whites, grays, light browns. In small towns, many people lived in equally simple row houses. Even the worst of Dublin's slums were often semiconcealed behind Georgian facades. It is true that harshly ornate red-brick Victorian architecture appealed to some of the upwardly mobile, and it is certainly true that the wretched poverty in which many people lived was undisguised in the grim and dilapidated tenements of Limerick or Derry or Belfast. But on the whole, Irish architecture was aesthetically pleasing; its lines and colors suited the grays and greens of the landscape.

As prosperity came to Ireland, so did the desire for modern housing, central heating, and electric appliances. Most families had relatives in the United States, and the suburban taste of New Jersey and California made its way back to Ireland, carrying an aura of success and prosperity. Jack Fitzsimons's influential *Bungalow Bliss,* first published in 1972 and reissued several times, convinced thousands of people to adopt new styles. Bright colors, huge picture windows, tile roofs, and stone facings in garish new patterns, including one known locally as "crazy paving," became the rule. Had they been built in the United States, such houses would have been clustered together in subdivisions, hidden from the eye of casual visitors. But small Irish towns had always been built on a single street, and as new houses were added, they often went up along the main road into town: urban straggle, if not quite urban sprawl. And as cloverleafs and bypasses are largely unknown, that main street was almost always the only road in and out of town. Travelers from Galway to Dublin would be forced to slow down to 25 miles an hour every time they encountered a village. Such pauses gave them plenty of time to focus on the defects of local taste and to lament the passing of the traditional landscape.

And indeed the rapid expansion of bungalow Ireland created problems for the environment and for the tourist industry. A stretch of Atlantic Coast north of Galway has almost been blocked from view by new construction, which includes holiday houses and trailer camps, as well as local housing. One could hardly ask people to live in damp cold cottages because tourists find them picturesque, but neither could one count on the free market to keep Ireland beautiful. In 1990, the state tourist board published a pamphlet for would-be home builders entitled *Building Sensitively in Ireland's Landscapes.* Focusing on Connemara, the authors made a number of recommendations intended to discourage people from building houses that obstruct scenic views and to encourage them to imitate the simple lines, soft colors, and native materials of traditional Irish houses. Noting the wisdom of traditional builders who protected houses by building them in recessed or sheltered areas, the authors provide advice for choosing sites and constructing inconspicuous driveways.

In-Between House in Ballinamore, County Leitrim, built in 2003 and designed by Dominic Stevens, provides a good example of this recommended approach. When a couple who worked at home decided to move to a hillside over a lake, the architect decided to built a house in "a collection of pieces" that could sit "in the landscape"; he wanted it to have the "scale and material simplicity ... [of] rural Irish vernacular houses."[61] From a distance one sees a grouping of white-washed, one-story buildings that might well be a farm cottage with its various outbuildings, although close inspection reveals that each building has a contemporary roofline that slants down sharply between back and front walls of unequal heights. The architects not only intended to make the house fit in the landscape and preserve distinctively Irish lines, but they wanted it to allow the couple to separate their work and living areas. Between the houses, they provided both open and glassed-in "in-between" spaces that would be "charged with atmosphere" but not defined in terms of their use: "hillside becomes entrance space becomes reading corner becomes gathering space." A team of reviewers found fault with details but seemed to agree that the project represents "social . . . and political courage."[62]

HOUSING FOR THE POOR

However much one may cringe at seeing a mustard-colored pile with a Spanish tile roof and a large satellite dish near the banks of the Shannon, the Celtic Tiger has raised the standard of housing for many people. Current property prices, however, are high. In this respect, the greater Dublin area resembles California's Bay Area, and although prices are less inflated elsewhere, a couple looking for a four-bedroom house in Limerick is likely to pay twice as much as they would in the American Midwest. When a three-bedroom bungalow costs half a million dollars, even schoolteachers, nurses, and police officers may be unable to live near the places they work, and only charity or a government subsidy can protect the unskilled or unemployed from homelessness. Moreover, a tax structure similar in most respects to that in the United States has enabled the Republic to attain the highest rate of home ownership in the Economic Union, almost 80 percent in 1997.[63] The result is a tight rental market in which the needs of the poor can be addressed only through public housing and grants. In recent years, when demand for decent housing has exceeded supply, public housing is increasingly the domain of those with the highest incidence of unemployment, psychiatric disorders, and addictions. Another problem, again not unique to Ireland, is the clustering of people with the lowest incomes and worst problems in blocks of publicly owned apartments that breed crime and low expectations. In 1998, more than 150,000 persons were in dire need of housing and the situation is similar today.[64]

The Irish have no more solved this problem than have other prosperous societies, but there have been a few encouraging developments. Many people believe that the Temple Bar model, where the inner-city combines living, working, and shopping space, not only offers the best solution to the commuting problems of the middle class, but the best model for humane public housing. It is of interest, then, that one of projects receiving a special mention in 2004's Irish architectural competition was Allinett's Lane Apartments in Cork city, a "local authority" or public housing project. An "urban infill project," the two buildings harmonize perfectly with older painted plaster buildings on one of the city's steep streets. M. V. Cullinan Architects set out to prove that "higher-density development" need not result in "loss of privacy or amenity."[65] As in some of the expensive Temple Bar renovations, the back of the building has been turned into a courtyard. Each apartment has large windows facing out on the courtyard, enabling the residents to enjoy some of the advantages of contemporary building without disrupting the appearance of the street. Small balconies off each apartment provide "drying racks" for laundry, and there is screened-in space for bicycles. Although experts note that the detailing and exterior suffer from the builder's low budget, the building is attractive and appears to anticipate its residents' needs; an American architect, for example, might have assumed that low-income families have access to a clothes drier.

The state has also moved to improve housing for travellers. In 1993, a partnership between architects, government officials, and travellers in the Republic and Northern Ireland produced a series of designs for new open housing sites. The architects who entered the President Robinson competition for the design of Travellers' accommodation recognized that attempts to force travellers into housing projects had often failed. They knew they would need to understand the travellers' cultural identity, which meant not only nomadism but an emphasis on "the extended family and the combination of living and working space."[66] As in the Temple Bar designs, modern requirements for safety and comfort would need to be balanced against respect for a tradition. One award-winning design created a private space for each family with "bermed earth." Each space contained a "large roof covering the main living space and caravan

Many travellers still live in squalid housing. © *Irish Times*.

(mobile home)." Another semicircular plan combined six bays to accommodate 12 caravans, with a "facilities buildings" containing kitchen, bathroom, and laundry between each of the bays.[67] Landscaping provided additional privacy and, in most cases, concealed mobile homes from passers-by.

Two years after the competition, in 1995, the Irish government accepted a report from its Task Force on the Travelling Community and committed itself to construct accommodation for more than 3,000 families in a five-year plan. Partly because of the animus of the settled community against such projects, this plan proved far too optimistic. By 2000, only 99 units had actually been provided.[68] Perhaps Mary Robinson's goal, that the plans produced for the competition should also serve as "blueprints for a better understanding ... between our settled way of life and this fascinating and different culture that must be valued before it is understood," will be achieved in the twenty-first century.[69]

NOTES

1. The painting is reproduced in Kenneth McConkey, *A Free Spirit: Irish Art 1860–1960,* Antique Collectors' Club (London: Pyms Gallery, 1990), 106.

2. A full-page color reproduction of *The Man of Aranmore* (sometimes called *The Man of Inishmore*) is on page 61 of John Booth's *A Vision of Ireland* (Nairn, Scotland: Thomas and Lochar, 1992).

3. John Synge, *The Aran Islands,* with drawings by Jack B. Yeats (Belfast: Blackstaff, [1906] 1988). Image opposite 56; quotation from 57.

4. The oil painting is reproduced in McConkey, 159. The quotation from Henry comes from McConkey, 160.

5. Brian P. Kennedy, *Irish Painting* (Dublin: Town House and Country House, 1993), 35. The quotation in the sentence that follows is from the same page.

6. Kennedy, 34.

7. Kelly, 13. He is quoting Robert Ballagh on Keating's "exoticism."

8. McGonagle, 11.

9. James M. Smith, "Retelling Stories; Exposing Mother Ireland in Kathy Prendergast's *Body Map Series* and Mary Leland's *The Killeen*." In *Re/Dressing Cathleen: Contemporary Works from Irish Women Artists,* Jennifer Grinnell and Alston Conley, eds. (Boston: McMullen Museum of Art, Boston College, 1997), 44. I am indebted to Smith for much of the analysis that follows.

10. Smith, 45.

11. Christina Bridgwater, "Poetic Land–Political Territory," in *Poetic Land–Political Territory* (Sunderland: Northern Centre for Contemporary Art, 1995). The text is unpaginated and no editor is specified. A full-page color reproduction of O'Dowd's "Over by Clogher Bay" is included in the book.

12. Christina Bridgwater, Christina. "Poetic Land–Political Territory." The text is unpaginated. "Enclosure on a Mountain" is reproduced in the book.

13. Bruce Arnold, *Mainie Jellett and the Modern Movement in Ireland* (New Haven, Conn.: Yale University Press, 1991), 204.

14. Arnold, 53.

15. Arnold, 56.

16. Arnold, 64.

17. Arnold, 80.

18. Quoted from a lecture on French painting given in October 1939 for the opening of Jack Longford's Exhibition of Contemporary Paintings in Dublin, Arnold, 169.

19. *Three Irish Women Painters,* 2. No author given.

20. The terms "Grey Period" and "White Paintings" are used by Smith, 12–13.

21. Alistair Smith, "Louis le Brocquy: On the Spiritual in Art," in Brenda Mc Parland, et al., *Louis le Brocquy: Paintings 1939–1996* (Dublin: Irish Museum of Modern Art, 1996), 33. "Family"(1951) is reproduced in full color on 22; "Man Writing" (1951) on 18; "A Sickness"/"Family Illness"(1951) on 19. All are oil paintings on canvas.

22. Quoted in Smith, 36.

23. Quoted in Smith, 13.

24. This discussion of "shadow" as a theme and technique is drawn from Smith, 13.

25. Smith, 16.

26. Smith, 37–41 provides a discussion of le Brocquy's interest in "head cults," from which the paragraph that follows is drawn.

27. Quoted in Smith, 41.

28. Walker, 127.

29. Jean Fisher, *The Enigma of the Hero in the Work of James Coleman* (Dublin: Orchard Gallery, 1983), 10.

30. Walker, 138.

31. "Sean Scully interviewed by Irving Sandler," in *Sean Scully: Paintings* (Manchester: Manchester City Art Galleries, 1997), 42.

32. Armine Zweite, "To Humanize Abstract Painting: Reflections on Sean Scully's "'Stone Light,'" in *Sean Scully: Twenty Years, 1976–1995,* ed. Ned Rifkin (London: Thames and Hudson, 1995), 22.

33. Quoted in Carter Ratcliff, "Sean Scully: The Constitutive Stripe," 9.

34. Mark Glazebrook, *Sean Scully: The Catherine Paintings* (Fort Worth, Tex.: Modern Museum of Fort Worth, 1993).

35. Zweite, 22. See also "Sean Scully: Summarising Living and Painting," in *Sean Scully Paintings* (Manchester: Manchester City Art Galleries, 1997), 8, 9.

36. "Interview with Sean Scully," 20 May 1994, Ned Rifkin, ed., in Ned Rifkin, *Sean Scully: Twenty Years, 1976–1995* (London: Thames and Hudson, 1995), 66.

37. Colin Coulter, *Contemporary Northern Irish Society: An Introduction* (London: Pluto, 1999), 72.

38. "Thinking North," foreword to Liam Kelly, *Thinking Long: Contemporary Art in the North of Ireland,* Gandon Editions (Kinsale, County Cork: Oysterhaven, 1996), 6. O'Doherty paints under the name "Patrick Ireland."

39. See Neil Jarman, "Painting Landscapes: the Place of Murals in the Symbolic Construction of Urban Space," in Anthony Buckley, *Symbols in Northern Ireland*

(Belfast: Institute of Irish Studies, Queen's University, 1998), 84, 85. In the eyes of the local authorities, these were subversive symbols of a foreign power. An American visitor to Belfast in 1997, accustomed to viewing the Irish tricolor flag as a benign ethnic symbol, expressed surprise at seeing armed police and soldiers taking it away from unarmed demonstrators. To soldiers and police, however, it seemed a deliberate provocation, akin to waving the flag of Castro's Cuba in the heart of Miami's Little Havana.

40. Murals are of course vulnerable to weather and urban renewal. Some have also been painted over. This figure comes from Neil Jarman, to whom I am also indebted for the description of how contemporary mural painters work.

41. Oona Woods, *Seeing Is Believing? Murals in Derry* (Derry: Guildhall Press, 1995). The mural described in the next sentence appears on page 34 of Woods' book.

42. Artists Belfast, *Glimpse: Contemporary Visual Art by Artists Based in the Belfast Studio Complexes* (Belfast: Queens Street Studios, 1999), 12.

43. Declan McGonagle, "Renegotiating the Given," in Declan McGonagle et al., *Irish Art Now: From the Poetic to the Political* (London: Merrell Holberton, 1999), 12.

44. McGonagle, 11.

45. Dorothy Walker, *Modern Art in Ireland* (Dublin: Lilliput, 1997), 189.

46. Judith Hill, *Irish Public Sculpture: A History* (Dublin: Four Courts), 1998.

47. Frank McDonald, *The Construction of Dublin* (Kinsale: Gandon, 2000), 98

48. Vera Ryan, "An Interview with Conor Fallon," in *Conor Fallon: Monograph 1* (Kinsale: Gandon, 1996), 21, 22.

49. Joanne McMahon and Jack Roberts, *The Sheela-na-gigs of Ireland and Britain: The Divine Hag of the Christian Celts* (Cork: Mercier Press, 2000), 15, 16. Sheela is Irish for "Julia"; "na" probably is the possessive pronoun, "of the." But "gig" has no precise equivalent in Irish Gaelic.

50. Pamela Berger, "Modern Propagators of Ancient Legends and Traditions: Mythic Memory or Serendipity?" in Grinnell, 60. Berger's comment is based on an interview with O'Connell.

51. Herbert Ypma, *Irish Georgian* (London: Thames and Hudson, 1998), 56.

52. Ypma, 34.

53. Ypma, 13.

54. Ypma, 91.

55. Temple Bar Properties Ltd. *Dublin's Cultural Quarter: Temple Bar* (Dublin: Temple Bar Properties, 2002), 13.

56. McDonald, 292.

57. McDonald, 103.

58. Mary Corcoran, "The Re-enchantment of Temple Bar," in *Encounters with Modern Ireland: A Sociological Chronicle 1995–1996,* ed. Michel Peillon and Eamonn Slater (Dublin: Institute of Public Administration, 1998), 13.

59. Corcoran, 10.

60. Mc Donald, 282. It must be a sign of increased cultural confidence that an Irish journalist feels comfortable stereotyping alcoholics as British.

61. *New Irish Architecture 19. AAI Awards 2004.* "In-Between House, Ballinamore, Co. Leitrim," 192. The quotation in the next sentence is also from this page.

62. *New Irish Architecture,* 19, 196.

63. P. J. Drudy and Michael Punch, "Housing and Inequality in Ireland," in *Rich and Poor: Perspectives on Tackling Inequality in Ireland,* ed. Sara Cantillon et al. (Dublin: Oak Tree, 2002), 237.

64. Drudy, 245.

65. "Allinett's Lane Apartments, Cork," in *New Irish Architecture* 19 (2004): 146–151.

66. John O'Connell, "Travellers' Accommodation—Past and Present," in *The President Robinson Awards for the Design of Travellers' Accommodation* (Dublin: Pavee Point Publications, 1993), 11.

67. *The President Robinson Awards,* 24, 26.

68. Sean O'Riain, *Solidarity with Travellers: A Story of Settled People Making a Stand for Travellers* (Dublin: Roadside Books, 2000).

69. Mary Robinson, "Preface," *The President Robinson Awards,* 5.

Glossary

Belfast Agreement   Also known as the "Good Friday agreement." Plan for a peaceful Northern Ireland with its own Assembly elected by proportional representation.

Dail Eireann   Lower house of the Parliament of the Republic. Like the British House of Commons, it is popularly elected and holds most of the legislative power.

DUP   Democratic Unionist Party. Founded by Ian Paisley, a conservative movement attracting primarily Protestants who find the Ulster Unionist Party too liberal.

the Emergency   War years, 1939–1945, when Eire remained neutral.

Erin   Poetic name for Ireland, from the Irish Éirinn.

Feis   Step-dancing competition.

Fianna Fail   Bills itself as "the Republican party."   Emerged from the anti-Treaty side in the civil war; in practice a centrist conservative party.

Fine Gael   Republic's second largest party; formed from a coalition that included the pro-Treaty Cumann na nGhaedhael party and several others, including the fascist Blue Shirts. In practice, a centrist conservative party.

the Free State   1922–1937; designation for the 26 counties of Ireland that formed an independent state after the Treaty of 1922. The name was changed to Eire in the new constitution of 1937; the name Republic of Ireland was adopted in 1949.

gaeltacht   Officially designated Irish speaking areas of the Republic of Ireland, mostly in the West

garda   Garda Síochána, "The Guardians of the Peace." Police force of the Republic.

loyalist   Person loyal to the British government; used by more radical Unionists in Northern Ireland, often actively hostile to the Catholic Church and the Republic of Ireland.

nationalist   Person who wishes Ireland to be an independent country. In today's North a synonym for "Catholic," although historically nationalists came from all of the Irish communities.

Oireachtas   Legislature, consisting of two houses, Dail Eireann and Seanad Eireann.

Orange Order   An interdenominational Protestant fraternal order established in the eighteenth century

the Pale   First used in 14th century for fortified area around Dublin subject to English rule. Borders shifted with political events but "beyond the Pale" designates areas under the control of the Irish chieftains in the sixteenth and seventeenth centuries.

Republican   In popular use, synonymous with "nationalist"; someone who wants a separate Irish Republic

RTE   Radio Telefís Eireann, the Republic's state-sponsored television and radio service.

SDLP   Northern Ireland's Social Democratic and Labour Party. A nationalist party that supports the Belfast Agreement.

The Seanad   Senate. An advisory body loosely comparable to the British House of Lords: 11 of its members are selected by the Taoiseach; 6 are elected by graduates of Ireland's two largest universities; the remaining 43 are popularly elected from five panels of experts in such fields as education and agriculture nominated by members of the Dail, senators, and local officials.

sean-nos   Old style.

Sinn Fein   "Ourselves alone," in early twentieth century, revolutionary party associated with IRA; in 2005 displaced the SDLP as the majority party of Catholics in Northern Ireland

Taoiseach   Irish for "chieftain," the Irish prime minister.

Troubles   Euphemism used for the civil war (1922–1923) between victorious Republicans, which followed Independence. In contemporary usage, refers to violence between Catholics and Protestants in Northern Ireland that broke out in 1969.

Unionist   Person loyal to the British government. Today's moderate Unionists advocate incorporating the North into the political culture of England, Scotland, and Wales, that is, into a multicultural, liberal, and, for all practical purposes, secular state.

UUP   Ulster Unionist Party; traditional party of most Protestants in Northern Ireland; in power for most of Northern Ireland's history.

Bibliography

Allen, Darina. *The Complete Book of Irish Country Cooking*. New York: Penguin, 1995.

Aretxaga, Begoña. *Shattering Silence: Women, Nationalism, and Political Subjectivity in Northern Ireland*. Princeton, N.J.: Princeton University Press, 1997.

Arnold, Bruce. *Irish Art: A Concise History*. Rev. ed. London: Thames and Hudson, 1989.

Arnold, Bruce. *Mainie Jellett and the Modern Movement in Ireland*. New Haven, Conn.: Yale University Press, 1991.

Arts Council/An Chomhairle Ealaion. *Irish Art: The European Dimension*. Dublin: Boethius, 1990.

Artists Belfast. *Glimpse: Contemporary Visual Art by Artists Based in the Belfast Studio Complexes*. Belfast: Queens Street Studios, 1999.

Asbee, Sue. *Flann O'Brien*. Boston: Twayne, 1991.

Barton, Ruth. *Irish National Cinema*. London: Routledge, 2004.

Barton, Ruth, and Harvey O'Brien, eds. *Keeping It Real: Irish Film and Television*. London: Wallflower P, 2004.

Becker, Annette, et al. *Twentieth-Century Architecture: Ireland*. Munich: Prestel, 1997.

Beckett, Samuel. *Krapp's Last Tape: Modern Irish Drama*. Ed. John P. Harrington. New York: Norton, 1991.

Bolger, Dermot. *The Journey Home*. London: Flamingo-HarperCollins, 2003.

Booth, John. *A Vision of Ireland*. Nairn, Scotland: Thomas and Lochar, 1992.

Bradley, Anthony, and Maryann Gialanella Valiulis, eds. *Gender and Sexuality in Modern Ireland*. Amherst: University of Massachusetts Press, 1997.

Bridgwater, Christina. *Poetic Land—Political Territory*. Sunderland: Northern Centre for Contemporary Art, 1995.

Broderick, Desmond, and Garry Shiel. *Diet and Activity Patterns of Children in Primary Schools in Ireland.* Dublin: St. Patrick's College, 2000.

Brown, William. *An Army with Banners: The Real Face of Orangeism.* Belfast: Beyond the Pale, 2003.

Bryan, Dominic. *Orange Parades: The Politics of Ritual, Tradition and Control.* London: Pluto, 2000.

Buckley, Anthony, ed. *Symbols in Northern Ireland.* Belfast: Institute of Irish Studies, Queen's University, 1998.

Burton, Frank. *The Politics of Legitimacy: Struggles in a Belfast Community.* London: Routledge and Kegan Paul, 1978.

Byrne, Terry. *Power in the Eye: An Introduction to Contemporary Irish Film.* Lanham, Md.: Scarecrow, 1997.

Campbell, Matthew. *The Cambridge Companion to Contemporary Irish Poetry.* Cambridge: Cambridge University Press, 2003.

Canning, Veronica. *Working Women in Ireland: Your Guide to Coping with Pregnancy and Motherhood.* Dublin: Blackhall, 1998.

Cantillon, Sara et al. *Rich and Poor: Perspectives on Tackling Inequality in Ireland.* Dublin: Oak Tree, 2001.

Carr, Marina. *By the Bog of Cats.* Loughcrew, Ireland: The Gallery Press, 1998.

Carroll, Michael P. *Irish Pilgrimage: Holy Wells and Popular Catholic Devotion.* Baltimore: Johns Hopkins University Press, 1999.

Clayton-Lea, Tony, and Richie Taylor. *Irish Rock: Where It's Come from, Where It's At, Where It's Going.* London: Sidgwick and Jackson, 1992.

Cleary, Joe, and Claire Connolly, eds. *The Cambridge Companion to Modern Irish Culture.* Cambridge: Cambridge University Press, 2005.

Coakley, John, ed. *Changing Shades of Orange and Green: Redefining the Union and the Nation in Contemporary Ireland.* Dublin: University College Dublin Press, 2002.

Cohen, Marilyn, and Nancy J. Curtin, eds. *Reclaiming Gender: Transgressive Identities in Modern Ireland.* London: Macmillan, 1999.

Colgan, Karina. *You Have to Scream with Your Mouth Shut: Violence in the Home.* Dublin: Marino-Mercier, 1995.

Comerford, R. V. *Ireland.* Inventing the Nation Series. London: Arnold, 2003.

Connolly, Claire, ed. *Theorizing Ireland.* Readers in Cultural Criticism. Basingstoke, Hampshire: Palgrave, 2003.

Connolly, S. J. *The Oxford Companion to Irish History.* 2nd edition. Oxford: Oxford University Press, 2002.

Connor, Sean. *Youth Sport in Ireland: The Sporting, Leisure and Lifestyle Patterns of Irish Adolescents.* Dublin: Liffey, 2003.

Coogan, Tim Pat. *Ireland in the Twentieth Century.* London: Hutchinson-Random, 2003.

Cooke, Dennis. *Persecuting Zeal: A Portrait of Ian Paisley.* Dingle, Co. Kerry, Ireland: Brandon, 1996.

Corcoran, Farrel. *RTE and the Globalisation of Irish Television.* Bristol: Intellect, 2004.

Corcoran, Mary. "The Re-enchantment of Temple Bar." In *Encounters with Modern Ireland: A Sociological Chronicle 1995–1996,* ed. Michel Peillon and Eammon Slater. Dublin: Institute of Public Administration, 1998.

Corcoran, Mary, and Mark O'Brien, eds. *Democratic Censorship and the Democratic State.* Dublin: Four Courts, 2005.

Corcoran, Neil. *After Yeats and Joyce: Reading Modern Irish Literature.* Oxford: Oxford University Press, 1997.

Coulter, Colin. *Contemporary Northern Irish Society: An Introduction.* London: Pluto, 1999.

Cullen, Paul. *Refugees and Asylum Seekers in Ireland.* Cork: Cork University Press, 2000.

Daly, Mary E. *Women and Work in Ireland: Studies in Irish Economic and Social History.* Dublin: Dundalgan, 1997.

Davies, Gordon L. Herries. "The Concept of Ireland." In *The Shaping of Ireland: The Geographical Perspective,* edited by William Nolan. Dublin: Mercier, 1986.

Davis, E., and R. Sinnot. *Attitudes in the Republic of Ireland Relevant to the Northern Ireland Problem.* Dublin: Economic and Social Research Institute, 1979.

Deane, Seamus. *The Field Day Anthology of Irish Writing.* 3 vols. Derry: Field Day Publications, 1991.

Doyle, Paddy. *The God Squad: A Remarkable True Story.* London: Corgi, 1988.

Duddy, Thomas. *A History of Irish Thought.* London: Routledge, 2002.

Eagleton, Terry. *The Truth about the Irish.* Dublin: New Island, 1999.

Edwards, Ruth Dudley. *The Faithful Tribe: An Intimate Portrait of the Loyal Institutions.* London: HarperCollins, 1999.

Fahey, Tony, and Dorothy Watson. *An Analysis of Social Housing Need.* Dublin: The Economic and Social Research Institute, 1995.

Fahey, Tony, and John Fitz Gerald. *Welfare Implications of Demographic Trends.* Dublin: Oak Tree, 1997.

Fahey, Tony, and Maureen Lyons. *Marital Breakdown and Family Law in Ireland: A Sociological Study.* Dublin: Oak Tree, 1995.

Fallon, Brian. *Irish Art 1830–1990.* Belfast: Appletree, 1994.

Fallon, Peter, and Derek Mahon, eds. *The Penguin Book of Contemporary Irish Poetry.* London: Penguin, 1990.

Fallon, Peter, and Sean Golden, eds. *Soft Day: A Miscellany of Contemporary Irish Writing.* Notre Dame, Ind. University of Notre Dame Press, 1980.

Fanning, Bryan. *Racism and Social Change in the Republic of Ireland.* Manchester: Manchester University Press, 2002.

Farrell, Antony et al., eds. *My Generation: Rock'n'Roll Remembered: An Imperfect History.* Dublin: Lilliput, 1996.

Ferriter, Diarmaid. *A Nation of Extremes: The Pioneers in Twentieth-Century Ireland.* Dublin: Irish Academic Press, 1999.

Finnegan, Frances. *Do Penance or Perish: A Study of Magdalen Asylums in Ireland.* Piltown, Co. Kerry: Congrave Press, 2001.

Finnegan, Richard B., and Edward T. McCarron. *Ireland: Historical Echoes, Contemporary Politics.* Boulder, Col.: Westview, 2000.

Fisher, Jean. *The Enigma of the Hero in the Work of James Coleman.* Dublin: Orchard Gallery, 1983.

FitzGerald, Garret. *Reflections on the Irish State.* Dublin: Irish Academic Press, 2003.

Flannery, Tony. *From the Inside: A Priest's View of the Catholic Church.* Cork: Mercier, 1999.

Forkner, Ben, ed. *Modern Irish Short Stories.* Middlesex, England: Penguin, 1980.

Friel, Brian. *Translations.* London: Faber and Faber, 1981.

Fuller, Louise. *Irish Catholicism since 1950: The Undoing of a Culture.* Dublin: Gill and Macmillan, 2002.

Geoghegan, Philip et al. *Building Sensitively in Ireland's Landscape.* Dublin: Bord Failte, 1990.

Gibbons, Luke. *Transformation in Irish Culture.* Critical Conditions: Field Day Essays. Notre Dame, Ind.: University of Notre Dame Press, 1996.

Gillespie, Raymond, and Brian P. Kennedy. *Ireland: Art into History.* Niwot, Col.: Roberts Rinehart, 1994.

Gillmor, Desmond, ed. *The Irish Countryside: Landscape, Wildlife, History, People.* Dublin: Wolfhound, 1989.

Glazebrook, Mark. *Sean Scully: The Catherine Paintings.* Fort Worth, Tex.: Modern Museum of Fort Worth, 1993.

Gowran, Sandra. *Counted Out: Challenging Poverty and Social Exclusion.* City of Dublin Curriculum Development Unit. Dublin: Folens, 2002.

Graham, Brian, ed. *In Search of Ireland: A Cultural Geography.* London: Routledge, 1997.

Gray, A. M. et al. *Social Attitudes in Northern Ireland: The Eighth Report.* London: Pluto, 2002.

Greenwood, Amanda. *Edna O'Brien.* Tavistock, England: Northcote House, 2003.

Grene, Nicholas. *The Politics of Irish Drama: Plays in Context from Boucicault to Friel.* Cambridge: Cambridge University Press, 1999.

Grinnell, Jennifer, and Alston Conley, eds. *Re/Dressing Cathleen: Contemporary Works from Irish Women Artists.* Boston: McMullen Museum of Art, Boston College, 1997.

Haddick-Flynn, Kevin. *A Short History of Orangeism.* Cork: Mercier, 2002.

Hanafin, Patrick. *Constituting Identity: Political Identity Formation and the Constitution in Post-Independence Ireland.* Burlington, Vt.: Ashgate-Dartmouth, 2001.

Hand, Derek. *John Banville: Exploring Fictions.* Dublin: Liffey, 2002.

Harrington, John P. *Modern Irish Drama.* New York: Norton, 1991.

Harrington, John P., and Elizabeth J. Mitchell, eds. *Politics and Performance in Contemporary Northern Ireland.* Amherst: University of Massachusetts Press, 1999.

Harris, Nick. *Dublin's Little Jerusalem.* Dublin: A&A Farmar, 2002.

Hartnett, Michael. *Inchicore Haiku.* Dublin: Raven Arts, 1985.

Hayes, Alan, and Diane Urquhart. *The Women's History Reader.* New York: Routledge, 2001.

Heaney, Seamus. *Finders Keepers: Selected Prose 1971–2001*. New York: Farrar Straus, 2002.

Heaney, Seamus. *Opened Ground: Selected Poems 1966–1996*. New York: Farrar Straus, 1998.

Helleiner, Jane Leslie. *Irish Travellers: Racism and the Politics of Culture*. Toronto University Press, 2000.

Hemry, Mark, ed. *Chasing Danny Boy: Powerful Stories of Celtic Eros*. San Francisco: Palm Drive, 1999.

Hill, Judith. *Irish Public Sculpture: A History*. Dublin: Four Courts, 1998.

Horgan, John. *Broadcasting and Public Life: RTE News and Current Affairs: 1926–1997*. Dublin: Four Courts, 2004.

Horgan, John. *Irish Media: A Critical History Since 1922*. London: Routledge, 2001.

Houen, Alex. *Terrorism and Modern Literature, from Joseph Conrad to Ciaran Carson*. Oxford: Oxford University Press, 2002.

Hug, Chrystel. *The Politics of Sexual Morality in Ireland*. New York: St. Martin's, 1999.

Hyndman, Marilyn. *Further Afield: Journeys from a Protestant Past*. Belfast: Beyond the Pale, 1996.

Inglis, Tom. *Lessons in Irish Sexuality*. Dublin: UCD Press, 1998.

Inglis, Tom. *Moral Monopoly: The Rise and Fall of the Catholic Church in Modern Ireland*. Dublin: University College Dublin Press, 1998.

Irish Family Planning Association. *The Irish Journey: Women's Stories of Abortion*. Dublin: IFPA, 2000.

Johnson, James H. *The Human Geography of Ireland*. New York: John Wiley, 1994.

Johnson, Margaret M. *The Irish Heritage Cookbook*. San Francisco: Chronicle Books, 1999.

Joyce, James. *Dubliners: Text, Criticism, and Notes*. Ed. Scholes, Robert, and A. Walton Litz Harmondsworth, England: Penguin, 1968.

Kavanagh, Patrick. *Collected Poems*. New York: Norton, 1964.

Kearns, Kevin. *Dublin Pub Life and Lore: An Oral History*. Niwot, Colo: Roberts Rinehart, 1997.

Kelly, Aaron, and Alan A. Gillis, eds. *Critical Ireland: New Essays in Literature and Culture*. Dublin: Four Courts, 2001.

Kelly, Liam. *Thinking Long: Contemporary Art in the North of Ireland*. Oysterhaven, Kinsale, County Cork: 1996.

Kenny, Mary. *Abortion: The Whole Story*. London: Quartet Books, 1986.

Kenny, Mary. *Goodbye to Catholic Ireland: A Personal, Social, and Cultural History from the Fall of Parnell to the Realm of Mary Robinson*. London: Sinclair-Stevenson, 1997.

Kenny, Mary. *Goodbye to Catholic Ireland*. Rev. ed. Dublin: New Island, 2000.

Kiberd, Declan. *Inventing Ireland: The Literature of the Modern Nation*. Cambridge, Mass. Harvard University Press, 1996.

Kiberd, Declan. *Irish Classics*. Cambridge, Mass.: Harvard University Press, 2002.

Kiely, Gabriel, and Valerie Richardson. *Family Policy in Ireland–1993.* Report to European Observatory of National Family Policies. Brussels, Belgium: European Commission, 1994.

Kirby, Peadar, Luke Gibbons, and Michael Cronin, eds. *Reinventing Ireland: Culture, Society, and the Global Economy,* 3rd ed. London: Pluto, 2002.

Knight, Susan, ed. *Where the Grass Is Greener: Voices of Immigrant Women in Ireland.* Dublin: Oak Tree, 2001.

Knowles, Roderic. *Contemporary Irish Art: A Documentation.* Dublin: Wolfhound, 1982.

Lalor, Brian, ed. *The Encyclopedia of Ireland.* New Haven: Yale University Press, 2003.

Lentin, Ronit, ed. *Emerging Irish Identities.* Proceedings of a Seminar held in Trinity College Dublin, 27 November 1999. 2000.

Longley, Edna, and Declan Kiberd. *Multi-Culturalism: The View from the Two Irelands.* Cork: Cork University Press, 2001.

Love, Mervyn T. *Peace Building through Reconciliation in Northern Ireland.* Aldershot, England: Avebury, 1995.

Lydon, James. *The Making of Ireland: From Ancient Time to the Present.* London: Routledge, 1998.

Maclachlan, Malcolm, and Caroline Smyth, eds. *Binge Drinking and Youth Culture: Alternative Perspectives.* Dublin: Liffey, 2004.

MacLauglin, Jim. *Travellers and Ireland: Whose Country, Whose History?* Cork: Cork University Press, 1995.

MacManus, Seumas. *The Story of the Irish Race,* rev. ed. Old Greenwich, Conn.: Devin-Adair, 1921.

McBride, Ian. *History and Memory in Modern Ireland.* Cambridge: Cambridge University Press, 2001.

McBride, Lawrence. *Images, Icons, and the Irish Nationalist Imagination.* Dublin: Four Courts, 1999.

McBride, Simon. *Private Ireland: Irish Living and Irish Style Today.* New York: St. Martin's, 1999.

McCarthy, Imelda Colgan, ed. *Irish Family Studies: Selected Papers.* Dublin: Family Studies Centre, University College Dublin: 1995.

McConkey, Kenneth. *A Free Spirit: Irish Art 1860–1960.* Antique Collectors' Club. London: Pyms Gallery, 1990.

McCann, Eamonn. *Dear God: The Price of Religion in Ireland.* London: Bookmarks, 1999.

McDonagh, Martin. "The Beauty Queen of Leenane." In *Plays I.* London: Methuen, 1999.

McDonald, Frank. *The Construction of Dublin.* Dublin: Gandon, 2000.

McGahern, John. *By the Lake.* New York: Knopf, 2002.

McGonagle, Declan. *Irish Art Now: From the Poetic to the Political.* London: Merrell Holbertson, 1999.

McGuinness, Frank. *Observe the Sons of Ulster Marching Towards the Somme. Frank McGuinness: Plays One.* London: Faber and Faber, 1996.

McIlroy, Brian. *Irish Film: An Illustrated History*. Dublin: Anna Livia, 1988.

McIlroy, Brian. *Shooting to Kill: Filmmaking and the 'Troubles' in Northern Ireland*. Richmond, British Columbia: Steveson Press, 2001.

McLoone, Martin. *Irish Film :The Emergence of a Contemporary Cinema*. London: British Film Institute, 2000.

McLoone, Martin, and John MacMahon, eds. *Television and Irish Society: 21 Years of Irish Television*. Dublin: RTE-Irish Film Institute, 1984.

McMahon, Joanne, and Jack Roberts. *The Sheela-na-gigs of Ireland and Britain: The Divine Hag of the Christian Celts*. Cork: Mercier Press, 2000.

McParland, Brenda et al., *Louis le Brocquy: Paintings 1939–1996*. Dublin: Irish Museum of Modern Art, 1996.

Maher, Eamon. *John McGahern: From the Local to the Universal*. Dublin: Liffey, 2003.

Maher, Sean. *The Road to God Knows Where: A Memoir of a Travelling Boyhood*. Dublin: Veritas, 1998.

Mahon, Brid. *Land of Milk and Honey: The Story of Traditional Irish Food and Drink*. Dublin: Poolbeg, 1991.

Megahey, Alan. *The Irish Protestant Churches in the Twentieth Century*. New York: St. Martin's, 2000.

Milne, Kenneth. *A Short History of the Church of Ireland*, 4th edition. Dublin: Columba, 2003.

Montgomery-Massingberd, Hugh and Christopher Simon Sykes. *Great Houses of Ireland*. New York: Rizzoli International, 1999.

Murphy, Colin, and Lynne Adair. *Untold Stories: Protestants in the Republic of Ireland: 1992–2002*. Dublin: Liffey, 2003.

Murray, Christopher. *Twentieth-Century Irish Drama: Mirror up to a Nation*. 1997. Syracuse, N.Y.: Syracuse University Press, 2000.

New Irish Architecture 19. *AAI Awards 2004*. Kinsale: Architectural Association of Ireland-Gandon, 2004.

O'Brien, Edna. *The Country Girls*. New York: Knopf, 1960.

O'Brien, Edna. *Down by the River*. London: Weidenfeld and Nicolson, 1996.

O'Brien, Edna. *In the Forest*. London: Weidenfeld and Nicolson, 1996.

O'Brien, Edna. *Mother Ireland*. New York: Harcourt Brace, 1976.

O'Brien, Peggy, ed. *The Wake Forest Book of Irish Women's Poetry 1967–2000*. Winston-Salem, N.C.: Wake Forest University Press, 1999.

O'Carroll, Ide, and Eoin Collins. *Lesbian and Gay Visions of Ireland: Towards the Twenty-First Century*. London: Cassell, 1995.

O'Casey, Sean. *The Shadow of a Gunman*. 1923. *Literature: The Human Experience*. Eds. Richard Abcarian and Marvin Klotz, 4th edition. New York: St. Martin's, 1986. 287–323.

O'Connell, John. "Travellers' Accommodation–Past and Present." In *The President Robinson Awards for the Design of Travellers' Accommodation*. Dublin: Pavee Point Publications, 1993.

O'Connell, Michael. *Changed Utterly: Ireland and the New Irish Psyche*. Dublin: Liffey, 2001.

O'Connor, Frank. "Guests of the Nation." In *Stories by Frank O'Connor*. New York: Vintage, 1956.

O'Connor, Joseph. *Star of the Sea*. New York: Harcourt, 2002.

O'Dowd, Liam, ed. *On Intellectuals and Intellectual Life in Ireland: International, Comparative and Historical Contexts*. Belfast: Institute of Irish Studies, Queen's University and The Royal Irish Academy, 1996.

O'Faolain, Nuala. *My Dream of You*. New York: Riverhead, 2001.

O'Riain, Sean. *Solidarity with Travellers: A Story of Settled People Making a Stand for Travellers*. Dublin: Roadside Books, 2000.

Ormsby, Frank, ed. *Poets from the North of Ireland*, 2nd edition. Belfast: Blackstaff, 1990.

O'Toole, Fintan. *Critical Moments: Fintan O'Toole on Modern Irish Theatre*. Ed. Julia Furay and Redmond O'Hanlon. Dublin: Carysfort Press, 2003.

O'Toole Fintan. *The Ex-Isle of Erin: Images of a Global Ireland*. Dublin: New Island Books, 1997.

Parkinson, Alan F. *Ulster Loyalism and the British Media*. Dublin: Four Courts, 1998.

Patterson, Glenn. *Number 5*. London: Penguin, 2003.

Peillon, Michel. *Contemporary Irish Society: An Introduction*. Dublin: Gill and Macmillan, 1982.

Pettit, Lance. *Screening Ireland: Film and Television Representation*. Manchester: Manchester University Press, 2000.

Polley, Derek. *Home Ground: A Geography of Northern Ireland*. Newtownards, NI: Colour Books, 1999.

Pringle, Dennis G. et al., eds. *Poor People, Poor Places: A Geography of Poverty and Deprivation in Ireland*. Dublin: Oak Tree, 1999.

Raftery, Mary, and Eoin O'Sullivan. *Suffer the Little Children: The Inside Story of Ireland's Industrial Schools, 1999*. New York: Continuum, 2001.

Richards, Shaun, ed. *The Cambridge Companion to Twentieth-Century Irish Drama*. Cambridge: Cambridge University Press, 2004.

Rifkin, Ned. *Sean Scully: Twenty Years, 1976–1995*. London: Thames and Hudson, 1995.

Rivlin, Ray. *Shalom Ireland: A Social History of Jews in Modern Ireland*. Dublin: Gill and Macmillan, 2003

Rockett, Kevin. *Still Irish: A Century of the Irish in Film*. Dún Laoghaire, Ireland: Red Mountain P, 1995.

Rockett, Kevin et al. *Cinema and Ireland*. Syracuse, N.Y.: Syracuse University Press, 1988.

Rolston, Bill. *Drawing Support 2: Murals of War and Peace*. Belfast: Beyond the Pale, 1995.

Rolston, Bill, and Michael Shannon. *Encounters: How Racism Came to Ireland*. Belfast: Beyond the Pale, 2002.

Rose, Kieran. *Diverse Communities: The Evolution of Lesbian and Gay Politics in Ireland*. Cork: Cork University Press, 1994.

Ross, Ruth Isabel. *Irish Family Food*. Dublin: Gill and Macmillan, 1996.

Rossiter, Ann, and Mary Sexton. *The Other Irish Journey: A Survey Update of Northern Irish Women Attending British Abortion Clinics, 2000–2001.* London: Marie Stopes International, 2001.

Ryan, Vera. "An Interview with Conor Fallon." In *Conor Fallon: Monograph 1.* Kinsale: Gandon, 1996.

Ryder, Chris and Vincent Kearney. *Drumcree: The Orange Order's Last Stand.* London: Methuen, 2001.

Sales, Rosemary. *Women Divided: Gender, Religion, and Politics in Northern Ireland.* New York: Routledge, 1997.

Savage, Robert J. Jr., ed. *Ireland in the New Century: Politics, Culture and Identity.* Dublin: Four Courts, 2003.

Sean Scully: Paintings. Manchester: Manchester City Art Galleries, 1997.

Shannon, Elizabeth. *I am of Ireland: Women of the North Speak Out.* Rev. ed. Amherst: University of Massachusetts Press, 1997.

Shannon, Geoffrey, ed. *The Divorce Act in Practice.* Dublin: Round Hall, 1999.

Sheehan, Helena. *The Continuing Story of Irish Television Drama: Tracking the Tiger.* Dublin: Four Courts, 2004.

Sheehan, Helena. *Irish Television Drama: A Society and Its Stories.* Dublin: RTE, 1987.

Sheehy, Jean. *The Rediscovery of Ireland's Past: the Celtic Revival 1830–1930.* London: Thames and Hudson, 1980.

Smith, Ailbhe. *Wildish Things: An Anthology of New Irish Women's Writing.* Dublin: Attic Press, 1989.

Smith, Suzanne and Fidèle Mutwarasibo. African Cultural Project. Dublin http://africansmagazine.com/africanseire.html

Smyth, Aibhe. *The Abortion Papers: Ireland.* Dublin: Attic, 1992.

Storey, Earl. *Traditional Roots: Towards an Appropriate Relationship between the Church of Ireland and the Orange Order.* Dublin: Columba, 2002.

Sullivan, Megan. *Women in Northern Ireland: Cultural Studies and Material Conditions.* Gainesville: University Press of Florida, 1999.

Synge, John. *The Aran Islands.* With drawings by Jack B. Yeats. 1906. Belfast: Blackstaff, 1988.

Synge, John. *The Complete Plays of John Synge.* New York: Vintage, 1960.

Temple Bar Properties Ltd. *Dublin's Cultural Quarter: Temple Bar.* Dublin: Temple Bar Properties, 2002.

Toibin, Colm. *The Blackwater Lightship.* London: Picador, 1999.

Toibin, Colm. *The Penguin Book of Irish Fiction.* New York: Viking, 2000.

Toibin, Colm. *Seeing Is Believing: Moving Statues in Ireland.* Dublin: Pilgrim, 1985.

Toibin, Colm. *The Trial of the Generals: Selected Journalism 1980–1990.* Dublin: Raven Arts, 1990.

Townsend, Charles. *Ireland: The 20th Century.* London: Arnold, 1999.

Trevor, William, ed. *The Oxford Book of Irish Short Stories.* Oxford: Oxford University Press, 1989.

Trotter, Mary. *Ireland's National Theaters: Political Performance and the Origins of the Irish Dramatic Movement.* Syracuse, N.Y.: Syracuse University Press, 2001.

Valiulis, Maryann. *Gender and Sexuality in Modern Ireland.* Amherst: University of Massachusetts Press, 1997, 158.

Walker, Dorothy. *Modern Art in Ireland.* Foreword by Seamus Heaney. Dublin: Lilliput, 1997.

Walshe, Eibhear, ed. *Sex, Nation and Dissent in Irish Writing.* Cork: Cork University Press, 1997.

Watson, Iarfhlaith. *Broadcast in Irish: Minority Language, Radio, Television and Identity.* Dublin: Four Courts, 2003.

Whelan, Thomas R., ed. *The Stranger in Our Midst: Refugees in Ireland: Causes, Experiences, Responses.* Dublin: Kimmage Mission Institute of Theology and Cultures, 2001.

White, Tony. *Investing in People: Higher Education in Ireland from 1960 to 2000.* Dublin: Institute of Public Affairs, 2001.

Wichert, Sabine. *Northern Ireland since 1947,* 2nd edition. New York: Longman, 1999.

Wilson, Robert McLiam. *Eureka Street: A Novel of Ireland Like No Other.* New York: Arcade-Little, Brown, 1997.

Wood, Ian S. *Ireland During the Second World War.* London: Caxton Editions, 2002.

Woods, Oona. *Seeing Is Believing?: Murals in Derry.* Derry: Guildhall Press, 1985.

Ypma, Herbert. *Irish Georgian.* London: Thames and Hudson, 1998.

WEB SITES

http://www.belfasttelegraph.co.uk/, Belfast Telegraph; leading newspaper in Northern Ireland.

http://www.browseireland.com, browse Ireland.com; art, entertainment, general information.

http://cain.ulst.ac.uk/, rich archive of material on Troubles.

http://www.catholicireland.net, Catholic Church in Ireland.

http://www.cso.ie/, Central Statistics Office, Dublin.

http://www.garda.ie, Garda Siochana, Irish police. Crime statistics and more.

http://www.ireland.com, gateway to *Irish Times* and general information.

http://www.irishchurches.org/, Irish Council of Churches (Protestant, Anglican).

http://www.irishcultureandcustoms.com, Irish Culture and Customs.

http://www.irishtouristboard.com, Irish Tourist Board; links to cultural sites.

http://www.irlgov.ie/, Republic of Ireland.

http://www.linkireland.com/, links to every Irish county: events, museums, information.

http://www.luminarium.org/mythology/ireland/, Irish folklore and mythology; newspapers.

http://www.museum.ie/, National Museum of Ireland.

http://www.nics.gov.uk/, Government of Northern Ireland.

http://www.niwc.org/, Northern Ireland Women's Coalition.

http://www.nwci.ie/, National Women's Council of Ireland; useful links.

http://www.orangenet.org/, Orange Order.

http://www.psni.police.uk/, Northern Ireland's police. Crime statistics and more.

http://www.sluggerotoole.com/, Slugger O'Toole's long-running forum for discussion of politics and culture in Northern Ireland.

Index

Abbey Theatre, 6, 19, 149, 173–75, 178, 180

abortion: and availability in England, 66, 80; and constitution of the Republic, 39, 79–80, 86; illegal in Republic, 25, 41, 70, 77–80, 86, 191; Northern Ireland, 41, 80, 152–54

abuse: child, 72, 73, 101, 157; domestic, 82, 83

Act of Union, 15

Adams, Gerry, 54, 145

addiction, 2, 154, 156

Ahern, Bert, 74

AIDS, 84–86, 120, 141

Alcoholism, 2, 42, 100–103, 110, 117, 183

Allen, Darina, 90–93

Allen, Joan, 155

Altan, 168

Anglicanism, 24, 43–45, 53. *See also* Church of Ireland

Antrim, 4, 12, 99

Aran Islands, 3, 8, 19, 147, 148, 174, 188, 189

architecture, 6, 184, 187, 206–13

Ardmore Studios, 6, 149

Armagh, 4, 51, 198

Ascendancy, 14

Asian immigrants, 11–13, 55, 93

asylum, 11, 12, 71, 72

B-specials, 27

Banville, John, 93, 116, 139

BBC, 5, 12, 55, 133, 134, 137, 139, 147, 201

Beckett, Mary, 118

Beckett, Samuel, 115, 175, 176

Behan, Brendan, 100

Belfast, 5, 118, 198–200

Belfast Agreement, 25–29, 47, 48, 53, 217. *See also* Good Friday Agreement

Belfast Telegraph, 49, 144, 146

birth rate, 9, 41, 76, 77

Black and Tans, 22, 27

Bloody Sunday, 5, 27, 123, 142, 170, 200

bog, 4, 112, 123, 180–182

Boland, Eavan, 126

Bolger, Dermot, 119, 139
Boyne, Battle of, 2, 14, 33, 48, 49, 179, 201
British Army, 5, 178
broadcasting, 133–38, 141–43
Broadcasting Authority. *See* Radio Telefis Eireann
Bruen, Ken, 119
Buddhists, 55
Byrne, Gay, 138, 154

Cahill, Martin, 154, 155
Calvin, John, 45
Carleton, William, 109
Carr, Marina, 180–82
Carson, Ciaran, 125–28
Carson, Edward, 47
Casey, Eamonn, 42
Castletown, 208
Cathleen ni Houlihan, 19, 110, 126, 173, 182, 190
Catholic Church: declining numbers, 41; and education, 72–73; history in Ireland, 34–35; influence in Free State and Republic, 23, 24, 33, 34, 40–43, 85, 86; in popular culture, 36–30; sexual abuse by clergy, 42, 43, 157; teaching on sex, 67–80; theology, 35, 39–41. *See also* abortion; divorce
Cavan, 6, 103
Celtic New Age music, 169, 170
Celtic Tiger, 1, 2, 213
censorship, 23, 33, 36, 115, 120, 133, 137, 141–43
Charabanc Theatre Company, 179, 180
Chieftains, 13, 168
Church of Ireland, 14, 43, 44, 48, 50–54, 171, 174
Churchill, Winston, 23, 24, 29, 137, 176
civil rights, Catholic, 27, 34, 47, 123, 142

Clancy Brothers, 165, 167, 168
Clannad, 169, 170
Cleary, Michael, 40, 42
Coca-Cola, 95
Coleman, James, 196–98
Collins, Michael, 21, 119, 151
Comiskey, Brendan, 42
Commonwealth, 12, 24
Connolly, James, 19, 20, 46, 203
constitution, 21, 33, 39–41, 57, 68, 70, 76–78, 80, 85
contraception, 25, 33, 40, 76, 78
Cork (city), 6, 7, 90–93, 213
Corkery, Daniel, 111, 115
Craig, James, 23, 33
crime, 2, 6, 26, 95, 119, 154, 156, 213
Cromwell, Oliver, 2, 14, 43, 56, 89
Cuchulain, 109, 169

Dail, 10, 21, 22, 41, 68, 76, 77, 82, 141–43
Daly, Cahal, 42, 54
dance, 69, 140, 161–64, 179
Davitt, Michael, 17, 127
De Humanae Vitae, 40, 41, 76
de Valera, Eamonn, 21, 23, 57, 59, 137, 138
Deane, Seamus, 176
Democratic Unionist Party, 29, 47, 48
Derry, 4–5, 27, 82, 117, 170, 176, 177, 198, 211; Siege of, 14, 49
Derry Film and Video Collective, 152, 153
diet, 15–17, 69, 89, 90, 92, 93, 95
discrimination, legal protections against, 1, 11, 27, 80–82, 85
divorce, 73–75
Doherty, Willie, 190, 191, 201, 202
Donegal, 4, 7, 8, 37, 152, 163, 169
Donoghue, Emma, 120
Doyle, Roddy, 101, 119, 139, 153, 156
drama, 110, 114, 137–141, 161, 171–77, 181, 182

drink, 89, 98–103
Drumcree, 50–54
Dublin, 1, 2

Easter Rising, 20, 21, 134, 174, 178, 200, 203
economic growth, 1–3, 5, 24–26, 58, 59
ecumenism, 48
education, 8–10, 26, 72, 81; for peace 54, 55, 59
electricity, 7, 8, 189
Emancipation, Catholic, 3, 15, 43
Enya, 161, 170
EU, 81, 146, 163, 213. See also European Union
European Court of Human Rights, 25, 27, 84, 85
European Court of Justice, 25
European Parliament, 25
European Union, 4, 9, 13, 24, 25, 95, 120, 209. See also EU

Fallon, Conor, 204
Fallon, Peter, 123–25, 128
Falls Road, 54
family, 8, 9; ideology of, 24, 65, 66–70, 84, 85, 137
famine, history of, 15–17; depicted, 109, 116, 117, 203, 204; long-term effects on diet, 89, 90, 92; long-term effects on marriage, 67; long-term effects on traditional music, 162, 163, 165, 166
farming, 3–7, 16; idealization of, 111–13; portrayed realistically, 121–23, 139
Faulkner, Brian, 5, 27
feminism, 13, 39, 68, 69, 82, 101
feminists, 76, 78–80, 117, 126, 150, 180
Fenians, 17, 20
Fermanagh, 4
Fianna Fail, 42, 74

Field Day, 143, 176–78, 180
film, 65, 133, 136, 147–57, 178. See also Irish Film Board; Irish Film Centre
Fine Gael, 73
FitzGerald, Garret, 27, 73
Flaherty, Robert, 147, 148
Flatley, Michael, 161, 163, 164, 168
Flead, 163
Football, 19, 26, 35, 89, 98, 103–5, 136, 162
France, 13, 15, 20, 35, 45, 110, 115, 135, 189, 195
Frears, Stephen, 153
Free Presbyterians, 45–47
Free State, 4, 22–24; relation with Catholic Church, 33, 67–70, 137, 142, 162, 163, 205
Friel, Brian, 139, 176

Gaelic (Irish language), 8, 13, 80, 174; contemporary writing in 127–28
Gaelic Athletic Association, 19, 35, 103
Gaelic League, 3, 19, 20, 23, 109, 134, 162, 165
Gaeltacht, 8, 26, 128, 134–36, 141, 152, 153
Garda Siochana, 2, 77, 119
gay rights, 25, 81, 83–85. See also homosexuality
gender, 65–68, 70, 81, 82, 86, 100, 101
Georgian architecture, 6, 145, 187, 207–11
Gillespie, Rowan, 203
Gilligan, 2, 140, 156
globalization, 13, 41, 58, 86, 146, 147
Goldsmith, Oliver, 109
Gonne, Maud, 20, 173
Good Friday Agreement, 28, 83. See also Belfast Agreement
Great Britain, 3, 137
Gregory, Lady Augusta, 19, 109, 110, 172, 174

Guerin, Veronica, 2, 144, 154–56
Guinness, 6, 92, 99, 101, 179, 207, 208

Harkin, Margo, 152
Hartnett, Michael, 101, 128
Haughey, Charles, 76, 141
Health, 24, 78, 85, 94, 95, 102, 103, 145
Heaney, Seamus, 12, 118, 123–26, 128, 176, 180
Henry II, 13, 196
Henry VIII, 13, 43
Henry, Paul, 121, 189, 192, 193
heroin, 2, 127, 155
Higgins, 117, 127
Hindus, 55
holiday, 33, 54, 96, 97, 212
Holocaust, 57
Home Rule, 3, 4, 18, 125, 178
homosexuality, 66, 70, 84, 85, 120
housing: discrimination in Northern Ireland, 26, 33, 34, 51–54, 58; progress in improving, 69, 207, 211–15; substandard, 6, 10, 155, 207
Hume, John, 54
hurling, 19, 89, 98, 103–5, 162
Hyde, Douglas, 3, 19, 134, 187

immigrants: to America from Ireland, 105, 115, 157, 165; to Ireland, 6, 9, 11, 12, 55–58, 93, 155
Industrial Development Authority, 80
industrial schools, 70, 72
Internet, 58, 135, 136, 143, 147, 184, 200, 202, 207
Irish Catholic Church, 35
Irish Film Board, 149
Irish Film Centre, 209
Irish Independent, 10, 144, 154
Irish Renaissance, 19, 109, 110, 126, 187, 188, 192, 205
Irish Republican Army (IRA), 17, 19–22, 111, 207; attitudes toward

in Republic, 25, 142, 143; fictional representations of, 117, 118; 1969–present, 27, 28, 52, 54; wall paintings, 200
Irish Republican Brotherhood, 3, 17, 19
Irish Tenors, 161, 167
Irish Times, 144
Irish Volunteers, 20
Islam, 55, 125

James I, 2, 13
Jellett, Mainie, 192, 193
Jews, 33, 55–58
jobs, 5, 7, 9, 10, 12, 24, 34, 70, 81, 149, 151
John Paul II, 40, 41
Jones, Marie, 179, 180
Jordan, Neal, 139, 150, 151
Joyce, James, 10, 18, 90, 109–11, 115, 116, 176; illustrations, 198; portraits, 196, 204

Kavanagh, Patrick, 100, 121
Keating, Sean, 121, 189
Kerry, 7, 91, 92, 97, 163
Kerry Babies Tribunal, 153, 154
Kiberd, Declan, 12
Kiely, Benedict, 101
Kilroy, Thomas, 139, 176
Kinsella, Thomas, 122, 123
Knock, 36, 37, 113

labor force, 9, 80–82
Land League, 3, 17, 18
Late, Late Show, 138
le Brocquy, Louis, 193–95, 204
le Brocquy, Sybil, 192
Leenane, 182, 183
Leinster, 1, 4, 6–8, 13, 196
leisure, 89, 103
Lemass, Sean, 24, 141
lesbians, 6, 83–85, 117, 120, 139
Limerick, 6, 7, 35, 56, 157, 211, 213
Londonderry, 4, 5. See also Derry

Longley, Edna, 177
Longley, Michael, 124, 125
Lough Derg, 37, 123
Lovett, Ann, 153
Loyalists and anti-immigrant violence,
    12; painting by, 200, 201; violence
    against Catholics, 25, 34, 52,
    150, 179
Luther, Martin, 45

MacColuim, 162, 163
MacNeice, Louis, 122
magazines, 99, 145–47, 154
Magdalen laundries, 65, 66, 70–72,
    194, 214, 215
Mahon, Derek, 124, 125, 177
marriage, 36, 65–70
Mathews, Aidan Carl, 127
Maxton, Hugh, 124
McCabe, Eugene, 112, 139, 176
McCabe, Patrick, 119, 139
McCafferty, Nell, 39
McCormick, John, 165, 166, 168, 169
McCourt, Frank, 90
McDonagh, Martin, 182–84
McGahern, John, 112–14, 180
McGuckian, Medbh, 126–28
McGuinness, Frank, 178, 179, 193
McKinty, Adrian, 119
McQuaid, John, 40, 42
media, 10, 40, 42, 59, 133–47
Meehan, Paula, 127
minorities, 10–13, 34
Modernization, 8–10, 23–26, 41, 65,
    95, 178, 207, 209
Monaghan, 6, 25, 103, 121
Montague, John, 128
Moore, Thomas, 165, 166, 169, 172
Morrison, Van, 161, 168, 171
Muldoon, Paul, 124, 128
Munster, 4, 6–8
murals. *See* wall paintings
murder, 2, 27, 80, 117, 119, 124, 153,
    155, 156, 182

Murdoch, Iris, 207
Muslims, 9, 55

nationalists, 18–20, 172–74
Neeson, Liam, 151
newspapers, 133, 137, 140, 143–46
Ní Dhomhnaill, Nuala, 127, 128
Normans, 13
Northern Ireland, 4, 5, 22, 23, 26–29,
    33, 34, 46–55; Travellers in, 12,
    13, 214; women in 80–85. *See also*
    Troubles
Northern Ireland Assembly, 29, 48, 54
Northern Ireland Police, 48

Ó Searcaigh, Cathal, 127
O'Brien, Conor Cruise, 24, 142, 143
O'Brien, Dermod, 188
O'Brien, Edna, 36, 114, 115,
    120, 180
O'Brien, Flann, 100, 115, 116, 145
O'Casey, Sean, 139, 174
O'Connell, Daniel, 15, 17
O'Connor, Frank, 111, 139
O'Connor, Joseph, 116, 117
O'Connor, Sinead, 78, 161, 171
O'Dowd, Gwen, 191, 192
O'Faolain, Nuala, 79, 102
O'Faolain, Sean, 112
O'Flaherty, Liam, 100, 112, 139
O'Malley, Mary, 127
O'Neill, Hugh, 13
O'Neill, Terence, 27, 47
O'Reilly, Tony, 144
O'Sullivan, Thaddeus, 72, 133, 223
O'Toole, Fintan, 26, 42, 58, 59, 115,
    180, 182
obesity, 95
Orange Order, 45, 46, 48–53, 79
Osborne, Danny, 204

painting, 187–93, 195–201
Paisley, Ian, 29, 46–48, 52, 79, 84
Pale, 6, 8, 13

Parnell, Charles Stuart, 3, 17, 18, 71, 83, 142, 203
Patterson, Glenn, 118
Paulin, Tom, 125, 126, 176
pay, 16, 25, 34, 81, 82, 96, 156, 191
Peace People, 48, 83
peace process, 27, 51, 54, 83
peat, 1, 4, 123
penal laws, 2, 14, 15
pilgrimage, 36, 37, 97, 123
pill, 40, 76
Pius XII, 34, 137, 153
Plantation, 2, 46, 51, 120
population figures, 4–8, 16
potato, 3, 15, 16, 89–92, 95, 116, 177, 189
poverty: before Independence, 56, 99, 110, 119, 127; contemporary, 2, 3, 10, 117; linked to alcoholism, 101; mid-twentieth century, 23, 99, 157, 211. *See also* famine
Prendergast, Kathy, 190, 191
Presbyterian Church, 45–47, 59, 209, 210, 216. *See also* Free Presbyterian
prison, 20, 77, 151, 194, 200
pubs, 98–101

Quakers, 16. *See also* Society of Friends

radio, 101, 133–38, 144, 176, 184
Radio Telefís Eireann, 137, 141, 143
Raidió na Gaeltachta, 8, 135
Rain, 3, 36, 120, 157, 170
Rea, Stephen, 149, 150, 161, 176
refugees in Ireland, 11, 12, 57
Republic of Ireland: government, 4, 42, 57, 72–86, 102–3, 141–44, 209; origins of name, 13, 24
Riverdance, 12, 161, 164
Robinson, Mary, 25, 71, 73, 78, 83, 86, 221
rock music, 1, 119, 128, 150, 161, 168–70
Ros na Rún, 136

Rosc, 196, 197
Royal Irish Constabulary, 22, 176
Royal Ulster Constabulary, 26, 27
RTE, 6, 70, 135, 136, 138–41, 143, 145, 147, 152. *See also* Radio Telefís Eireann
rugby, 19, 89, 103–5
Russborough House, 155, 208

Scottish, 2, 14, 165
Scully, Sean, 187, 197, 198, 224
sculpture, 187, 202–4, 206
SDLP, 54, 217
Seanad, 82
sectarianism, 52–54, 82, 83, 119, 200
Section, 31 141–43
secularization, 41, 58
sexuality, 36, 65–68, 70, 71, 80, 114, 120, 138, 152–54
Shannon (river), 2, 3, 7, 17, 189
Shannon Free Zone, 7
Shaw, 109, 172, 174
Sheela-na-gig, 205
Simmons, 124
Simonds-Gooding, Maria, 191
singer, 145, 171, 184
Sinn Fein, 3–5, 19, 21, 28, 29, 54, 68, 143
smoking ban, 101
soccer, 19, 89, 103–5, 119, 153
Socialist Democratic Labor, 29
Society of Friends, 54, 209
software, 9
Somme, Battle of, 4, 49, 53, 125, 178, 179, 200
Spain, 13, 89, 103, 195
sports, 19, 89, 100–105, 135, 137, 162
St. Patrick, 98
St. Patrick's Day, 3, 23, 97, 98
Status, 5, 11, 41, 58, 68, 74, 76, 80, 81, 166
Stembridge, Gerard, 133
step-dancing, 162
Stormont, 5, 27, 50

storytelling, 161, 171, 172
Strongbow, 1, 13, 196–98
students, 8, 9, 12, 27, 40, 58, 73, 140, 192
suicide, 78, 79, 103
Supreme Court, 76–79, 85
Swift, Jonathan, 6, 109
Synge, John, 19, 109, 110, 148, 174, 182, 188, 189

technology, 7
Teilifís na Gaeltachta, 135
television: American, 58, 168; British, 58, 169; Catholic Church and, 40, 42; Irish, 8, 52, 103, 105, 133–48
Temple Bar, 1, 2, 93, 151, 208–10, 213, 214
terror, 10, 34, 126, 181
TG4, 105, 136, 147
Thatcher, Margaret, 27, 48
theater, 5, 6, 139, 149, 172, 175, 177, 179, 180, 209
Titanic, 5, 124, 167
Toibin, Colm, 39
tourism, 5, 7, 29, 37, 93, 99, 102, 120
tourists, 1, 90, 98, 119, 148, 200, 210, 212
traditional music, 50, 165, 167, 168
Travellers, 10, 11, 140, 182, 195, 214
Trimble, David, 29, 52
Trinity College, 6, 10, 46, 58, 76, 85, 126, 164
troubles, 25–27; economic impact of, 5; in film, 150–52; in literature, 117, 118; reporting of, 141–43; in theater, 176, 177; in visual art, 123, 124, 198–202; and women, 82, 83
turf, 4, 24. *See also* peat
Tyrone, 4, 13

U2, 161, 170
UDA, 48, 100. *See also* Ulster Defense Association
Ulster Defense Association, 27, 52

Ulster Freedom Fighters, 27
Ulster Volunteer Force, 3, 18, 27. *See also* UVF
underclass, 2, 6, 10, 117, 154
unemployment, 5, 10, 213
union movement, 19
Unionism, 13, 176
United Irishmen, 2, 15, 46, 166
United Kingdom, 4, 9, 18, 23, 27, 28, 66, 76, 79, 102, 144, 146. *See also* Act of Union
United Nations, 4, 24, 25, 81, 86, 142
UVF, 3, 4, 48, 100, 200. *See also* Ulster Volunteer Force

Vatican II, 39, 40
Vikings, 6, 210

wall paintings, 59, 125, 199–201
Waterford, 6
wells, holy, 37, 38
Wilde, Oscar, 109, 172, 174, 205
William of Orange, 14
Williams, Betty, 83
Williams, Raymond, 140
Wilson, Robert McLiam, 118
Wolfe Tone, 15, 172
women: magazines targeted to, 146; as poets, 126, 127; and sexuality, 67–71, 138, 152, 153; in theater, 179–82; and workforce, 9, 25, 80–82
World Cup (soccer), 91, 103
World War I, 18, 20, 23, 69, 178. *See also* Somme, Battle of
World War II: Eire neutral during, 23–25, 80, 125, 137–80, 207; Northern Ireland, 23, 54

X case, 77–79, 114

Yeats, Jack B., 188, 189, 192
Yeats, William Butler, 19, 20, 109–11, 115, 121–23, 172, 174; portrait, 198

About the Author

MARGARET SCANLAN is Professor of English at Indiana University, Bloomington.

Recent Titles in
Culture and Customs of Europe